BEST DEVELOPMENT PRACTICES

Doing the Right Thing and Making Money at the Same Time

By Reid Ewing

With
MaryBeth DeAnna
Christine C. Heflin
Douglas R. Porter

Published in cooperation with the Urban Land Institute, the Florida Department of Community Affairs, and the Florida Atlantic University/Florida International University Joint Center for Environmental and Urban Problems

Planners Press
American Planning Association
Chicago, Illinois • Washington, D.C.

Published by:
American Planning Association
122 S. Michigan Ave., Suite 1600
Chicago, IL 60603

Copyright 1996 by the State of Florida. This book was originally prepared for the Florida
Department of Community Affairs with funding from the Florida Energy Office.

ISBN (paperback edition): 1-884829-10-4
ISBN (hardbound edition): 1-884829-11-2

Library of Congress Catalog Card Number: 95-83253

CONTENTS

Acknowledgments

This treatise on development is the product of many talented people. Direction was provided by a hands-on Advisory Committee:

Ben Starrett (Chairman)
Florida Department of Community Affairs

John DeGrove (Vice-Chairman)
FAU/FIU Joint Center for Environmental and Urban Problems

Tara Bartee
Florida Department of Transportation

Thomas Beck
Florida Department of Community Affairs

Craig Benedict
City of Coconut Creek
(representing the Florida League of Cities)

David Blodgett
Florida Department of Transportation

James Charlier
Charlier Associates, Inc.

Wayne Daltry
Southwest Florida Regional Planning Council
(representing the Florida Regional Councils Association)

Victor Dover
Dover, Kohl & Partners

Lee Einsweiler
Siemon, Larsen, & Marsh

Patti McKay
1000 Friends of Florida

Robert Pennock
Florida Department of Community Affairs

Jan Rickey
Florida Energy Office

Frank Folsom Smith
The Folsom Group

Bruce Wilson
Broward County Metropolitan Planning Organization
(representing the Florida MPO Advisory Committee)

If this document stands out from others, it is because it is informed by the experiences of some of Florida's finest developers. Developers of featured communities commented candidly on their successes and failures, shared documents best measured by the pound, showed me around their projects in the style of proud parents (and rightly so), and set me straight on many points as they reviewed drafts. The group consisted of *Raimund Herden* of Bluewater Bay; *Bob Kramer* of Haile Plantation; *Michael McAfee* of The Hammocks; *Roger Gatlin* of Hunter's Creek; *Stuart Wyllie* of Miami Lakes; *Randy Chastain* of Oakbridge; and *Jim Paulmann* of Palmer Ranch.

Sara Forelle of the FAU/FIU Joint Center conducted an initial review of the environmental literature. Compensating for our lack of specialized expertise were many environmental reviewers, among the top in their fields:

Stormwater Management

John Cox, Department of Environmental Protection, Tallahassee

Bruce Ferguson, School of Environmental Design, University of Georgia, Athens

Martin Wanielista, College of Engineering, University of Central Florida, Orlando

Biological Conservation/Wildlife Management

Brad Hartman, Office of Environmental Services, Florida Game and Freshwater Fish Commission, Tallahassee

Bill Hamilton, Conservation Consultants, Inc., Sarasota

James Lynch, Zoologist, Smithsonian Environmental Resource Center, Edgewater, Maryland

Xeriscaping

Lou Kavouras, Southwest Florida Water Management District, Brooksville

Douglas Welsch, Department of Horticulture and Forestry, Texas A & M University, College Station

Wetlands

Mark Brown, Center for Wetlands, University of Florida, Gainesville

Kevin Erwin, Kevin L. Erwin Consulting Ecologist, Inc., Fort Myers, Florida

Robert Robbins, South Florida Water Management District, West Palm Beach

Integrated Pest Management

Arthur Hornsby, Florida Soil and Water Sciences Department, University of Florida, Gainesville

Ann Leslie, Office of Pesticide Programs, Environmental Protection Agency, Washington, D.C.

Michael Raupp, Cooperative Extension Service, University of Maryland, College Park

Wastewater Reuse

Donald Brandes, St. Johns River Water Management District, Palatka, Florida

James Crook, Black and Veatch, Cambridge, Massachusetts

Kenneth Miller, CH2M-Hill, Denver, Colorado

Habitat Rehabilitation and Enhancement

James Gore, The Conservancy, Naples, Florida

Christine Heflin, then with the FAU/FIU Joint Center and now with the City of Coral Springs, co-authored the *Best Housing Practices*. *Marc Smith* of the Shimberg Center for Affordable Housing, University of Florida, and *Robin Vieira* of Florida Solar Energy Center, served as our expert reviewers.

Christine Heflin also took the lead on the various surveys within the State of Florida. *Doug Porter* conducted the survey of state growth management programs. Porter is President of the Growth Management Institute in Chevy Chase, Maryland. He was formerly Director of Policy Research at the Urban Land Institute in Washington, D.C.

MaryBeth DeAnna brought the project to closure by checking citations, supplying missing information, and generating missing graphics. DeAnna is a Research Associate at the FAU/FIU Joint Center for Environmental and Urban Problems in Fort Lauderdale, Florida.

Shamoon Mohammed digitized hundreds of photos and figures and helped analyze travel data from the Palm Beach County household travel survey, U.S. Census of Population and Housing, and Nationwide Personal Transportation Survey. *Suzanne Lambert* (with an assist from MaryBeth DeAnna) did a superb job on the layout. The enormity of her task, and the quality of her work, can only be fully appreciated by other desktop publishers; what made it so difficult was the high ratio of photos and figures to text, the need to keep photos and figures on the same page as text (in the absence of figure numbers), and the desire to avoid large blank spaces in the middle of chapters.

My heartfelt thanks to these individuals.

Reid Ewing
Fort Lauderdale
January 1996

I. INTRODUCTION

Florida is expected to grow by five million people over the next 20 years. Without changes in development policy and practice, this growth will take the form of urban sprawl, sprawl being Florida's now-dominant development pattern. The economic and social costs will be enormous.[1]

In *Best Development Practices*, we define good community development, as distinct from sprawl, in operational terms. Public purposes loom large, though not at the expense of market considerations. Recommendations go to the enlightened edge of current development practices, but not beyond where we might lose our target audience, the development community. The public purposes pursued though these best practices—affordable housing, energy efficiency, and preservation of natural areas, among others—make good business sense.

Recommendations are also directed to government planners and public officials. Set forth are broad principles upon which to base comprehensive plans and land development regulations, benchmarks against which to judge development proposals, and ample justification for good development practices that may have been advocated all along by knowledgable officials.

While conceived for new communities, and illustrated with examples from seven new communities, nearly all of our best practices apply to smaller planned communities in the 300- to 500-acre range. Many practices also apply to residential subdivisions, commercial centers, and other stand-alone projects. This is significant because smaller developments greatly outnumber large ones.

While conceived for "green field" sites, our best practices may be useful in assessing the quality of existing development or giving direction to redevelopment plans. The underlying principles of good development are that basic and universal.

Our recommendations cover four aspects of development—*land use*, *transportation*, *environment*, and *housing*. The emphasis is on the physical environment (without taking anything away from the important social, economic, and political forces at work in communities). A fifth aspect of development—*urban/suburban design*—is the subject of complementary guidelines to be published later.[2]

WHAT CONCEIVABLE PURPOSE?

Development in Florida is already subject to endless rules and regulations. What conceivable purpose is served by additional development guidelines?

Existing rules and regulations mostly tell developers what not to do. When they say what to do, it is in the form of minimum requirements. *Do*

Florida's Future?

Source: *Sunshine: The Magazine of South Florida,* Cover illustration by Tim Reilly, February 6, 1994.

not encroach into wetlands, but if you do, mitigate your impacts by creating, enhancing, or restoring other wetlands. Do not dump traffic onto already congested roads, but if you do, mitigate your impact by helping pay for road improvements. At best, these rules prevent things from getting much worse as Florida continues to grow.

We can do better. For 50 years or more, leading developers, planners, designers, environmentalists, and others have pointed the way toward better development. The National Association of Home Builders, Urban Land Institute, American

Planning Association, and many others have published volumes on the subject.[3] What is required is a synthesis and dissemination of their collective wisdom.

BREAKING NEW GROUND

This is not the first attempt to formulate development guidelines (see Appendix A). We borrow liberally from the best of earlier efforts.

We also break new ground. These recommendations blend *contemporary* and *traditional* design principles. Andres Duany, Peter Calthorpe, and other neo-traditionalists (or "new urbanists," to use the trendy term) raise powerful objections to current development practices. They advocate a return to design principles of pre-automotive times. But the automobile is a fact of life, and the low-density lifestyles that are both cause and effect of auto-dependence clearly appeal to most Americans. Surely, there is some middle ground or some mix of contemporary and traditional designs that is preferable to either alone.

These recommendations are the first with the imprimatur of a state government upon them. A survey of the nation's eight other "growth management" states uncovered two that put large-scale developments through a special review process, two more that authorize new communities in statute or state plan, but none that has standards or guidelines for such places (Appendix B).

Finally, these recommendations are more deeply rooted in empirical research than any to date. We draw upon the technical literature in dozens of fields, from landscape ecology to environmental psychology; from transit-oriented design to crime prevention through design. For real-world examples, we look to the best contemporary developments and traditional towns in Florida (Appendices C and D).

POLICY BASIS

These best practices are grounded in the State Comprehensive Plan and State Land Development Plan, the seminal documents of growth management in Florida.[4] The State Comprehensive Plan, enacted by Florida Legislature in 1985, outlines goals and policies for growth within the state. All regional and local plans must comport with the state plan. The State Land Development Plan translates these general goals into more specific objectives. The objectives are to be given weight by state and regional agencies as they prepare their plans and review development proposals.

The best practices that follow represent a further translation. The purposes pursued in the state plans are translated into planning and design recommendations for developers and the agencies that regulate them.

Public Purposes Served by Best Development Practices

Purpose	State Comprehensive Plan
Housing Affordability	Goal (5)
Crime Prevention	Goal (7), Policies 9 and 11
Water Conservation	Goal (8), Policies 9-11
Natural Area Protection	Goal (8), Policy 8
	Goal (10)
	Goal (16), Policies 2 and 6
Air Quality	Goal (11), Policy 2
Energy Efficiency	Goal (12)
Personal Mobility	Goal (4), Policy 10
	Goal (12), Policies 3-4
	Goal (20), Policies 8-10 and 15
Accessibility	Goal (16), Policies 1 and 3
	Goal (20), Policy 9
	Goal (25), Policy 5

Two additional public purposes—discouraging urban sprawl and creating vibrant communities—are implicit in the State Comprehensive Plan. For vibrant communities, our best practices emphasize diversity, street life, sense of place, and other aspects of livability. To discourage sprawl, our best practices give specificity to many of the anti-sprawl provisions of Florida's Local Government Comprehensive Planning Rule.[5]

Anti-Sprawl Provisions Implemented through Best Development Practices

Open space requirements	✔
Clustering requirements	✔
Minimum densities/intensities	✔
Phasing controls	✔
Full cost pricing of facilities/services	
Transfer of development rights and purchase of development rights	
Planned unit development requirements	
Provision for traditional neighborhood developments	
Provision for mixed land uses	✔
Jobs-housing balance requirements	✔
Provision for new towns and rural villages	
Buffering requirements	✔
Urban service/growth boundaries	
Access management measures	✔

ENDNOTES

[1] See R. Ewing, "Characteristics, Causes, and Effects of Sprawl: A Literature Review," *Environmental and Urban Issues*, Vol. 21, Winter 1994, pp. 1-15.

[2] A transit-oriented design manual, prepared for the Florida Department of Transportation by the FAU/FIU Joint Center for Environmental and Urban Problems, is due out in 1996.

[3] The more recent and comprehensive guides to development include: National Association of Home Builders, *Cost Effective Site Planning: Single-Family Development*, Washington, D.C., 1986; National Association of Home Builders, *Land Development*, Washington, D.C., 1987; R.D. Yaro et al., *A Design Manual for Conservation and Development*, Lincoln Institute of Land Policy, Cambridge, MA, 1988; D. Listokin and C. Walker, *The Subdivision and Site Plan Handbook*, Center for Urban Policy Research, Rutgers University, New Brunswick, NJ, 1989; R. Ewing, *Developing Successful New Communities*, Urban Land Institute, Washington, D.C., 1991; and F.D. Jarvis, *Site Planning and Community Design for Great Neighborhoods*, National Association of Home Builders, Washington, D.C., 1993.

[4] The State Land Development Plan is being revised and retitled the State Land Plan. The authors of the revised plan inform us that our best practices are consistent with the new plan.

[5] Rule 9J-5.006(5), Florida Administrative Code.

II. QUEST FOR THE BEST

When it comes to development guidelines, visionary is good, utopian is not. If guidelines are viewed as utopian, they will be dismissed by the naturally conservative and results-oriented development industry. Others have suffered this fate.

This manual looks to established, successful Florida developments for *Best Development Practices*. After an exhaustive search, seven contemporary developments were selected as exemplary, not in every way but in many ways. These places serve as a reality check. They show what can reasonably be expected of developers. They prove that developers can incorporate quality features and still make a profit.

For comparative purposes, five traditional towns were also selected as exemplary and then surveyed and studied.

SCREENING CRITERIA

To screen contemporary developments for possible selection and study, rules of thumb were crafted. The rules allowed candidate developments to be assessed with short telephone interviews, followed in many cases by brief site visits.

(1) Market Success

Developments had to be successful in the marketplace. While some promising new developments are going up around the state, such as Southlake in Orlando and Windsor Park in Jacksonville, we sought developments that had already proven themselves by capturing impressive shares of new home sales in their markets. Developments that had defaulted on financial obligations, disposed of assets to remain solvent, or changed hands under unfavorable circumstances were automatically disqualified even if they have since become profitable.

(2) Shopping and Recreational Opportunities

Developments had to offer shopping and recreational opportunities on-site. The presence of on-site facilities keeps some daily trips off the external road network. It adds to the sense of community. It can be a big plus for those who do not drive. Off-site facilities are seldom as accessible on foot, as approachable by back roads, or as identified with the development and hence patronized loyally by residents.

(3) Environmental Themes

Developments had to preserve significant natural features of pristine sites, or restore some of the environmental values of environmentally degraded sites. Marketing literature was reviewed for environmental themes and tangible actions—such as use of reclaimed wastewater and reliance on open, natural drainage systems.

(4) "Affordable" Housing with Amenities

Florida has hundreds of affordable developments without amenities, and dozens of luxury home developments with lavish amenities. We wanted developments with housing for people of moderate means, and at the same time, amenities good enough to attract the affluent. "Amenities" had to include ample open space, attractive landscaping and signage, and design controls.

(5) Road Connections

We looked for multiple connections to the regional road network, and gave credit when subdivisions connected to more than one external street. This is in contrast to many contemporary developments that have only one way in and out. With multiple connections, traffic is dispersed rather than concentrated. Trips are shorter, which makes walking and biking more attractive and auto trips less polluting and fuel consuming.

There had to be more street life than is typical of suburbia. Active street life may be the best indication of good urban/suburban design. The casual contacts that create a sense of community occur when people are out and about on foot, not when they are racing around in their cars. People are inclined to spend time outside only if the environment is safe, pleasant, and relatively interesting.

BEST OF THE NEW

The search for Florida's best contemporary developments began with a review of Florida Quality Developments (Developments of Regional Impact or DRIs meeting special criteria) and of Florida Association of Realtors' ENVY (environmental) Award winners. These are all good developments, of course. But only Bluewater Bay, Hunter's Creek, and Palmer Ranch—all ENVY winners—met all screening criteria.

This was followed by telephone calls to the 11 regional planning councils. These interviews tended to focus on giant DRIs that had consumed much regional planning council time during the DRI review process. Bluewater Bay and Palmer Ranch showed up again, and Haile Plantation, Miami Lakes, and Oakbridge were mentioned for the first time. Miami Lakes, one of the nation's most acclaimed new communities, would have made the list in any event.

Locations of Featured Developments

△ — Featured Contemporary Developments

Finally, county planning staffs were contacted on the theory that they would be aware of smaller exemplary projects overlooked by the regional planning councils. Survey results make interesting reading. It is surprising how few developments in Florida even mix land uses and housing types, let alone meet all screening criteria. Bluewater Bay, Hunter's Creek, Oakbridge, and Palmer Ranch were cited again. Haile Plantation came up twice, and The Hammocks was mentioned for the first time.

Developments that appeared promising from the surveys were contacted for brochures, master development plans, and status-of-development information; surveyed by telephone to check on specific features; and later visited if they appeared to meet all screening criteria. In this way, seven exemplary developments were selected for further study. A questionnaire was completed for each project covering all aspects of development for which best practices are recommended (Appendix C). The seven are profiled in the next section.

Summary Statistics for Featured Developments

	Year	Acreage	Population Mid-1994	Population Build-Out
Bluewater Bay	1978	1,990	7,000	10,500
Haile Plantation*	1981	1,073	4,000	7,300
Hammocks	1978	1,097	15,900	16,500
Hunter's Creek	1986	3,995	6,000	22,800
Miami Lakes	1962	2,500	14,900	16,900
Oakbridge	1987	1,419	1,800	7,500
Palmer Ranch	1987	5,119	4,200	23,100

* Statistics for Haile Plantation do not reflect the recent addition of 543 acres contiguous to and north of the original site.

opment of energy-efficient aerated concrete block homes; a commercial center with a front entrance on a state highway, a back entrance into the community, and parking areas dispersed and visually screened; and a marina and golf course (Northwest Florida's number 1 rated course) that blend in with nature.

Natural Marina at Bluewater Bay

INTRODUCTION TO FEATURED DEVELOPMENTS

Bluewater Bay is located in Florida's Panhandle midway between Panama City and Pensacola and a short drive from the Emerald Coast. It is an island of development amidst the spectacular natural beauty of a state park, the Eglin Reservation, and Choctawhatchee Bay. While rated one of America's top ten family vacation resorts (according to *Family Circle* magazine) and Florida's top tennis resort (according to *World Tennis Magazine*), Bluewater Bay is not your typical resort community. It is mainly populated by year-round residents, and these residents, by design, are of all ages and widely varying incomes. Among the stand-out features of Bluewater Bay are a traditional neighborhood of porch homes and picket fences; a new neighborhood of "alley homes" offering outstanding streetscapes; a beachfront devel-

Haile Plantation is just four miles southwest of the University of Florida in Gainesville, on what was once a plantation owned by (surprise) the Haile family. The plantation theme runs though the development, from the entry with its pasture land, grazing horses, and community farm plots; along the community's principal roads with their wooded buffers hiding development; to the housing stock of wood-frame porch homes surrounded by old oaks and native landscaping. Neighborhoods are given a sense of place by their small scale, distinctive layouts and housing types, buffered separation from one another, and (in some cases) central commons around which homes are arranged. Other notable features include: home designs that save energy; a signature golf course that wraps around tree stands, uses reclaimed wastewater and integrated pest management, and preserves gopher tortoise habitat along fairways; an emerging village center of shops, offices, apartments, and townhouses; and a newly acquired 500-plus acre site that is being planned along more traditional lines than the original site, that is, with a more grid-like street network, a variety of lot sizes within each neighborhood, and a central activity area within five minutes walking time of all homes.

Recreation Center in the Characteristic Style of Haile Plantation

The Hammocks is southwest of Miami, on what was once a featureless and nearly treeless agricultural site that now abounds with parks, lakes, and mature trees. Planned in the 1970s, The Hammocks has the same cellular design as the best-known new communities of its era: Columbia, Maryland, and Reston, Virginia. Diverse neighborhoods are grouped into villages, each to have its own convenience shopping center and elementary school/park combination. Of the featured developments, The Hammocks achieves by far the highest net residential densities and, consequently, is the most affordable, most socioeconomically integrated, and the most transit-friendly. Yet the community does not feel crowded thanks to pocket parks and landscaped courtyards within neighborhoods, and to a central lake and greenway system to-

Heavily Used Greenway at The Hammocks

ward which nearly all neighborhoods are oriented. A 10-mile network of internal pathways (most of which can be walked or biked without crossing a single road) is unmatched in its connections, lake views, natural surveillance, and hence high level of resident use. The Hammocks Town Center, while lacking pedestrian amenities, contains a commendable mix of uses: a community shopping center, regional library, junior high school, and fire station.

Hunter's Creek provides much-needed housing on the job-rich south side of Orlando, already home to Disney World and expected to generate an additional 10,000 jobs per year. The community has been a winner in the competitive Orlando real estate market, recording the highest dollar volume of new home sales of any master planned community. Its success is due to location, housing value, and the convenience of on-site facilities. Hunter's Creek is located at the junction of a new parkway and the newly opened Orlando beltway's southern leg, giving it easy access to the rest of the region. With respect to value, the community has a "country club" image at home prices more typical of middle-income subdivisions. In terms of convenience, only eight years into development, Hunter's Creek already has three shopping areas, three parks, and two public schools. Other distinctions include: the Orlando area's only Florida Association of Realtors' ENVY (environmental) Award; and first place awards in its category from the Mid-Florida Home Builders Association and the East Central Florida Regional Planning Council.

Country-Club Living at Subdivision Prices in Hunter's Creek

Miami Lakes is a community of fine neighborhoods, shopping areas, business parks, and recreational facilities in a not-so-fine part of the Miami metropolitan area. It has withstood the blight around it thanks to a good master plan and an ongoing commitment by the family who once ran a dairy farm on the land, then developed it, and now manage it and live there themselves. The master plan features 22 man-made lakes, with neighborhoods wrapped around them, parks and beaches along them, and scenic views across them from passing roadways. At its heart is a town center with courtyards, fountains, sidewalk cafes, apartments set above shops, corporate offices on the periphery, and a theater and four-star hotel anchoring Main Street. It is an urban and urbane place in the suburbs. Miami Lakes comes as close to being self-contained as any featured development, having more jobs than resident workers and its own public schools, public library, police and fire stations, and convenience and neighborhood shopping centers. Its design and amenities have earned the community numerous awards and citations, including write ups in such prestigious publications as *Planning*, *Builder*, and *The Atlantic Monthly*.

High Density Housing on One of 22 Lakes at Miami Lakes

Oakbridge lies on a reclaimed phosphate mine and landfill just three minutes south of Downtown Lakeland. When development began, the site's environmental problems were extreme; the landfill was on the Superfund list, and the phosphate mine, even with fill, produced radon gas at levels requiring airtight home construction. These problems had caused the site to be passed over by development and left a hole in Lakeland's urban fabric. But now, in a near-miracle of engineering and marketing, Oakbridge provides the Lakeland area with its only luxury housing for corporate executives, its nicest apartments for corporate workers, its only private equity golf course, and the likely site of its first fashion mall. In efforts to attract new industry, Oakbridge is the first stop on the Economic Development Council's tours. Oakbridge also serves as home to sandhill cranes, great blue herons, American alligators, and other species of concern in created wet-

Habitat and Scenic Beauty on a Reclaimed Phosphate Mine at Oakbridge

lands and stormwater ponds. This combination of economic development and environmental restoration won Oakbridge the 1990 award for environmental planning at the Industrial Development Research Council's World Congress.

Palmer Ranch, southeast of Sarasota, is the largest of the featured developments, with more than 5,000 acres under development and another 5,000 in reserve. Its size allows Palmer Ranch to set aside 40 percent of its acreage as open space and still have enough land for a self-contained community, complete with a planned town center and commerce park. Its forte is environmental innovation. Created wetlands at Palmer Ranch are models of successful mitigation. Oversized eagle protection zones respect

Championship Golf, Created Wetland, and Clustered Housing at Palmer Ranch

Rate-of-Return on Quality

Recently, the Urban Land Institute (ULI) attempted to quantify the dollars returned vs. dollars invested in high-quality site planning, landscaping, and amenities.[1] The conclusion: Quality creates long-term value and more than pays for itself. While our concept of quality is a little different than ULI's, our conclusion is the same.

Development activity at all sites selected as exemplary has continued for years uninterrupted and at a good pace. With two exceptions, the same master developer has been involved for the duration, this in an industry known for its bankruptcies and foreclosures. The exceptions, The Hammocks and Hunter's Creek, were owned by the same foreign corporation which sold its profitable U.S. real estate holdings. Ownership changed hands again when one corporate partner bought out the other. Both changes in ownership were prompted by strategic considerations, not financial losses.

Additional evidence of financial success includes:

- Despite a $10 million up-front investment in land reclamation, Oakbridge expects to break even about 10 years into its development program. Land that was once next-to-worthless due to its environmental problems now sells for up to $350,000/acre.

- While experiencing losses in some early years, Miami Lakes reports 20 straight years of operating profit. The family-held company has done well enough to shun outside investors and retain all of its assets except a few industrial, office, or multifamily housing parcels.

- Hunter's Creek is the most successful project in American General's portfolio of 10 large-scale developments. Since the project opened eight years ago, gross profit margins have run from 20-30% annually and housing starts have never fallen below 200 units per year.

- With 500 lots sold in 1994, Palmer Ranch accounted for 30% of the Sarasota new home market; the developer has experienced positive cash flows every year since the project opened.

- With 120 housing starts in 1994, Haile Plantation captured 14% of the Gainesville market. Figures like this are all the more impressive in light of the old rule of thumb—that a single developer is lucky to claim a 5% market share.

flight patterns and preserve perching sites. The plan for the east side of the ranch, based on a landmark environmental systems analysis, preserves 98 percent of the wetland acreage. Palmer Ranch was the first large-scale development in the state to be planned in its entirety under the *master development approval process*; the first to negotiate the sale of environmentally sensitive lands under Preservation 2000; one of the first to install dual water lines for domestic wastewater reuse; and one of the first to blend contemporary and traditional design principles in a single development, the Rivendell project. Its planning innovations have won Palmer Ranch awards from the American Planning Association and the Florida Planning and Zoning Association.

BEST OF THE OLD

The best contemporary developments do certain things very well, among them preserve natural areas and create safe environments for families. On the other hand, traditional towns seem to do some things better than even the best contemporary developments, such as handle traffic and encourage street life. We figured that valuable lessons for the design of new communities could be learned by studying the best of the old. Naturally, the focus was on physical design, for this is where traditional towns excel.

Traditional towns, while founded at different times in Florida's history, share the same basic design features that served urban America so well until the automobile came along. A whole "new"

Traditional Town—16th Century

Neo-Traditional Development— 20th Century

planning paradigm, *neo-traditionalism*, has evolved from the study of such towns.[2]

Our search for the best traditional towns focused on places that were well-established before the automobile age and have not grown into full-blown cities since then.[3] Of the dozens of towns visited, a few have all 10 traditional features enumerated in the accompanying feature box. Many more have some traditional features but not others. Several otherwise classic small towns were disqualified by state highways slicing through their centers. The highways have been widened and strip development has taken over, replacing main streets or rendering them a quaint afterthought.

A Disqualifier - State Highway Widening Through Downtown Inverness

Based upon their traditional designs, five towns were selected as exemplary: Apalachicola, Arcadia, Dade City, DeLand, and Key West. Four of the five are part of Florida's *Main Street* program for historic places. All five have designated historic districts. One was cited recently as one of *The 100 Best Small Towns in America*.[4]

The questionnaire used to study these towns is reproduced in Appendix D. The questionnaire first establishes the extent of traditional design features and then assesses how well the features work in today's auto-oriented world. Selected information about the five is presented on the following page.

Traditional Design Features[5]

(1) A well-defined edge of town.

(2) A main street lined with stores, on-street parking, and all other parking in back.

(3) Prominent public buildings and public places (town squares, village greens, etc.) that serve as focal points.

(4) Narrow streets and short blocks in a basic grid pattern.

(5) Commercial, residential, and public uses on the same streets.

(6) Housing of different types and sizes in the same blocks.

(7) Small setbacks of buildings from the street.

(8) Houses with connections (porches, stoops, walks) to the street.

(9) Accessory apartments behind homes and above shops.

(10) Alleys (at least in downtown) that permit narrow lots, small setbacks, and uninterrupted sidewalks.

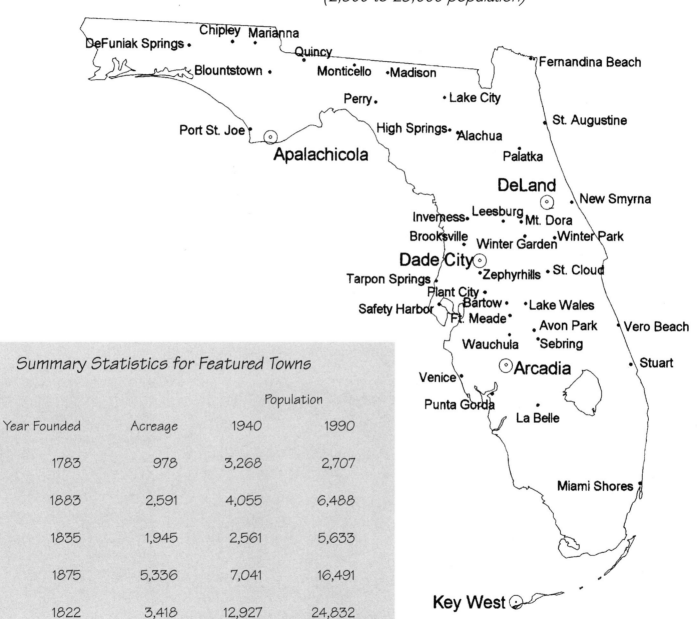

Traditional Towns Visited
(2,500 to 25,000 population)

Chipley · Marianna
DeFuniak Springs ·
Quincy
Blountstown · Monticello · Madison
Perry · · Lake City
Port St. Joe · High Springs · Alachua
Apalachicola Palatka
DeLand
Inverness · Leesburg · Mt. Dora · New Smyrna
Brooksville Winter Park
Winter Garden
Dade City · Zephyrhills · St. Cloud
Tarpon Springs
Plant City · Bartow · Lake Wales
Safety Harbor Ft. Meade · Avon Park · Vero Beach
Wauchula · Sebring
Arcadia Stuart
Venice
Punta Gorda
La Belle
Fernandina Beach
St. Augustine

Miami Shores

Key West

Summary Statistics for Featured Towns

	Year Founded	Acreage	Population 1940	Population 1990
Apalachicola	1783	978	3,268	2,707
Arcadia	1883	2,591	4,055	6,488
Dade City	1835	1,945	2,561	5,633
DeLand	1875	5,336	7,041	16,491
Key West	1822	3,418	12,927	24,832

13

TRADITIONAL DESIGN FEATURES

Well-Defined Edge - DeLand

Main Street - DeLand

Public Focal Point - Dade City

Apartment Above Shop - Key West

Home-Street Connection - Dade City

Alley for Rear Access - Key West

ENDNOTES

[1] L.W. Bookout, "Valuing Landscape, Site Planning, and Amenities," *Urban Land*, Vol. 53, November 1994, pp. 39-43.

[2] Neo-traditional developments around the United States are profiled and beautifully illustrated with photos, plans, and sketches in P. Katz, *The New Urbanism—Toward an Architecture of Community*, McGraw-Hill, New York, 1994.

[3] To qualify as "traditional," places had to have at least 2,500 residents in 1940, the threshold population for an "urban place" in the U.S. Census. To qualify as "towns," they could have no more than 25,000 population in 1990, the threshold population of a "central city" in the old U.S. Census classification scheme.

[4] The one is Arcadia, cited in N. Crampton, *The 100 Best Small Towns in America*, Prentice Hall, New York, 1993, pp. 21-23.

[5] These features are gleaned from the neo-traditional literature: A. Duany and E. Plater-Zyberk, "The Second Coming of the American Small Town," *The Wilson Quarterly*, Vol. 16, Winter 1992, pp. 19-48; A. Duany, E. Plater-Zyberk, and R. Shearer, "Zoning for Traditional Neighborhoods," *Land Development*, Vol. 5, Fall 1992, pp. 20-26; P.H. Brown, "Rootless in Urban America—Toward 'New Tradition' Communities for the 21st Century," Presented at the Annual Meeting of the Colorado Chapter, American Institute of Architects, September 1992; E. Lerner-Lam, "Neo-Traditional Neighborhood Design and Its Implications for Traffic Engineering," *ITE Journal*, Vol. 62, January 1992, pp. 17-25; L.W. Bookout, "Neotraditional Town Planning—A New Vision For the Suburbs?" *Urban Land*, Vol. 51, January 1992, pp. 20-26; and P. Calthorpe, *The Next American Metropolis—Ecology, Community and the American Dream*, Princeton Architectural Press, New York, 1993, pp. 21-24. Long after the list of traditional features was compiled, a fine book on traditional small towns (not neo-traditional but the real thing) came to our attention. While primarily concerned with small town culture and commerce, the book also describes the physical design of small towns before the automobile became common, and after it transformed small town life and physical form. J.A. Jakle, *The American Small Town—Twentieth-Century Place Images*, Archon Books, Hamden, Conn., 1982.

III. BEST LAND USE PRACTICES

Practice 1: Keep vehicle miles of travel (VMT) below the area average.

Practice 2: Contribute to the area's jobs-housing balance.

Practice 3: Mix land uses at the finest grain the market will bear and include civic uses in the mix.

Practice 4: Develop in clusters and keep the clusters small.

Practice 5: Place higher density housing near commercial centers, transit lines, and parks.

Practice 6: Phase convenience shopping and recreational opportunities to keep pace with housing.

Practice 7: Make subdivisions into neighborhoods with well-defined centers and edges.

Practice 8: Reserve school sites and donate them if necessary to attract new schools.

Practice 9: Concentrate commercial development in compact centers or districts (rather than letting it spread out in strips).

Practice 10: Make shopping centers and business parks into all-purpose activity centers.

Practice 11: Tame auto-oriented land uses, or at least separate them from pedestrian-oriented uses.

This first set of best practices offers guidance regarding both the mix of land uses and the layout of uses in relation to one another.

Our overriding goal is to arrest urban sprawl. Whatever form it takes—whether scattered, strip, or spread development—sprawl is characterized by poor accessibility and lack of common open space.[1] Here, we strive to promote *good accessibility* of workers to jobs, students to schools, transit users to transit lines, etc. Good accessibility translates into higher property values, less time wasted in travel, less auto-dependence and related air pollution and fuel consumption. A landmark study of planned communities vs. conventional suburbs found residents more satisfied with the former, and the main reason was better accessibility to daily activities outside the home.[2]

We also promote the set aside of *ample open space*. Natural areas support wildlife, enhance water quality, recharge groundwater supplies, hold stormwater, and provide views and recreational opportunities. Well-designed and well-located public spaces give otherwise monotonous subdivisions a sense of place and draw residents out of their private realms to recreate and socialize. In the aforementioned study, second only to accessibility as a source of resident satisfaction were the "trees, hills, lakes, etc." and "plenty of space."[3]

Getting Around Palm Beach County

As input to *Best Land Use Practices*, we analyzed travel patterns in Palm Beach County in relationship to land use patterns. Households in a sprawling suburb spend two-thirds more vehicle hours (VHT) per person traveling than do comparable households in a traditional city. Excess travel amounts to about 250 vehicle hours per person per year. While a staggering figure, this is still less than one might expect given the ten-fold difference in accessibility between the communities. What saves the outlying community of Wellington from inordinately high VHT per person is the large number of internal shopping and recreational trips. What keeps the sprawling community of Jupiter Farms from being an unmitigated traffic disaster is the large number of time-saving "tours" taken by residents. A tour is a string of trips completed in a single outing. Study methods, results, and policy implications are discussed in Appendix E.

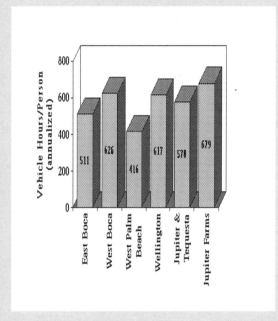

Vehicle Hours Per Person in Palm Beach County Communities
(annualized)

Practice 1: Keep vehicle miles of travel (VMT) below the area average.

Between 1983 and 1990, vehicle miles of travel (VMT) in the U.S. grew by a whopping 42 percent.[4] That is about seven times the growth of population during the same period. Sprawl has left most of us with no alternative to frequent, long-distance trips by automobile. The out-of-pocket costs are substantial; the social costs in air pollution, time delay, uninsured accidents, and parking subsidies are even higher.[5]

To arrest the VMT spiral, *Land Use Practice 1* sets an overall target for exemplary developments: At the end of each phase of development, VMT per capita should be no higher than the area average. Infill projects will have an easy time with this. Edge developments will find it a little harder, and satellite developments will find it harder still. The more remote the development, the more *self-contained* it must be to stay below the area-average VMT per capita.

Unlike many other best practices, this one cannot be administered by simply checking a master development plan or phasing program. Instead, a regional travel model must be run with and without the proposed development, and summary statistics compared. The Florida Standard Urban Transportation Model Structure (FSUTMS) is available for all urbanized and some nonurbanized areas within the state. It is routinely run by Metropolitan Planning Organizations (MPOs), cities, counties, and consulting firms. FSUTMS has been used to analyze traffic impacts of Bluewater Bay, Haile Plantation, and increments of Palmer Ranch; it is no trouble to analyze VMT impacts as well.

Even if a development performs poorly in initial runs, it may be possible to stay below the area-average VMT per capita by modifying the mix of land uses, redesigning the street network, postponing development for a number of years, or incorporating travel demand management measures into the overall plan.[6]

This first practice sets an overall target. The remaining best practices help ensure that the target is met or exceeded.

State of Regional Travel Modeling

Two limitations of FSUTMS and other conventional travel models must be acknowledged.[7] First, their estimates and forecasts are approximate, and particularly so for individual facilities or small subareas. Second, these models cannot represent micro-mixing of land uses and associated walk-bike trips. We would only note that regional travel models are the best tools available today for predicting travel impacts of large-scale developments, and that these models are constantly being upgraded.[8]

Practice 2: Contribute to the area's jobs-housing balance.

New communities often market themselves as places where people can both live and work.

It is a good selling point and a worthy goal. At the scale of a new community (thousands of acres), a jobs-housing balance becomes achievable. That is, jobs and workers can be brought into numerical balance, usually at somewhere

Before We Write Off Jobs-Housing Balance...

While the concept of jobs-housing balance has its supporters, its detractors seem to be winning the war of words.[9] To help inform the debate, journey-to-work data from the 1990 U.S. Census of Population and Housing were used to compute the proportion of work trips that remain within each of Florida's more than 500 cities, towns, and census designated places; this proportion is commonly referred to as the rate of internal capture.[10] Using regression analysis, INTERNAL CAPTURE was related to the number of jobs within a locality (INTERNAL JOBS); the number of jobs elsewhere in the same metropolitan area or nonmetropolitan county (EXTERNAL JOBS); the degree to which local jobs and working residents are numerically in balance (JOB BALANCE); and two variables relating local earnings to housing costs.[11] The resulting best-fit equation is:

$$\text{Internal Capture} = 0.35 \times \text{Internal Jobs}^{+0.21} \times \text{External Jobs}^{-0.19} \times \text{Job Balance}^{+0.28}$$

All explanatory variables enter with the expected signs and are highly significant; together, they explain 59% of the variation in rates of internal capture.[12] Internal capture increases with the number of local jobs, and declines with the number of jobs elsewhere in the same labor market. Controlling for these variables, a numerical balance of local workers and local jobs results in a significantly higher rate of internal capture.

To illustrate the use of this equation, in 1990, Miami Lakes had 13,469 jobs out of a metropolitan total of 940,397 jobs. As home to 7,631 working residents, Miami Lakes would be expected to capture 17% of all work trips internally, not too far from the actual rate of 11% (derived from the 1990 Census). The overestimate is probably due to the rise in housing costs relative to worker earnings as Miami Lakes has become a "choice" place to live.

between 1.3 and 1.7 jobs per household; and housing prices can at least somewhat match worker incomes.[13] The most successful new communities manage to capture upwards of a third of all work trips internally.[14]

For smaller-scale projects, it becomes less practical to match jobs and housing, and even when a nominal match is achieved, a smaller proportion of work trips will likely remain on-site. Thus, this best practice emphasizes jobs-housing balance in the larger subregion of which a project is a part, rather than striving for balance within each and every project.

Geographers speak of an "indifference region" around work places. Workers are equally happy living anywhere within this area, but are inclined to move closer to their work places if they live at greater distances. By various estimates, such areas range from three to 20 miles in extent.[15] Absent a consensus, it seems safest to assume a small indifference region and strive for a jobs-housing balance within say, a three-to-five mile area around a development site.[16] Any development that helps bring jobs and housing into better balance within such an area should reduce average commute lengths, thereby reducing VMT.[17]

Hunter's Creek was selected as exemplary over other planned communities in the Orlando area because it supplies middle-income housing on the "side of town" with a surplus of middle-income jobs.

Hunter's Creek in Relation to Disney and Other Employment Centers

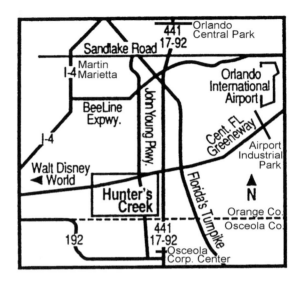

Marketing to Moderate and Upper Incomes at Hunter's Creek

Low $100's

High $300's

Practice 3: Mix land uses at the finest grain the market will bear and include civic uses in the mix.

For 20 years now, in one publication after another, the Urban Land Institute (representing the development industry) and National Association of Home Builders have proclaimed the advantages of mixed-use development.[18] One advantage is the ability to capture some trips that would otherwise end up on external roads.[19] Another is the relative freedom afforded those who cannot drive when destinations are within walking distance.[20] Additional benefits include: a positive fiscal impact on local governments when commercial development is part of the mix;[21] a positive impact on residential property values when commercial and civic uses are close by (though not next door);[22] greater street security when people are coming and going at all hours, as they do in mixed-use developments;[23] and a greater sense of community when commercial and civic uses are mixed in with residential and when public places exist for residents to have casual social contact.[24]

All contemporary developments featured in this document have at least some commercial uses as well as residential and recreational. This, perhaps more than anything else, is what makes them "exemplary." Mixed-use development is rare in Florida, as we discovered in our survey of county planning departments.

Contributions to Sense of Community

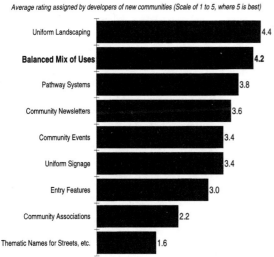

Average rating assigned by developers of new communities (Scale of 1 to 5, where 5 is best)

Uniform Landscaping	4.4
Balanced Mix of Uses	**4.2**
Pathway Systems	3.8
Community Newsletters	3.6
Community Events	3.4
Uniform Signage	3.4
Entry Features	3.0
Community Associations	2.2
Thematic Names for Streets, etc.	1.6

Source: R. Ewing, *Developing Successful New Communities*, Urban Land Institute, Washington, D. C., 1991, p. 66.

Planned Land Uses in Contemporary Developments (% of total acres)

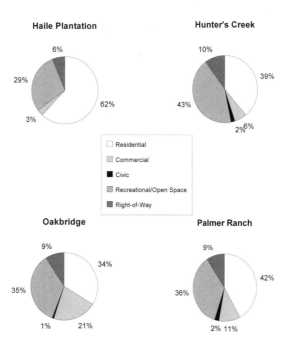

Existing Land Uses in Traditional Towns (% of total acres)

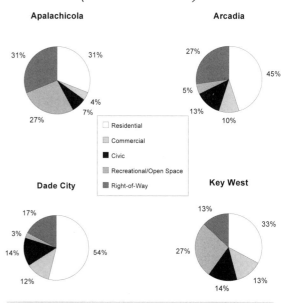

Projected Internal Capture Rates

(% of daily vehicle trips remaining within the development at build-out)

Haile Plantation	16%
Hunter's Creek	25
Oakbridge	13
Palmer Ranch	28

Sources: For all but Hunter's Creek, values are taken from their respective Applications for Development Approval or Notices of Proposed Change to DRIs. The internal capture rate for Hunter's Creek comes from Kimley-Horn and Associates, Inc., *Traffic Distribution Analysis - Hunter's Creek*, Orlando, FL, 1991.

Yet, even these exemplary developments fall short of traditional towns in a couple respects. First, they have few schools, churches, libraries, and other civic uses compared to traditional towns (see pie charts on previous page). Miami Lakes has the best assortment of such uses, and not coincidentally, feels most like a "real town." Civic uses are the glue that binds a community together; they should be sought after by contemporary developers.

Second, contemporary developments have relatively coarse (large-grained) patterns of land use that limit walkability. Traditional towns integrate land uses at the scale of the block, lot, or even individual building. Grand houses sit next to humble ones. Rental units, in the form of backyard cottages or garage apartments, co-exist with single-family houses. Individual businesses, and not just those serving the immediate neighborhood, are nestled in among homes. Churches and schools are located within neighborhoods. Different land uses interface "seamlessly." From our surveys of traditional towns, these arrangements work well in context.[25]

Nonresidential Uses in Miami Lakes

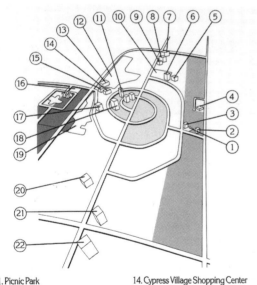

1. Picnic Park
2. Police
3. Lake Katherine Shopping Center
4. Miami Lakes Technical Education Center
5. Miami Lakes Montessori School
6. Miami Lakes Junior High School
7. Fire Station
8. Library
9. Windmill Gate Shopping Center
10. School Park
11. Main Street Shopping
12. Championship 18-hole Golf Course
13. Miami Lakes Golf Resort
14. Cypress Village Shopping Center
15. Miami Lakes Community Center
16. 10-Acre Park
17. Miami Lakes Athletic Club
18. Miami Lakes Inn
19. Lighted Executive Golf Course
20. Miami Lakes Elementary School
21. Lake Patricia Shopping Center
22. Hialeah/Miami Lakes High School

■ Miami Lakes Business Park East
■ Miami Lakes Business Park West
□ Town Center

Fine-Grained Development in Apalachicola

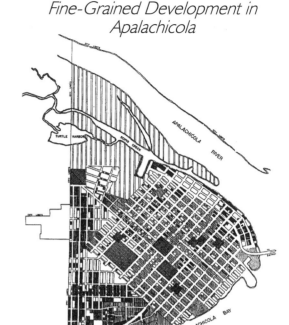

Example of Mixed Uses in Apalachicola

Whether the contemporary market is ready for such a fine-grained mix of uses is anyone's guess.[26] But the market is clearly receptive to a finer mix than normally found in the suburbs. Miami Lakes has five convenience centers dispersed among its neighborhoods. It has a mixed-use town center with apartments above shops and offices, a hotel, and a movie theater sprinkled in. Haile Plantation has small clusters of townhouses, patio homes, and custom homes, all within a five-minute walk of the Haile Village Center. The plan for the Village Center includes apartments and shops back-to-back. At the relatively fine grain of these developments, different land uses do not overwhelm each other and can easily be buffered or made architecturally compatible.[27]

Small Clusters at Haile Plantation

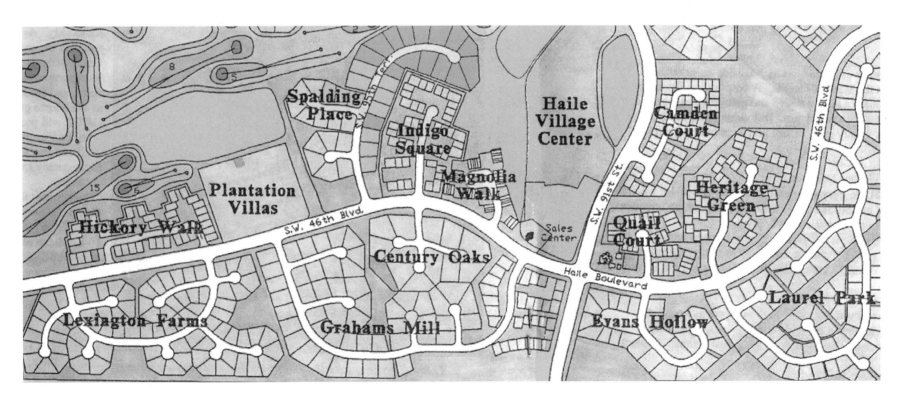

Rivendell at Palmer Ranch

When it comes to mixing land uses, the state-of-the-art may be Rivendell at Palmer Ranch. Often described as neo-traditional, the project is, in fact, more of a hybrid. It will have clusters of apartments, townhouses, "village homes," and quarter-acre detached homes, adjacent to one another or separated by narrow buffers. The clusters will be organized around a curvi-linear street system of loops and occasional cul-de-sacs. A village center will feature a restaurant/bed and breakfast, community center, library, and child care center. All of this will be contained on a site of only 380 acres.

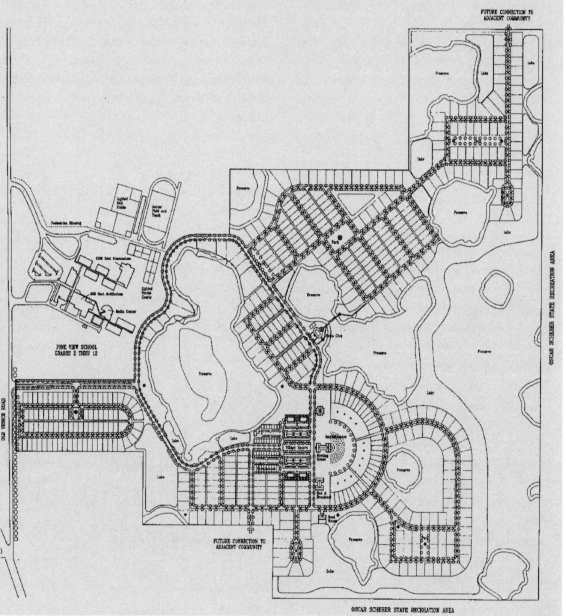

Practice 4: Develop in clusters and keep the clusters small.

For as long as ULI and NAHB have promoted mixed-use development, they have also championed cluster development.[28] The two go hand-in-hand. Cluster development provides natural separations between land uses that would otherwise be incompatible (see accompanying figure). The result may not be the "seamless" development advocated by neo-traditional planners, but it can be sufficiently fine-grained for walkability.

Cluster developments are built at *gross densities* comparable to conventional developments, but leave more open space by reducing lot sizes. This saves money by limiting site clearing and grading to certain areas, reducing the lineal feet of residential streets and utilities, and permitting the use of swales in lieu of costly curbs and gutters, inlets, and underground storm sewers.[29] Air conditioning loads are moderated by retained green spaces, stormwater runoff volumes are moderated by permeable surfaces, and landscape irrigation requirements are moderated by smaller lots and lawns.[30] Valuable natural fea-

tures can be preserved. Opportunities are created for separate and contrasting neighborhood identities.

In addition, open spaces enhance the value of developable lands around them, allowing cluster to command a premium in the residential real estate market.[31] Designed as public spaces, they provide a setting for planned and casual interactions among neighbors, contributing to the sense of neighborliness and community.[32]

Yet, inexplicably, true cluster development is hard to find in Florida. There are small-lot subdivisions that lack the dedicated open spaces characteristic of cluster. There are large-lot subdivisions that have open spaces in the form of wetlands or golf courses. But where are the intimate neighborhoods with central commons? And where are the compact developments with uplands running through them or wrapping around them?

As with mixed use, cluster development patterns can be fine- or coarse-grained. A fine-grained pattern is preferred for several reasons. Small housing clusters look less like "projects" and more like places.[33] Small housing clusters are safer than large ones because residents can identify "outsiders" and are more apt to exercise territorial control.[34] Small increments of development minimize carrying costs and risks associated with economic downturn; developers and builders can learn from small rather than big mistakes.[35]

Natural Separation of Clusters at Palmer Ranch

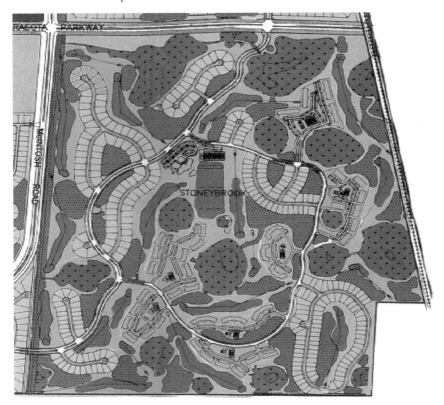

At The Hammocks, all single-family housing has been built under cluster zoning. This has meant that green spaces could be incorpo-

Greenway Down the Middle of The Hammocks

Housing Clusters Separated by Woods and Fairways at Haile Plantation

rated into neighborhoods and a splendid greenway system could be maintained between the neighborhoods and lakes. The Hammocks achieves an average net residential density of 11.5 units per acre, twice its gross density.

Neighborhood Built Around Landscaped Courtyards at The Hammocks

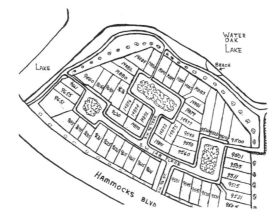

Homes on a Green at Haile Plantation

At Haile Plantation, cluster is an option for all single-family subdivisions. Gross density is limited to three units per acre regardless, but lots can be either 8,500 square feet or 3,500 square foot, the latter with offsetting common areas. The cluster option has been exercised liberally, which has allowed the community to retain wooded buffers between its clusters. Haile achieves an average net residential density of 4.0 units per acre, almost twice its gross density.

Both The Hammocks and Haile Plantation have relatively small housing clusters in fine-grained patterns. Both benefit from good neighborhood identity and sense of place (see feature box).

How Small Is a "Small" Housing Cluster?

The size of housing clusters varies considerably among featured developments. Compare average acreages and dwelling unit counts for single-family detached home clusters (where clusters are defined by common access roads and common lot sizes).

	Average Acreage	Average Unit Count
Haile Plantation	27	46
Hammocks	14	86
Hunter's Creek	49	158

Villages of Harden Park

When it comes to cluster development, state-of-the-art may be the Villages of Harden Park at Oakbridge. The development will cluster housing and use various government incentives to keep single-family home prices below $70,000, townhouse prices below $50,000, and apartment rents below market. To minimize site development costs, over two-thirds of the site will remain as park or common open space. The project may fall victim to competing uses for the same site, but if it survives, it will be an interesting one to watch.

Conceptual Plan for Harden Park

Practice 5: Place higher density and senior housing near commercial centers, transit lines, and community facilities.

In a mixed-use development, we must decide how uses will be arranged in relation to each other. Euclidian zoning emphasizes separation of incompatible uses. Compatibility is not much of an issue, though, in the absence of heavy industry and big-box retail. Other uses can be made compatible by developing in small clusters and applying blanket design controls.[36]

With design controls in place, the overriding consideration in land planning becomes *accessibility*. It is well-established that auto ownership declines as residential densities rise.[37] The willingness to walk, bike, or ride transit thus increases with density. By placing higher density and senior housing near commercial centers, transit lines, and community facilities, we provide travel opportunities for the least mobile residents.

We also, indirectly, make housing more affordable. As leading neo-traditionalists say, the best affordable housing program is one that eliminates the need for a second car. Back in 1988, it was estimated that owning and operating a second car cost about $3,000 per year, or $1,750 net of transit fares. With the savings from shedding a car, the typical household at that time could afford $14,000 more in a home mortgage.[38] A more recent, though less rigorous, estimate of the net savings through car shedding is $3,000; a household with a "one car mort-

gage" has an additional $25,000 in home buying power.[39]

Following this practice, small commercial centers—which have trouble competing for automobile traffic—suddenly become viable because pedestrian traffic always favors nearby stores.[40] This is why corner stores can thrive in cities but not in low-density, auto-dependent suburbs; in the suburbs, auto users pass by small stores for better prices and variety at distant, larger stores and centers. That is not all bad, of course, but it does generate more travel than necessary.[41]

Bus service—which is predominately accessed on foot—also becomes viable when higher density and senior housing are placed within easy walking distance of stops. Transit-oriented development manuals recommend that density gradients be established along transit lines, with higher densities located adjacent to arterials or collectors along which buses operate.[42]

Walking distances for different trip purposes have been estimated with data from the *Nationwide Personal Transportation Survey*. The following figures display both frequency distributions and median walking distances. They can be used to delineate areas around commercial centers, transit stops, and community facilities that would be most suitable for higher density and senior housing.

Density Gradient Along a Transit Route

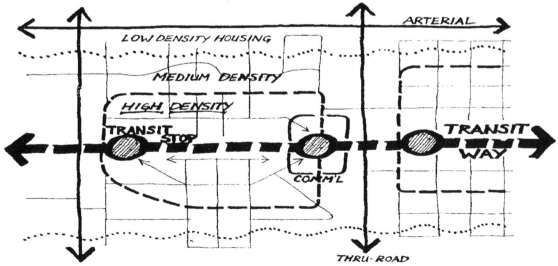

Source: H. Rabinowitz and E. Beimborn, *The New Suburb*, Technology Sharing Program, U.S. Department of Transportation, Washington, D.C., 1991, cover graphic.

Walking Distances for Different Purposes

Shopping Trips

Median Trip Length= .30 Miles

Number of Trips

Distance in Miles

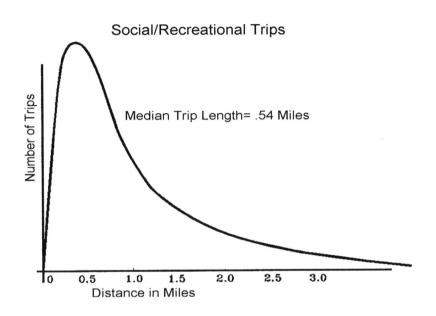

Social/Recreational Trips

Median Trip Length= .54 Miles

Number of Trips

Distance in Miles

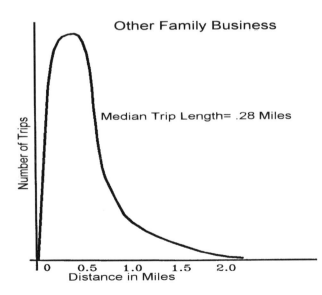

Other Family Business

Median Trip Length= .28 Miles

Number of Trips

Distance in Miles

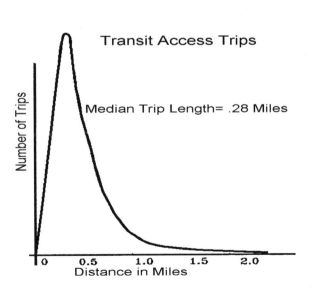

Transit Access Trips

Median Trip Length= .28 Miles

Number of Trips

Distance in Miles

Source: Tabulations from the 1990 Nationwide Personal Transportation Survey (NPTS). Walking distances were estimated from reported travel times, assuming everyone walked at the NPTS average speed of 3.16 mph. Curves were smoothed to account for people's tendency to round off travel times.

The Hammocks, Hunter's Creek, and Miami Lakes have placed their highest densities around their town centers. Palmer Ranch has its multifamily and senior housing across from a regional mall. Rivendell at Palmer Ranch will have a "step down" density pattern moving outward from the village center; its lowest densities will buffer existing low-density neighborhoods north of the development site and a state park east and south of the site.

Practice 6: Phase commercial and recreational facilities to keep pace with housing.

In their literature and advertising, developers play up the availability of on-site commercial and recreational facilities. They know that these are valued amenities that translate into land and home sales.

They also translate into less external travel by residents. Our own analysis of Palm Beach County travel data says as much; on-site shopping and recreation save Wellington from inordinately high vehicle hours of travel (Appendix E). Another recent analysis, this one in the San Francisco Bay Area, showed that person-miles of travel for shopping purposes are 42 percent higher in areas with poor accessibility to shopping compared to those with good accessibility.[43]

This is not to suggest that residents always shop at the closest supermarket or play at the closest tennis courts. They do not. Accessibility is only one factor in the choice of destination, and some destinations are poor substitutes for others of the same type. Supermarkets, for example, are less substitutable than convenience stores due to greater price and quality differences and larger purchases made on individual shopping trips. Still, on average, the closer the trip attractions are, the shorter trips will be.[44]

Commercial and recreational facilities should be introduced as early as possible in the development process, and thereafter phased to keep pace with residential development. Large developments are built in phases or increments anyway, subject to a master development plan. Oakbridge has three phases, Hunter's Creek has five. Phases or increments can be structured such that facilities are provided when market or service thresholds are reached.

"Step Down" Density Pattern of Rivendell at Palmer Ranch

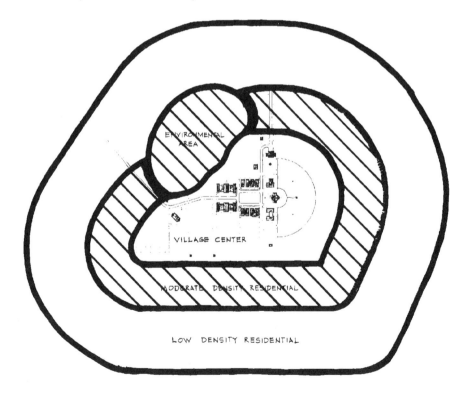

ENVIRONMENTAL AREA

VILLAGE CENTER

MODERATE DENSITY RESIDENTIAL

LOW DENSITY RESIDENTIAL

One of 3 Shopping Centers

One of 3 Parks

One of 2 Schools

Shopping Centers vs. Population in 58 New Communities

To check national benchmark figures, the number of shopping centers in each of 58 new communities surveyed for *Developing Successful New Communities* was related to the number of residents. From the resulting equations, we would expect the first shopping center to open when a community reaches just over 4,000 residents, and the first supermarket-anchored center to open at just under 10,000 residents. One variable alone, resident population, explains 90% of the variation in the number of supermarket-anchored centers across communities, and 70% of the variation in centers of all types. Of course, these equations assume a sort of static equilibrium in which the number of shopping centers supplied at a given time equals the number demanded by the resident population.

Population thresholds for different commercial and recreational facilities are set forth in the national literature or can be easily estimated from the national literature (see accompanying table). These are only benchmark figures, of course, meant to illustrate an approach. For any particular facility, demand will depend on conditions within the trade or service area.

Minimum Population Requirements[45]

Supermarket	6,500
Dry Cleaner	5,700
Video Rental	11,400
Beauty Salon	3,700
Book Store	22,400
Laundromat	5,800
Movie Theater	29,000
Tennis Courts	2,000 (per court)
Neighborhood Park	5,000
Public Swimming Pool	20,000

Sources: Derived from Urban Land Institute (ULI), *Dollars & Cents of Shopping Centers: 1993—A Study of Receipts and Expenses in Shopping Center Operations*, Washington, D.C., 1993; and R.A. Lancaster (ed.), *Recreation, Park and Open Space Standards and Guidelines*, National Recreation and Park Association, 1983, Alexandria, Va., pp. 55-60.

Practice 7: Make subdivisions into neighborhoods with well-defined centers and edges.

Suburban subdivisions are given colorful names, entry features, and distinctive landscaping and architecture in an effort to create neighborhood identity. Yet, lamentably, there is nothing neighborly about many of them. Neighbors have no need to interact and do not interact much. Their time is spent indoors. Neighborhood parks lie outside neighborhoods, serving several neighborhoods at driving distances. Neighborhood shops have been replaced by strip centers, neighborhood schools by district schools, neighborhood churches by regional churches, specialized by sect serving scattered congregations. Homes have become staging areas for activities at remote locations.

Most writings on neighborhood design harken back to Clarence Perry's brainchild, the *neighborhood unit*. For Perry and his successors, neighborhoods are conceived as fairly large areas (a half mile across, in Perry's scheme), with common facilities at their heart, internal streets for local traffic, external streets for through-traffic, and a variety of open spaces.[46]

We adopt the sociologist's more limited view of neighborhoods as small, usually homogeneous units, defined by physical features and social networks.[47] What makes the typical suburban subdivision something less than a neighborhood, in this sense, is the lack of a well-defined *center* and *edge*, and at the center, a *common area* within which neighbors can casually interact.[48] The center/commons may take the form of a pocket park, plaza, playground, tot lot, or recreation center. It does not matter what form it takes as long as the center/commons fits the population it is intended to serve.

Miami Lakes reportedly has more pocket parks per 1,000 population than any other community in the state. Every neighborhood has at least one, some have several. Other featured developments have central greens or pocket parks within certain neighborhoods to give them special character.

These greens and parks vary in quality. Some are more accessible, secure, comfortable, and interesting than others, and hence more heavily utilized. Even in a single community, such as Miami Lakes, some pocket parks are the focal points of their neighborhoods and have connections to the larger open space system of lakes; other pocket parks feel like leftover spaces. Rates of utilization seem to vary accordingly.

Neighborhoods also need well-defined edges, so people can perceive where one neighborhood ends and the next begins. Even the mention of edges may seem gratuitous, in that suburban subdivisions are often bounded by walls, lakes, or other physical barriers. If anything, their edges are too "hard" for good interplay with other parts of mixed-use developments. Symbolic barriers would suffice nicely in many cases where physical barriers are erected instead.

Pocket Parks as Focal Points at Miami Lakes

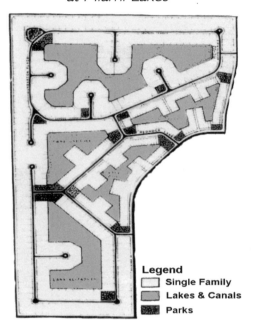

Legend
☐ **Single Family**
▨ **Lakes & Canals**
▩ **Parks**

Pocket Parks as Leftover Spaces at Miami Lakes

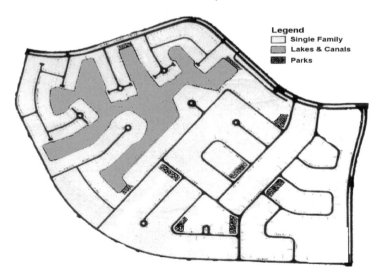

Legend
☐ **Single Family**
▨ **Lakes & Canals**
▩ **Parks**

However, in our frame of reference, a neighborhood is not always coincident with a subdivision. If development is fine-grained, as recommended in *Land Use Practice 3*, a subdivision may have several distinct neighborhoods with different housing types, landscape treatments, street layouts, etc. It is important that these neighborhoods have edges, too.

Without walling off a neighborhood, access can be subtly restricted by interrupting the street network at strategic points along the boundary. One source recommends that at least half of the streets at the boundary be so interrupted.[61] The remaining access points come to have special significance as gateways to the neighborhood. A common area may be placed at the interface between neighborhoods to both buffer and unify neighborhoods (unify where the common area is a park or other gathering place).

All featured developments create neighborhood identity by subtly or not-so-subtly restricting access. Miami Lakes, with its many short street sections ending at T-intersections, is the subtlest. Haile Plantation, with nearly all houses on cul-de-sacs and tree screens between neighborhoods, is probably the least subtle. For more on street network design, see *Transportation Practice 1*.

It has become common in neo-traditional plans to use alleys for separation between different housing types. In these plans, neighborhood identity is achieved without restricting access, simply by having like-properties face each other and unlike-properties back up to each other. It is an interesting approach that can be extended to different land uses in mixed-use developments.

Tree Screen Separating
Neighborhoods at Haile Plantation

Street Separating Single- and
Multifamily Neighborhoods
at Miami Lakes

Neo-Traditional Plan Using Alleys for Separation

High-Quality Public Spaces

The quality of neighborhood open space is more important than the quantity. Area-to-population requirements (e.g., 1.5 acres per 1,000 population) have tended to "dumb down" park planning.[49] Parks and other common areas need not take up much space, nor cost developers many lot sales. People actually prefer small, efficient spaces to large ones that seem underutilized.[50]

Among the important "quality" features of neighborhood public spaces are accessibility, visibility, safety, comfort, complexity, and linkage.[51] Neighborhood public spaces should be physically accessible to all—according to the experts, within about three minutes walking distance, or 750 feet of all residents. Use of small neighborhood parks begins to drop off at 200 to 400 feet and is minimal beyond 750 feet.[52]

Public spaces should be bordered by buildings, preferably with building entrances and windows facing them for natural surveillance.[53] Sight lines are important—if people cannot see common areas, or if they perceive them as leftover spaces, they will not use them. Having local streets converge on common areas solves this problem. "When there is good pedestrian and visual access...use does not drop off abruptly as distance increases."[54]

Public spaces should offer comfortable microclimates (both sun and shade) and comfortable seating arrangements (both gregarious and solitary).[55] They should be bounded spaces with definite shape, as many activity areas crammed into them as possible, and replete with sensuous elements (trees, water, sculpture, gentle slopes, and decorative pavements).[56] Whether hard architectural spaces or soft natural spaces, they appear more place-like when they contrast with their surroundings—soft on hard, formal amidst informal, etc.[57]

Play areas should be designed for challenge and novelty.[58] Conventional play areas, with their fixed and isolated play equipment, are less engaging for children than are "adventure" play areas that provide opportunities for choice, manipulation, learning, and linked play.[59]

Insofar as possible, public spaces should have direct physical and visual connections to one another. When such connections are made, the whole becomes greater than the sum of the parts, and utilization rates rise.[60] This is a fundamental principle of urban design that has been lost to contemporary developers, whose public spaces are isolated and inward-oriented.[61] One significant exception is The Hammocks, whose network of interrconnected pocket parks, greenways, and lakes generates exceptionally high rates of utilization.

CENTRAL GREENS AND POCKET PARKS IN NEIGHBORHOODS OF EXEMPLARY DEVELOPMENTS

Bluewater Bay

Haile Plantation

Practice 8: Reserve school sites and donate them if necessary to attract new schools.

This is a follow-up to *Land Use Practice 3*, which calls for civic uses as part of the mix in exemplary developments. Neighborhood schools are the principal civic institutions in communities lacking their own governments (that is, communities not incorporated as towns).[62]

In the face of declining enrollments, the trend over the past 20 years has been toward school consolidation. Neighborhood schools have gone the way of corner stores. The trend may be reversing itself, however, as it becomes apparent that links between schools and neighborhoods are beneficial to both.

Neighborhood schools provide a more supportive learning environment than do larger schools, with correspondingly higher student achievement scores and higher rates of participation in school activities.[63] They give neighborhoods an identity and cohesiveness that housing and recreational facilities alone cannot.[64] They raise property values, except in the immediate vicinity of school grounds.[65] They allow students to walk to school, to the benefit of parents and school districts alike.[66]

Walking is the preferred mode of travel when homes are within a quarter mile of

Effect of Distance on Mode of Travel to School

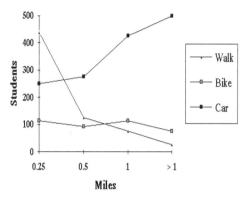

Source: E. M. Starnes et al., *Home-to-School Transportation Study-Executive Summary*, Department of Urban and Regional Planning, University of Florida, Gainesville, 1992, p. 8.

schools; walking and biking together are about as common as auto trips at a distance of a half mile.[67] Beyond that, the automobile and school bus dominate.

Miami Lakes has an elementary school and junior high; the community pioneered the now-common practice of shared parks/playgrounds, the school claiming them during the day and the community on evenings and weekends. The Hammocks has elementary schools in two of three villages and a junior high in the Town Center. Hunter's Creek and Bluewater Bay also have schools, and Haile Plantation will have one on its newly acquired land. The fleets of bicycles parked outside these schools, in this day and age, testify to the power of neighborhood schools as a determinant of students' travel choices.

Shared Park/Playground at The Hammocks

Bicycle Fleet Outside Bluewater Bay Elementary

36

After consultation with school authorities, school sites should be designated in the master plan and set aside for later sale or donation to the school district. While a sale may be preferable, donation is good, too. Where school impact fees are charged, the value of the donated sites must (by law) be credited against the fees.

The Hammocks, Hunter's Creek, and Palmer Ranch have all donated their school sites, while Bluewater Bay, Haile Plantation, and Miami Lakes sold theirs. Hunter's Creek has a credit against its school impact fees to be drawn down as building permits are issued. All six communities have or will have amenity packages that their smaller competitors cannot match.

Practice 9: Concentrate commercial development in compact centers or districts (rather than letting it spread out in strips).

Highway strip development is on everyone's list of undesirables. It is a type of "sprawl" explicitly discouraged by Florida's local comprehensive planning rule (Chapter 9J-5, Florida Administrative Code). It is also discouraged by Florida's strong highway access management rule (Chapter 14-97, Florida Administrative Code). Many of the businesses now located in strips or strip centers could just as well be in compact centers or districts, and public purposes would be better served.[68]

When asked, both planners and consumers by wide margins prefer shopping centers to commercial strips.[69] Aesthetics and shopping experience are only part of the reason. Scattered establishments along a strip disrupt through-traffic, compromising capacity and safety, as cars pull in and out of individual driveways.[70] If driveways are very close together (within 150 to 300 feet), drivers may face "overlapping conflicts" from cars accelerating out of one driveway and decelerating into the next. These same driveways and turn movements make it unpleasant and dangerous for pedestrians on the sidewalk system.[71]

Schools as a Marketing Point at Hunter's Creek

Extra Street Capacity with Access Management

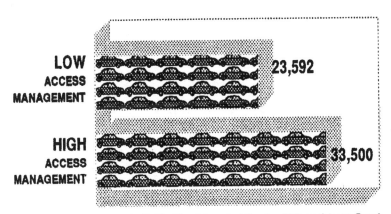

LOW ACCESS MANAGEMENT — 23,592

HIGH ACCESS MANAGEMENT — 33,500

Maximum Daily Traffic at Level of Service "D" on 4-Lane Road

Source: Florida Department of Transportation (FDOT), *Access Management—An Important Traffic Management Strategy*, Tallahassee, Fla., undated, p. 3.

Stores along a strip are usually too far apart to permit one-stop shopping and, in any case, have no functional relationship to one another (in contrast to stores in a center).[72] Scattered establishments along a strip may invite crime, or so it has been alleged. When establishments are concentrated in centers, storeowners and their customers can look out for one another.[73]

A refinement of this practice would limit highway-oriented commercial development to one side of the road—facing parks, offices, apartments, or other less intense traffic generators. One-sided commercial development eliminates conflicting crossover traffic. It reduces the need for median openings and intersections. It spreads traffic more evenly throughout the day since different uses have different peaking patterns.

The contemporary developments selected as exemplary have, with minor exceptions, escaped strip development. Nearly all commercial uses are placed in centers and access to them is strictly controlled by means of planted medians to restrict turning movements, widely spaced median openings, and relatively few driveways. Town Center at Hunter's Creek is limited to one right-in/right-out driveway off John Young Parkway; the driveway is 660 feet from the closest intersection, and the first median break is 660 feet further on. Oakbridge Center is also limited to one driveway off its principal road, this one 800 feet from the closest intersection. Bluewater Bay, The Hammocks, and Haile Plantation have, in addition, limited commercial development to one side of their principal roads.

One-Sided Commercial Development at Bluewater Bay

Only Entrance to Oakbridge Center from Harden Boulevard

Practice 10: Make shopping centers and business parks into all-purpose activity centers.

There is a growing consensus that what ails suburban shopping centers and business parks can be cured by enriching the mix of uses and designing them with the pedestrian amenities of downtown or main street.[74] The advantages of all-purpose centers are manifold:

- **Enlivenment of outdoor spaces.** Mixing uses animates centers and parks by generating pedestrian movement among buildings. In monolithic business parks, there is little interaction among occupants of different buildings; consequently, buildings are usually oriented toward parking areas rather than each other and pedestrian connections are foregone entirely.[75] Add other land uses and pedestrians suddenly have some place to go and some reason to go there.

- **Consolidation of trips.** By mixing uses, multipurpose *tours* are converted into multipurpose *trips*. At shopping centers, even a narrow range of uses can eliminate 25 percent of the trips shoppers would have made going to separate destinations.[76] At business parks, on-site services and shopping can eliminate 20 percent of the vehicle miles traveled by office workers.[77] The uses that belong in suburban activity centers are the same ones commonly linked to shopping and work trips on multipurpose tours. A business park, for example, should always offer on-site dining and banking facilities.

- **Encouragement of alternative modes.** Mixing uses encourages commuters to carpool, vanpool, or use transit (if available) since they have less need for a car to run errands. In commuter surveys, one of the main reasons cited for driving alone is the need to make stops or side trips. The proportion of workers carpooling to suburban employment centers rises when retail uses are mixed in.[78]

- **Moderation of peak demand.** Mixing uses spreads traffic on fronting roads more evenly throughout the day. It may cut parking requirements by up to 50 percent since hourly patterns of utilization are very different for, say, offices, restaurants, and cinemas in the same centers.[79] Land development codes should permit a corresponding reduction in off-street parking, something almost unheard of in Florida.[80]

All these public benefits are coupled with financial advantages for the developer. Mixing of uses enhances property values within centers, leads to faster land absorp-

Shared Retail/Restaurant Parking Economies

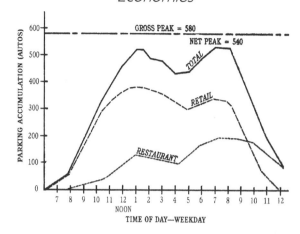

Source: Barton-Aschman Associates, Inc., *Shared Parking*, Urban Land Institute, Washington, D.C., 1983, p. 38.

Activities Linked to Work Trips in Palm Beach County

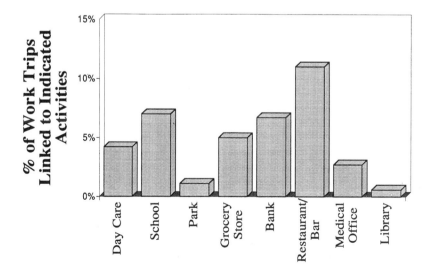

Source: Derived from the Palm Beach County Household Travel Survey, 1991.

Activities Linked to Shopping Trips in Palm Beach County

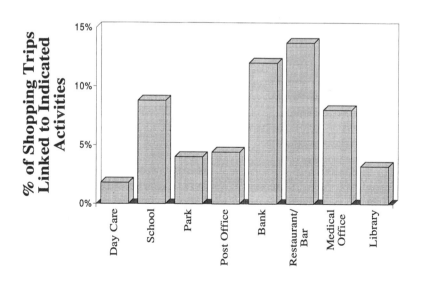

Source: Derived from the Palm Beach County Household Travel Survey, 1991.

tion, and produces operating economies of up to 20 percent.[81]

Among our exemplary developments, Miami Lakes offers the best examples of multi-purpose activity centers. The European-style Town Center combines retail, office, recreational, and residential uses; apartments sit atop shops, and a hotel and cineplex theater anchor the ends of Main Street. Cross parking easements keep total parking requirements to a minimum. Miami Lakes' Business Park East has a convenience shopping center, while Business Park West has a day care center. One of Miami Lakes' convenience shopping centers shares parking with the Miami Lakes Community Center; another, a four-sided center, devotes space on the back side to medical offices. What makes such arrangements possible is the very different visibility requirements of different uses.[82]

Other examples of multi-purpose centers include: Haile Village Center, with shops, professional offices, a day care center, a sheriff's substation, apartments, and townhouses; The Hammocks Town Center, which combines a community shopping center with a regional library, junior high school, and fire station; and Bluewater Bay's Merchants Walk and Marketplace, side-by-side centers that are beginning to approach main street DeLand in the range (if not number) of activities available.

Apartments, Shops, and a Theater in Miami Lakes Town Center

Day Care Center in Miami Lakes Business Park West

FOUR-SIDED CONVENIENCE CENTER AT MIAMI LAKES

Front

Back

Activities in Bluewater Bay's Merchants Walk/Marketplace

Retail	Services	Other
supermarket	banks (3)	post office
gas station/	day care center	business offices (17)
convenience	drycleaner	architect
store	travel agent	artist studio
restaurants (4)	realtors (3)	
florist	fitness center	
video rental	beauty salon	
gourmet food store	accountants (2)	
sports equipment	insurance/	
coin shop	financial services (2)	
gift shop	title companies (2)	
	doctors' offices (6)	
	dental offices (2)	
	optometrist	
	chiropractic office	
	orthopedic clinic	
	veterinarian	

Activities on DeLand's Main Street

Retail	Services	Other
supermarket	tailor	movie theater
restaurants (7)	printer	business offices (6)
bar	copy service	government offices (2)
florist/gift shops (4)	shoe repair (2)	newspaper offices (2)
video rental	photo studios (2)	non-profit
gourmet food store	dance studio	organizations (3)
kitchen appliances	fitness centers (2)	apartment buildings (2)
computer sales	beauty salon (2)	architect
clothing stores (11)	lawyers (5)	artist studio
jewelers (2)	realtors (2)	
bicycle shop	accountant	
book stores (4)	financial services (3)	
auto service center	insurance agents (4)	
auto parts/	family counselors (2)	
accessories (2)		
shoe stores (2)		
antiques (2)		
music stores (2)		
furniture/		
paint stores (4)		

Practice 11: Tame auto-oriented land uses, or at least separate them from pedestrian-oriented uses.

In an effort to preserve its small town character, Apalachicola has resisted the advances of drive-through restaurant chains and discount superstores. The community seems to do just fine without them. Most communities are not so discriminating. Even so, when they allow such uses in, it should be on the community's terms rather than the restaurant's or superstore's.

Some auto-oriented uses can be redesigned to be pedestrian-friendly. We have all seen fast-food restaurants and convenience stores that blend into traditional settings; small setbacks, parking behind buildings, wall-mounted signs, and compatible architecture make them almost indistinguishable from neighboring shops.

Other auto-oriented uses—discount department stores, warehouse clubs, and home improvement centers—have building masses and parking requirements that are plainly incompatible with the pedestrian. Communities have won concessions when they were willing to turn away these uses. Big-box retailers have agreed to one or more of the following: less square footage, smaller signs, more landscaping, more interest-ing architecture, more varied building materials, and shopping center sites rather than stand-alones.[83] But even at their best, superstores remain big boxes in a sea of asphalt. They must be relegated to locations where they will do the least harm to the community fabric.[84]

Both approaches are found in the best traditional towns. A fast-food restaurant in Key West conforms to the main street milieu. A major discount store in Arcadia is located outside town where, at least, it does not break up main street (though it unquestionably hurts main street businesses).

SUBDUED AUTO-ORIENTED USES ON MAIN STREET

DeLand

Key West

New Smyrna

In this regard, some exemplary developments have fared well and others have not. Miami Lakes' Town Center is truly pedestrian-oriented, and Haile Plantation's Village Center is becoming so. Miami Lakes' convenience centers have more sign control, more landscaping, more interrelation of buildings, and less dominant parking areas than typical of shopping centers. So does Merchants Walk at Bluewater Bay. But other exemplary developments have standard suburban shopping centers anchored by supermarkets and/or discount superstores that scream "access only by automobile."

The same principle applies to office and industrial uses. They should be tamed if possible, or otherwise relegated to harmless locations. A campus-style office or industrial park, while much more attractive than a commercial strip, is no less disruptive to the pedestrian fabric of a community.

We have all seen college campuses seamlessly integrated into their communities. Stetson University in DeLand is an example. The campus is wedged in between residential neighborhoods and downtown. Campus buildings are clustered and oriented toward one another or public streets. Parking areas are broken up and neatly hidden. The Stetson campus is in stark contrast to many contemporary university campuses in Florida which stand alone, indifferent to their surroundings.

It is the Stetson campus, not the contemporary university campuses, that we should emulate in the design of campus-style business parks (or more precisely, per *Land Use Practice 10*, all-purpose activity centers). Miami Lakes Business Park East probably comes as close to this ideal as any suburban business or office park in Florida (but for its lack of sidewalks, a serious oversight).

Haile Village Center

Small Landscaped Parking Areas at Bluewater Bay

Palmer Ranch's Auto-Oriented Community Shopping Center

Stetson University Campus in DeLand

CAMPUS-STYLE BUSINESS PARKS

Pedestrian-Scale at Miami Lakes   Auto-Scale at Oakbridge

ENDNOTES

[1] R. Ewing, "Characteristics, Causes and Effects of Sprawl: A Literature Review," *Environmental and Urban Issues*, Vol. 21, Winter 1994, pp. 1-15.

[2] J.B. Lansing, R.W. Marans, and R.B. Zehner, *Planned Residential Environments*, Survey Research Center, University of Michigan, 1970, pp. 45-50.

[3] Lansing et al., op. cit. On the relationship between residential satisfaction and open space generally, see R. Kaplan and S. Kaplan, *The Experience of Nature—A Psychological Perspective*, Cambridge University Press, New York, 1989, pp. 150-164, 216-291.

[4] A.E. Pisarski, *Travel Behavior Issues in the 90's*, Federal Highway Administration, Washington, D.C., 1992, p. 13.

[5] A dozen studies estimating the social costs of auto use are synthesized in R. Ewing, *Transportation & Land Use Innovations*, Department of Community Affairs, Tallahassee, Fla., pending.

[6] From simulation studies, daily VMT is 10 percent to 25 percent lower when development takes the form of neo-traditional neighborhoods or pedestrian pockets rather than conventional subdivisions. S.P. Gordon and J.B. Peers, "Designing a Community for Transportation Demand Management: The Laguna West Pedestrian Pocket," *Transportation Research Record 1321*, 1991, pp. 138-145; M.G. McNally and S. Ryan, "Comparative Assessment of Travel Characteristics for Neotraditional Designs," *Transportation Research Record 1400*, 1993, pp. 67-77; and M.G. McNally, "Regional Impacts of Neotraditional Neighborhood Development," *ITE 1993 Compendium of Technical Papers*, Institute of Transportation Engineers, Washington, D.C., 1993, pp. 463-467.

[7] State-of-the-practice in regional travel modeling relies on a structure developed decades ago, and largely unchanged for the past 15 years. Models were adequate for the purpose originally intended — the sizing of capital facilities (especially highways), but they fall short of what is required by the Clean Air Act, the Intermodal Surface Transportation Efficiency Act, and Florida's 1993 growth management act. For a critique of conventional models (given new demands), see G. Harvey and E. Deakin, *A Manual of Regional Transportation Modeling Practice for Air Quality Analysis*, National Association of Regional Councils, Washington, D.C., 1993, pp. 3-1 through 3-7.

[8] The Florida Department of Transportation has several ongoing projects aimed at enhancing and modernizing FSUTMS. See R. Ewing, M. DeAnna, and S. Li, "Travel Model Improvements—From Current Practice to State-of-the-Art," *ITE Journal*, scheduled for the June 1996 issue. Also see Cambridge Systematics, *Model Modifications—Volume 4*, 1000 Friends of Oregon, Portland, 1992; B.D. Spear, *New Approaches to Travel Forecasting Models—A Synthesis of Four Research Proposals*, Technology Sharing Program, U.S. Department of Transportation, Washington, D.C., 1994; and Texas Transportation Institute, *Travel Model Improvement Program*, College Station, Tex., undated.

[9] G. Giuliano, "Research Policy and Review 27. New Directions for Understanding Transportation and Land Use," *Environment and Planning A*, Vol. 21, 1989, pp. 145-159; L.W. Bookout, "Jobs and Housing—The Search for Balance," *Urban Land*, Vol. 49, October 1990, pp. 5-9; G. Giuliano, "Is Jobs-Housing Balance a Transportation Issue?" *Transportation Research Record 1305*, 1991, pp. 305-312; M. Wachs, "Thought Piece on the Jobs/Housing Balance," in *Achieving a Jobs-Housing Balance: Land Use Planning for Regional Growth*, Lincoln Institute of Land Policy, Cambridge, Mass., 1991; A. Downs, "Changing the Jobs-Housing Balance," *Stuck in Traffic—Coping with Peak-Hour Traffic Congestion*, The Brookings Institution, Washington, D.C., 1992, pp. 98-111; G. Giuliano and K. Small, "Is the Journey to Work Explained by Urban Structure?" *Urban Studies*, Vol. 30, 1993, pp. 1485-1500; and M. Wachs, "The Role of Land Use Strategies for Improving Transportation and Air Quality," Introductory remarks at the UCLA Extension Public Policy Program Symposium on the Transportation/Land Use/Air Quality Connection, Lake Arrowhead, Calif., 1993.

[10] The proportion of internally captured work trips is:

INTERNAL CAPTURE = (2 x employed persons both living and working in the locality) / (employed persons living in the locality + employed persons working in the locality)

The number of persons both living and working in a locality is multiplied by two because each person has two "trip ends," one at home and the other at work. If no one lives <u>and</u> works locally, INTERNAL CAPTURE will assume a value of 0; if everyone lives and works locally, INTERNAL CAPTURE will assume a value of 1.

[11] Our measure of JOB BALANCE is:

1 - Absolute Value (employed persons living in the locality - employed persons working in the locality) / (employed persons living in the locality + employed persons working in the locality)

JOB BALANCE ranges from 0 (with no balance) to 1 (with perfect balance).

Two variables measuring the degree of mismatch between earnings of workers in local jobs and housing costs in the locality were also derived and tested. Both were computed with U.S. Census data based on the old rule of thumb that people can afford housing two and one-half times their annual incomes:

Absolute Value (2.5 x median worker earnings - median value of owner-occupied housing units)

—and—

Absolute Value (proportion of workers earning > $30,000/year - proportion of owner-occupied housing units valued at > $75,000)

The former variable entered the regression equation with the "wrong" sign (+) and the latter proved insignificant.

[12] To estimate a power function using linear regression analysis, it is necessary to first take the logarithms of variables. The references in the text to the significance of variables and explanatory power of the equation refer to the logarithmic form of the equation, not to the power function reported.

[13] R. Cervero, "Jobs-Housing Balancing and Regional Mobility," *Journal of the American Planning Association*, Vol. 55, 1989, pp. 136-150.

[14] For a definition of internal capture, see the feature box on jobs-housing balance. Of the 11 new communities for which internal capture rates were computed with 1990 U.S. Census data, the highest internal capture rates are:

Peachtree City, Ga.	37%
Coral Springs, Fla.	34%
Columbia, Md.	31%

[15] A. Getis, "Residential Location and the Journey to Work," *Proceedings of the American Association of Geographers*, Vol. 1, 1969, pp. 55-59; P.L. Halvorson, "The Critical Isochrone: An Alternative Definition," *Proceedings of the American Association of Geographers*, Vol. 5, 1975, pp. 84-87; W.A.V. Clark and J.E. Burt, "The Impact of Workplace on Residential Relocation," *Annuals of the Association of American Geographers*, Vol. 70, 1980, pp. 59-67; and W.T. Watterson, "Dynamics of Job and Housing Locations and the Work Trip: Evidence from the Puget Sound Transportation Panel," Paper presented at the 73rd Annual Meeting, Transportation Research Board, Washington, D.C., 1994.

[16] Cervero, op. cit.

[17] Trip lengths in San Diego average 8.8 miles for commuters living in "sectors" with balanced jobs and housing, two miles less than the regional average. San Diego's sectors average less than three miles across, smaller than any estimate in the literature of indifference region size. San Diego Association of Governments, "Jobs/Housing Balance and Transportation Corridor Densities," Appendix 3 of *Regional Growth Management Strategy*, San Diego, Calif., 1991, p. 66. Also see W.W. Recker and H.J. Schuler, "An Integrated Analysis of Complex Travel Behavior and Urban Form Indicators," *Urban Geography*, Vol. 3, 1982, pp. 110-120; D.M. Nowlan and G. Stewart, "Downtown Population Growth and Commuting Trips—Recent Experience in Toronto," *Journal of the American Planning Association*, Vol. 57, 1991, pp. 165-182; J.C. Levine, "Decentralization of Jobs and the Emerging Suburban Commute," *Transportation Research Record 1364*, 1992, pp. 71-80; and L.D. Frank and G. Pivo, *Relationships Between Land Use and Travel Behavior in the Puget Sound Region*, Washington State Department of Transportation, Seattle, Wash., 1994, pp. 31-34.

[18] R. Witherspoon, J.P. Abbett, and R.M. Gladstone, *Mixed-Use Developments: New Ways of Land Use*, Urban Land Institute, Washington, D.C., 1976; D. Priest et al., *Large-Scale Development—Benefits, Constraints, and State and Local Policy Incentives*, Urban Land Institute, Washington, D.C., 1977; Council on Development Choices for the 80s, *The Affordable Community: Adapting Today's Communities to Tomorrow's Needs*, Urban Land Institute, Washington, D.C., 1981; David Jensen Associates, Inc., *Community Design Guidelines*, National Association of Home Builders, Washington, D.C., 1985; D. Schwanke et al., *Mixed-Use Development Handbook*, Urban Land Institute, Washington, D.C., 1987; and R. Ewing, *Developing Successful New Communities*, Urban Land Institute, Washington, D.C., 1991.

[19] One of the mainstays of the traffic engineering profession, *Trip Generation*, reports that fewer than half of all daily trips leave the mixed-use development of Brandermill, Virginia. It achieves this rate of internal capture even though Brandermill has fewer businesses than many mixed-use developments. Institute of Transportation Engineers, *Trip Generation*, 5th Edition, Washington, D.C., 1991, pp. I-42 and I-43.

[20] D. Popenoe, *The Suburban Environment—Sweden and the United States*, University of Chicago Press, Chicago, 1977, pp. 192-201; M. Berg and E.A. Medrich, "Children in Four Neighborhoods: The Physical Environment and Its Effect on Play and Play Patterns," *Environment and Behavior*, Vol. 12, 1980, pp. 320-348; A.J. Millas, "Planning for the Elderly within the Context of a Neighborhood," *Ekistics*, Vol. 283, 1980, pp. 264-273; and F.M. Carp, "Significance of Mobility for the Well-Being of the Elderly," in *Transportation in an Aging Society*, Special Report 218, Transportation Research Board, Washington, D.C., 1988, pp. 1-20.

[21] Office buildings, industrial plants, retail outlets, and high-density apartment buildings produce a fiscal surplus for local government, while lower-density residential uses produce a deficit. R.W. Burchell and D. Listokin, *Fiscal Impact Procedures—State of the Art: The Subset Questions of Nonresidential and Open Space Costs*, Center for Urban Policy Research, Rutgers University, New Brunswick, N.J., 1992, pp. 43-52.

[22] From various studies, we know that as long as the proportion of land devoted to nonresidential uses remains below 5 percent to 20 percent, and as long as nonresidential uses are not in the immediate vicinity of residences, their effect on residential property values is neutral or positive. We also know that small clusters of stores can escape any negative effect, even on their immediate surroundings, while commercial strips and large commercial centers cannot. J.F. Kain and J.M. Quigley, "Measuring the Value of Housing Quality," *Journal of the American Statistical Association*, Vol. 65, 1970, pp. 532-548; W.J. Stull, "Community Environment, Zoning, and the Market Value of Single-Family Homes," *Journal of Law and Economics*, Vol. 18, 1975, pp. 535-557; M.M. Li and H.J. Brown, "Micro-Neighborhood Externalities and Hedonic Housing Prices," *Land Economics*, Vol. 56, 1980, pp. 125-141; D.M. Grether and P. Mieszkowski, "The Effects of Nonresidential Land Uses on the Prices of Adjacent Housing: Some Estimates of Proximity Effects," *Journal of Urban Economics*, Vol. 8, 1980, pp. 1-15; G.D. Jud and J.M. Watts, "Schools and Housing Values," *Land Economics*, Vol. 57, 1981, pp. 459-470; and T.V. Cao and D.C. Cory, "Mixed Land Uses, Land-Use Externalities, and Residential Property Values: A Reevaluation," *Annals of Regional Science*, Vol. 16, 1982, pp. 1-24.

[23] This controversial proposition was first put forth in J. Jacobs, *Death and Life of Great American Cities*, Random House, New York, 1961. She argued that mixed-use areas generate pedestrian traffic at different hours, and this in turn generates "eyes on the street" at different hours. The eyes are those of the pedestrians themselves, plus the residents of houses and the proprietors of businesses fronting on a street. The residents and proprietors have an interest in the street specifically because there is street life. Once a street has good natural surveillance and active street life, Jacobs held that "the more the merrier" when it comes to strangers being drawn to a mixed-use area. While not disputing the value of active street life or natural surveillance, a comparative study of crime rates casts doubt on the notion that simply mixing commercial uses with residential will deter crime. Without good urban design, diversity of land uses may create more opportunity for crime—more potential perpetrators as well as more potential victims—without fostering street life and natural surveillance. S.W. Greenberg, W.M. Rohe, and J.R. Williams, "Safety in Urban Neighborhoods: A Comparison of Physical Characteristics and Informal Territorial Control in High and Low Crime Neighborhoods," *Population and Environment*, Vol. 5, 1982, pp. 141-165; and S.W. Greenberg and W.M. Rohe, "Neighborhood Design and Crime—A Test of Two Perspectives," *Journal of the American Planning Association*, Vol. 50, 1984, pp. 48-61.

[24] As one sociologist put it, "Houses alone do not a community make..." Typical suburban development has the effect of fragmenting the individual's world. He/she lives in one place, works or goes to school in another, shops in a third, recreates in a fourth, and cares deeply about none of these places. A sense of isolation results, particularly for children. R. Oldenberg, *The Great Good Place*, Paragon House, New York, 1989, pp. 3-19, 203-229.

[25] Only two concerns were voiced by officials of traditional towns: one, that commercial traffic was bothersome to neighboring residences and, two, that residential structures were vulnerable to conversion to commercial uses.

[26] Results of a 1989 housing survey are sobering. Homeshoppers were offered a choice between:

(a) homogeneous neighborhoods where expensive homes are separated from less expensive ones, where townhouses are separated from single-family houses, and where all houses are separated from stores and office buildings; and

(b) mixed neighborhoods where different types and sizes of houses are in the same general area and where small stores and other commercial activities are nearby.

Nationally, only 34 percent of homeshoppers preferred mixed neighborhoods, and the proportion was lowest in the southern states, a mere 28 percent. L.W. Bookout, "Neotraditional Town Planning—The Test of the Marketplace," *Urban Land*, Vol. 51, June 1992, pp. 12-17.

[27] In a fascinating study of single-family home prices in New Haven, researchers found that being adjacent to industry or commercial strips depresses home prices, but that "point commercial centers" (islands of small stores in the middle of residential areas) are "relatively harmless" in their price effects. Grether and Mieszkowski, op. cit.

[28] Council on Development Choices for the 80s, op. cit.; David Jensen Associates, op. cit.; Ewing, op. cit., 1991; Priest et al., op. cit.; Urban Land Institute, *New Approaches to Residential Land Development*, Technical Bulletin No. 40, Washington, D.C., 1961; Urban Land Institute, *Innovations vs. Traditions in Community Development*, Technical Bulletin No. 47, Washington, D.C., 1963; National Association of Home Builders, *Cost Effective Site Planning: Single-Family Development*, Washington, D.C., 1986; and F.D. Jarvis, *Site Planning and Community Design for Great Neighborhoods*, National Association of Home Builders, Washington, D.C., 1993.

[29] In one comparison, two neighborhoods were laid out on the same 166-acre site, one in a conventional pattern, the other in a cluster pattern. They had the same gross densities, 4 units per acre. But the cluster development preserved 20 percent of the land as open space, including all major wooded areas and natural drainage channels; it accommodated a small commercial center; and it cut development costs by a third, from $12,856 to $8,045 per unit. National Association of Home Builders, op. cit., pp.

113-120. Also see T.A. Kopf, "Cash Flow Analysis: A Decision Making Tool," *Land Development*, Vol. 2, Spring 1989, pp. 23-27.

[30] W.H. Whyte, *Cluster Development*, American Conservation Association, New York, 1964; Real Estate Research Corporation, *The Costs of Sprawl*, U.S. Government Printing Office, Washington, D.C., 1974; W. Sanders, *The Cluster Subdivision: A Cost-Effective Approach*, Planning Advisory Service Report Number 356, American Planning Association, Chicago, 1981; and W. Sanders and C. Thurow, *Water Conservation in Residential Development*, Planning Advisory Service Report Number 373, American Planning Association, Chicago, 1982.

[31] J. Lacy, *An Examination of Market Appreciation for Clustered Housing with Permanent Open Space*, Center for Rural Massachusetts, University of Massachusetts, Amherst, 1990. The impact on property values depends on the type of open space, distance from it, and orientation to it. J.W. Kitchen and W.S. Hendon, "Land Values Adjacent to an Urban Park," *Land Economics*, Vol. 43, 1967, pp. 357-360; W.S. Hendon, "The Park as a Determinant of Property Values," *American Journal of Economics and Sociology*, Vol. 30, 1971, pp. 289-296; A.H. Darling, "Measuring Benefits Generated by Urban Water Parks," *Land Economics*, Vol. 49, 1973, pp. 22-34; J.C. Weicher and R.H. Zerbst, "The Externalities of Neighborhood Parks: An Empirical Investigation," *Land Economics*, Vol. 49, 1973, pp. 99-105; T.R. Hammer, R.E. Coughlin, and E.T. Horn, "The Effect of a Large Urban Park on Real Estate Value," *Journal of the American Institute of Planners*, Vol. 40, 1974, pp. 274-277; G. Davies, "An Econometric Analysis of Residential Amenity," *Urban Studies*, Vol. 11, 1974, pp. 217-225; M.R. Correll, J.H. Lillydahl, and L.D. Singell, "The Effects of Greenbelts on Residential Property Values: Some Findings on the Political Economy of Open Space," *Land Economics*, Vol. 54, 1978, pp. 207-217; G. Blomquist and L. Worley, "Specifying the Demand for Housing Characteristics: The Exogeneity Issue," in D.B. Diamond and G.S. Tolley (eds.), *The Economics of Urban Amenities*, Academic Press, New York, 1982, pp. 89-102; J.K. Hagerty et al., "Benefits from Urban Open Space and Recreational Parks: A Case Study," *Journal of the Northeastern Agricultural Economics Council*, Vol. 11, Spring 1982, pp. 13-20; T.A. More, T. Stevens, and P.G. Allen, "The Economics of

Urban Parks—A Benefit/Cost Analysis," *Parks & Recreation*, Vol. 17, August 1982, pp. 31-33; R. Pollard, "View Amenities, Building Heights, and Housing Supply," in D.B. Diamond and G.S. Tolley (eds.), *The Economics of Urban Amenities*, Academic Press, New York, 1982, pp. 105-123; P.B. McLeod, "The Demand for Local Amenity: An Hedonic Price Analysis," *Environment and Planning A*, Vol. 16, 1984, pp. 389-400; B. Didato, "The Paths Less Traveled—A Wrapup on the Nation's Greenways," *Planning*, Vol. 56, January 1990, pp. 6-10; National Park Service, "Real Property Values," *Economic Impacts of Protecting Rivers, Trails, and Greenway Corridors*, San Francisco, 1990, pp. 1-1 through 1-18; D.A. King, J.L. White, and W.W. Shaw, "Influence of Urban Wildlife Habitats on the Value of Residential Properties," in L.W. Adams and D.L. Leedy (eds.), *Wildlife Conservation in Metropolitan Environments*, National Institute for Urban Wildlife, Columbia, Md., 1991, pp. 165-169 and P. Larsen, "Open Space That Sells," *Land Development*, Vol. 5, Spring-Summer 1992, pp. 22-25.

[32] T.J. Glynn, "Psychological Sense of Community: Measurement and Application," *Human Relations*, Vol. 34, 1981, pp. 789-818; B.L. Levine, "The Tragedy of the Commons and the Comedy of Community: The Commons in History," *Journal of Community Psychology*, Vol. 14, 1986, pp. 81-99; and S.E. Cochrun, "Understanding and Enhancing Neighborhood Sense of Community," *Journal of Planning Literature*, Vol. 9, 1994, pp. 92-99.

[33] P.G. Flachsbart, "Residential Site Planning and Perceived Densities," *Journal of the Urban Planning and Development Division*, Vol. 105, 1979, pp. 103-117.

[34] "Natural surveillance" and "territoriality" are fundamental to crime prevention through environmental design. Both factors favor small projects, the former because threats are more likely to be recognized as such and the latter because residents are more likely to defend against them. O. Newman, *Defensible Space—Crime Prevention Through Urban Design*, Collier Books, New York, 1972, pp. 71-79.

[35] Ewing, op. cit., 1991, pp. 108-109; and D.R. Jensen, *Zero Lot Line Housing*, Urban Land Institute, Washington, D.C., 1981, p. 68.

[36] It is through design review and design standards that master developers ensure compatibility of scale, architecture, landscaping, and signage. An entire chapter is devoted to the subject in Ewing, op. cit., 1991, pp. 88-97.

[37] H.S. Levinson and F.H. Wynn, "Effects of Density on Urban Transportation Requirements," *Highway Research Record 2*, 1963, pp. 38-64; Wilbur Smith and Associates, *Patterns of Car Ownership, Trip Generation and Trip Sharing in Urbanized Areas*, U.S. Department of Transportation, Washington, D.C., 1968, pp. 47-51; J.F. Kain and G.R. Fauth, *The Impact of Urban Development on Auto Ownership and Transit Use*, Discussion Paper D77-18, Department of City and Regional Planning, Harvard University, Cambridge, Mass., 1977; K. Neels et al., *An Empirical Investigation of the Effects of Land Use on Urban Travel*, The Urban Institute, Washington, D.C., 1977, pp. 54-56; P.D. Prevedouros and J.L. Schofer, "Factors Affecting Automobile Ownership and Use," *Transportation Research Record 1364*, 1992, pp. 152-160; R.T. Dunphy and K.M. Fisher, "Transportation, Congestion, and Density: New Insights," Paper presented at the 73rd Annual Meeting, Transportation Research Board, Washington, D.C., 1994; and J. Holtzclaw, *Using Residential Patterns and Transit to Decrease Auto Dependence and Costs*, Natural Resources Defense Council, San Francisco, 1994, pp. 19-20.

[38] P.H. Hare et al., "Making Housing Affordable by Giving Up the Second Car," in *Grass Roots to Green Modes*, 12th International Pedestrian Conference, City of Boulder, Colo., 1991, pp. 167-175.

[39] P.H. Hare, "One Car Mortgages, One Car Rents," in *Alternative Transportation: Planning, Design, Issues, Solutions*, Proceedings of the 14th International Pedestrian Conference, City of Boulder, Colo., 1993, pp. 135-139.

[40] According to one source, a net density of at least six units per acre is required to support a corner store. This is in line with the net densities recommended in *Housing Practice 2*. C. Alexander, S. Ishikawa, and M. Silverstein, *A Pattern Language—Towns · Buildings · Construction*, Oxford University Press, New York, 1977, pp. 440-443.

[41] To the extent that larger centers allow auto users to meet several shopping needs at once, converting multiple trips for one purpose each into one trip for multiple purposes, large centers may reduce total vehicle miles of travel. Thus, we are not arguing against larger centers but rather for a hierarchy of centers, some quite small and supported by pedestrian traffic from nearby dense developments. See R.W. Bacon, "An Approach to the Theory of Consumer Shopping Behavior," pp. 55-64; and H. Kohsaka, "An Optimization of the Central Place System in Terms of the Multipurpose Shopping Trip," *Geographical Analysis*, Vol. 16, 1984, pp. 250-269.

[42] See Municipality of Metropolitan Seattle, *Encouraging Public Transportation Through Effective Land Use Actions*, Seattle, 1987, p. 45; E. Beimborn and H. Rabinowitz, *Guidelines for Transit-Sensitive Suburban Land Use Design*, Urban Mass Transportation Administration, Washington, D. C., 1991, pp. 70-71; W. Bowes, M. Gravel, and G. Noxon, *Guide to Transit Considerations in the Subdivision Design and Approval Process*, Transportation Association of Canada, Ottawa, 1991, p. A-4; City of Winnepeg Transit Department, *Planning and Building Transit-Friendly Residential Subdivisions*, Winnipeg, 1991, p. 6; Calthorpe Associates, *Transit-Oriented Development Design Guidelines*, City of San Diego, Calif., 1992, pp. 45, 50-51; Orange County Transportation Authority, *Design Guidelines for Bus Facilities*, Santa Ana, Calif., 1992; Ontario Ministry of Transportation, *Transit-Supportive Land Use Planning Guidelines*, Toronto, 1992, pp. 18, 23, and 29; Tri-County Metropolitan Transportation District of Oregon, *Planning and Design for Transit*, Portland, Ore., 1993, p. 95; and BC Transit, *Transit Friendly Subdivision & Development Guidelines*, Victoria, B.C., undated, p. 7.

[43] S.L. Handy, "Regional Versus Local Accessibility: Implications for Nonwork Travel," *Transportation Research Record 1400*, 1993, pp. 58-66.

[44] Handy, op. cit.; W.A.V. Clark, "Consumer Travel Patterns and the Concept of Range," *Annuals of the American Association of Geographers*, Vol. 58, 1968, pp. 386-396; W.R. Bishop and E.H. Brown, "An Analysis of Spa-

tial Shopping Behavior," *Journal of Retailing*, Vol. 45, 1969, pp. 23-30; R.B. Zehner, *Access, Travel, and Transportation in New Communities*, Ballinger Publishing Company, Cambridge, Mass., 1977, pp. 12-13 and 39-45; W.W. Recker and L.P. Kostyniuk, "Factors Influencing Destination Choice for the Urban Grocery Shopping Trip," *Transportation*, Vol. 7, 1978, pp. 19-33; S. Hanson, "The Determinants of Daily Travel-Activity Patterns: Relative Location and Sociodemographic Factors," *Urban Geography*, Vol. 3, 1982, pp. 179-202; S. Hanson and M. Schwab, "Accessibility and Intraurban Travel," *Environment and Planning A*, Vol. 19, 1987, pp. 735-748; S. Tarry, "Accessibility Factors at the Neighborhood Level," in *Environmental Issues*, PTRC Education and Research Services Ltd., London, England, 1992, pp. 257-270; R. Ewing, P. Haliyur, and G.W. Page, "Getting Around a Traditional City, a Suburban PUD, and Everything In-Between," *Transportation Research Record 1466*, 1994, pp. 53-62; R. Ewing, "Beyond Density, Mode Choice, and Single-Purpose Trips," *Transportation Quarterly*, Vol. 49, 1995, pp. 15-24; and S. Handy, "Understanding the Link Between Urban Form and Travel Behavior," Paper presented at the 74th Annual Meeting, Transportation Research Board, Washington, D.C., 1995.

[45] Minimum population requirements for businesses were derived by dividing median annual sales (as reported by the Urban Land Institute for stores in neighborhood shopping centers) by average household expenditures for associated goods and services (as tabulated by Bureau of Labor Statistics, U.S. Department of Labor).

[46] Those who conceive neighborhoods this way include: Hillsborough County City-County Planning Commission, *Principles for Good Neighborhoods*, Tampa, Fla., 1992; Treasure Coast Regional Planning Council, *A Strategy for Encouraging Beneficial Development Types*, Palm City, Fla., February 1992 draft; Sasaki Associates, Inc., "Neighborhood Principles and Applications in Montgomery County," in *Transit and Pedestrian Oriented Neighborhood Study*, Maryland-National Capital Park and Planning Commission, Silver Spring, Md., 1993, pp. 55-79; and A. Duany and E. Plater-Zyberk, "The Neighborhood, the District, and the Corridor," in P. Katz, *The New Urbanism—Toward an Architecture of Community*, McGraw-Hill, New York, 1994, pp. xvii-xx.

[47] Our concept of neighborhood is more along the lines of T. Banerjee and W.C. Baer, "Toward a New Design Paradigm," *Beyond the Neighborhood Unit—Residential Environments and Public Policy*, Plenum Press, New York, 1984, pp. 171-198.

[48] The need for a neighborhood center and edge is an article of faith in the neighborhood literature. It is consistent with cognitive mapping studies showing that people's sense of place is enhanced by well-defined centers and edges. The need for common areas and facilities is also an article of faith. It is bolstered by surveys showing that some (not all) people have a need for "community" as well as privacy in their residential environment. Homes and yards provide the latter, common areas and facilities the former. A study of two otherwise comparable Washington, D.C., suburbs found greater "sense of community" and "community satisfaction" among residents of the one with well-defined boundaries, a central commons, and neighborhoods radiating out from the commons and connected to it by walkways. The design of this suburb fostered "both planned and casual citizen interaction" while the design of the conventional suburb did not. Glynn, op. cit. Also see Cochrun, op. cit.; S. Keller, *The Urban Neighborhood: A Sociological Perspective*, Random House, New York, 1968, pp. 87-106, 134-135, and 159-160; M.N. Corbett, *A Better Place to Live—New Designs for Tomorrow's Communities*, Rodale Press, Emmaus, Pa., 1981, pp. 103-108; M. Fried, "Residential Attachment: Sources of Residential and Community Satisfaction," *Journal of Social Issues*, Vol. 38, 1982, pp. 107-119; and J.I. Aragones and J.M. Arredondo, "Structure of Urban Cognitive Maps," *Journal of Environmental Psychology*, Vol. 5, 1985, pp. 197-212.

[49] J. Krohe, "Park Standards Are Up in the Air," *Planning*, Vol. 56, December 1990, pp. 10-13.

[50] Kaplan and Kaplan, op. cit., pp. 152-155. Also see Alexander et al., op. cit., pp. 304-313; W.H. Whyte, "Play Areas and Small Spaces," *The Last Landscape*, Doubleday & Company, Garden City, N.Y., 1968, pp. 260-270; and J.F. Talbot and R. Kaplan, "Judging the Sizes of Urban Open Areas: Is Bigger Always Better?" *Landscape Journal*, Vol. 5, 1986, pp. 83-92.

[51] See literature reviews by S.H. Crowhurst Lennard and H.L. Lennard, "Urban Space Design Principles," *Livable Cities—People and Places: Social and Design Principles for the Future of the City*, Center for Urban Well-Being, Southhampton, N.Y., 1987, pp. 9-37; M. Francis, "Urban Open Spaces," in E.H. Zube and G.T. Moore (eds.), *Advances in Environment, Behavior, and Design—Volume 1*, Plenum Press, New York, 1987, pp. 71-106; and C.C. Marcus and C. Francis (eds.), *People Places—Design Guidelines for Urban Open Space*, Van Nostrand Reinhold, New York, 1990 (particularly chapters on urban plazas, neighborhood parks, and miniparks).

[52] Alexander et al., op. cit., pp. 305-309; Kaplan and Kaplan, op. cit., pp. 150-161; H.P. Bangs and S. Mahler, "Users of Local Parks," *Journal of the American Institute of Planners*, Vol. 36, 1971, pp. 330-334; and T. Hiss, *The Experience of Place*, Alfred A. Knopf, New York, 1990, p. 18.

[53] Alexander et al., op. cit., pp. 518-523; S.N. Brower and P. Williamson, "Outdoor Recreation as a Function of the Urban Housing Environment," *Environment and Behavior*, Vol. 6, 1974, pp. 295-345; B. Hillier, "Against Enclosure," in N. Teymur, T.A. Markus, and T. Woolley (eds.), *Rehumanizing Housing*, Butterworths, London, 1988, pp. 63-88; P. Stollard, *Crime Prevention Through Housing Design*, E & F N Spon, London, 1991, pp. 21-26; and G.R. Wekerle and C. Whitzman, *Safe Cities—Guidelines for Planning, Design, and Management*, Van Nostrand Reinhold, New York, 1995, pp. 44-49..

[54] Bangs and Mahler, op. cit.

[55] Whyte, op. cit., pp. 112-128; N. Linday, "It All Comes Down to a Comfortable Place to Sit and Watch," *Landscape Architecture*, Vol. 68, 1978, pp. 492-497; and M. Chidister, "The Effect of Context on the Use of Urban Plazas," *Landscape Journal*, Vol. 5, 1986, pp. 115-127.

[56] Alexander et al., op. cit., pp. 517-523; Whyte, op. cit., pp. 132-140; S.D. Joardar and J.W. Neill, "The Subtle Differences in Configuration of Small Public Spaces," *Landscape Architecture*, Vol. 68, 1978, pp. 487-491; H.W. Schroeder, "Preferred Features of Urban Parks and For-

ests," *Journal of Arboriculture*, Vol. 8, 1982, pp. 317-322; K. Lynch and G. Hack, "The Sensed Landscape and Its Materials," *Site Planning*, MIT Press, Cambridge, Mass., 1984, pp. 153-192; and C.C. Marcus, "Miniparks and Vest-Pocket Parks," in C.C. Marcus and C. Francis (eds.), *People Places—Design Guidelines for Urban Open Space*, Van Nostrand Reinhold, New York, 1990, pp. 119-142.

[57] R. Trancik, *Finding Lost Space—Theories of Urban Design*, Van Nostrand Reinhold, New York, 1986, pp. 90-92.

[58] Whyte, op. cit., 1968; A. Bengtsson, *Environmental Planning for Children's Play*, Praeger Publishers, New York, 1970, pp. 154-219; M.P. Friedberg, *Play and Interplay*, The Macmillan Company, New York, 1970; S. Gold, "Nonuse of Neighborhood Parks," *Journal of the American Institute of Planners*, Vol. 38, 1972, pp. 369-378; R. Hart, *Children's Experience of Place*, Irvington Publishers, New York, 1979; P. Hill, "Toward the Perfect Play Experience," in P.F. Wilkinson (ed.), *Innovations in Play Environments*, St. Martin's Press, New York, 1980, pp. 23-33; and G.T. Moore, "State of the Art in Play Environment," in J.L. Frost and S. Sunderlin (eds.), *When Children Play—Proceedings of the International Conference on Play and Play Environments*, Association for Childhood Education International, Wheaton, Md., 1985, pp. 171-192.

[59] Much of the relevant literature is reviewed in Moore, op. cit. Also see the seminal work on adventure playgrounds, M.G. Allen, *Planning for Play*, MIT Press, Cambridge, Mass., 1968.

[60] Alexander et al., op. cit., pp. 557-560; Friedberg, op. cit., pp. 155-156; and Hillier, op. cit.

[61] Alexander et al., op. cit., pp. 86-90.

[62] The key role of neighborhood schools was acknowledged in the *neighborhood unit* concept. Elementary schools were placed at the very centers of neighborhoods. Other facilities might be incorporated as well, but the role of the school was paramount.

[63] A.C. Ornstein, "How Big Should Schools and Districts Be?" *The Education Digest*, Vol. 56, October 1990, pp. 45-47. Also see R.G. Barker and P.V. Gump, *Big School, Small School—High School Size and Student Behavior*, Stanford University Press, Palo Alto, Calif., 1964; and T.B. Gregory and G.R. Smith, *High Schools as Communities: The Small School Reconsidered*, Phi Delta Kappa Educational Foundation, Bloomington, Ind., 1987, pp. 59-76.

[64] "...participation in the activities centered on a neighborhood school broadens and deepens people's sense of being part of a neighborhood and their sense of belonging. In turn, it creates even stronger loyalties to the school itself. Neighborhood schools give rise to neighborhood PTAs; they provide neighborhood playgrounds; they become, on occasion, meeting places for other local organizations; and they serve, in many instances, as the first place where parents meet other parents in the 'neighborhood' who are not immediate 'neighbors'." P.W. Wood and W.L. Boyd, "Declining Enrollments and Suburban School Closing: The Problem of Neighborhoods and Neighborhood Schools," *Educational Administration Quarterly*, Vol. 17, 1981, pp. 98-119.

[65] P.F. Colwell and K.L. Guntermann, "The Value of Neighborhood Schools," *Economics of Education Review*, Vol. 3, 1984, pp. 177-182.

[66] Presently, only one-sixth of Florida's children walk or bike to school. Over one-third are driven to school by parents, adding to traffic congestion and hazardous conditions around schools for students who walk or bike. The remainder are bused to school, at a cost of $200 to $600 per student annually plus loss of valuable family and learning time on long bus rides. E.M. Starnes et al., *Home-to-School Transportation Study—Executive Summary*, Department of Urban and Regional Planning, University of Florida, Gainesville, 1992, p. 2.

[67] Starnes et al., op. cit. Walking distances are extended in countries with walking cultures, but even there, mode of travel to school abruptly shifts from walking to automobile when threshold distances are exceeded. M. Hillman, J. Adams, and J. Whitelegg, *One False Move...A Study of Children's Independent Mobility*, Policy Studies Institute, London, 1990, pp. 40-42, 67-68.

[68] Two thoughtful articles about strip development and the visibility and access requirements of businesses in strips are: F.W. Boal and D.B. Johnson, "Nondescript Streets," *Traffic Quarterly*, Vol. 22, 1968, pp. 329-344; and A. Achimore, "Putting the Community Back into Community Retail," *Urban Land*, Vol. 52, August 1993, pp. 33-38.

[69] D.A. Howe and W.A. Rabiega, "Beyond Strips and Centers—The Ideal Commercial Form," *Journal of the American Planning Association*, Vol. 58, 1992, pp. 213-219.

[70] Florida Department of Transportation, *Access Management—An Important Traffic Management Strategy*, Tallahassee, undated. Also see Roy Jorgensen Associates, *Cost and Safety Effectiveness of Highway Design Elements*, National Cooperative Highway Research Program Report 197, Transportation Research Board, Washington, D.C., 1978, pp. 78-80; V.G. Stover, S.C. Tignor, and M.J. Rosenbaum, "Access Control and Driveways,". *Synthesis of Safety Research Related to Traffic Control and Roadway Elements—Volume 1*, Federal Highway Administration, Washington, D.C., 1982, pp. 4-1 through 4-20; D. Ismart, "Access Management—State of the Art," 3rd National Conference on Transportation Planning Applications, Transportation Research Board, Washington, D.C., 1991; G. Long, C. Gan, and B.S. Morrison, *Safety Impacts of Selected Median and Access Design Features*, Transportation Research Center, University of Florida, Gainesville, 1993, pp. 36-59; P.S. Parsonson, M.G. Waters, and J.S. Fincher, "Effect on Safety of Replacing an Arterial Two-Way Left-Turn Lane with a Raised Median," Paper presented at the Access Management Conference, Transportation Research Board, Washington, D.C., 1993; and H.S. Levinson, "Access Management on Suburban Roads," *Transportation Quarterly*, Vol. 48, 1994, pp. 315-325.

[71] R.K. Untermann, *Accommodating the Pedestrian—Adapting Towns and Neighborhoods for Walking and Bicycling*, Van Nostrand Reinhold Company, New York, 1984, pp. 222-224; S.A. Smith et al., *Planning and Implementing Pedestrian Facilities in Suburban and Developing Rural Ar-*

eas—*Research Report*, National Cooperative Highway Research Program Report 294A, Transportation Research Board, Washington, D.C., 1987, p. 50; and Florida Department of Transportation, *Twelve Steps Toward Community Walkability*, Tallahassee, undated.

[72] F.N. Boal and D.B. Johnson, "The Functions of Retail and Service Establishments on Commercial Ribbons," in L.S. Bourne (ed.), *Internal Structure of the City*, Oxford University Press, New York, 1971, pp. 368-379; and J.A. Jakle and R.L. Mattson, "The Evolution of a Commercial Strip," *Journal of Cultural Geography*, Vol. 1, 1981, pp. 12-25.

[73] S. Angel, *Discouraging Crime Through City Planning*, Center for Planning and Development Research, University of California, Berkeley, 1968, pp. 20-33.

[74] See Achimore, op. cit.; T. Fisher, "Remaking Malls," *Progressive Architecture*, Vol. 69, November 1988, pp. 96-101; J.R. Molinaro, "Back on the Street: Street-level Retail an Important Addition to Office Development," *Land Development*, Vol. 2, Summer 1989, pp. 16-18; P. Langdon, "Pumping Up Suburban Downtowns," *Planning*, Vol. 56, July 1990, pp. 22-28; J.H. Kay, "Building a *There* There," *Planning*, Vol. 57, January 1991, pp. 4-8; J.R. Molinaro, "Creating a Vibrant Urban Core in the Suburbs," *Land Development*, Vol. 5, Winter 1993, pp. 16-20; D. Schwanke, T.J. Lassar, and M. Beyard, *Remaking the Shopping Center*, Urban Land Institute, Washington, D.C., 1994, pp. 31-89; I.F. Thomas, "Reinventing the Regional Mall," *Urban Land*, Vol. 53, February 1994, pp. 24-27; and T. Lassar, "Shopping Centers *Can* Be Good Neighbors, *Planning*, Vol. 61, October, 1995, pp. 14-19.

[75] W.R. Archer and M.T. Smith, "Why Do Suburban Offices Cluster?" *Geographical Analysis*, Vol. 25, 1993, pp. 53-64.

[76] Colorado/Wyoming Section Technical Committee, "Trip Generation for Mixed-Use Developments," *ITE Journal*, Vol. 57, 1987, pp. 27-32.

[77] D. Davidson, "The Role of Site Amenities as Transportation Demand Management Measures," Paper presented at the 74th Annual Meeting, Transportation Research Board, Washington, D.C., 1995.

[78] R. Cervero, "Land-Use Mixing and Suburban Mobility," *Transportation Quarterly*, Vol. 42, 1988, pp. 429-446; R. Cervero, *America's Suburban Centers—The Land Use-Transportation Link*, Unwin Hyman, Boston, 1989, pp. 138-140; and R. Cervero, "Land Uses and Travel at Suburban Activity Centers," *Transportation Quarterly*, Vol. 45, 1991, pp. 479-491.

[79] Barton-Aschman Associates, Inc., *Shared Parking*, Urban Land Institute, Washington, D.C., 1983; and T.P. Smith, *Flexible Parking Requirements*, American Planning Association, Washington, D.C., 1983.

[80] A review of 10 planned unit development (PUD) ordinances from around the State of Florida uncovered no case of credit for shared parking.

[81] Schwanke et al., op. cit., pp. 45-46; and R.F. Galehouse, "Mixed-Use Centers in Suburban Office Parks," *Urban Land*, Vol. 43, August 1984, pp. 10-13.

[82] Only retail anchors must be visible from passing roadways; smaller shops and offices can thrive on impulse buying and referrals. Achimore, op. cit.

[83] C.E. Beaumont, *How Superstore Sprawl Can Harm Communities—And What Communities Can Do About It*, National Trust for Historic Preservation, Washington, D.C., 1994, pp. 89-100; and S. Lewis, "When Wal-Mart Says 'Uncle'," *Planning*, Vol. 60, August 1994, pp. 14-19.

[84] Discount superstores have been labeled, quite fittingly, "sprawl-marts" because they contribute to downtown decline, extensive use of land, and suburban blight. As communities discover that most jobs and tax revenues generated by these national chains come at the expense of existing local businesses, and as teleshopping becomes more competitive in terms of price and convenience, one can only hope that communities exercise more discretion in approving sites for discount superstores, and that discount superstores, in turn, begin to offer more concessions to communities.

IV. BEST TRANSPORTATION PRACTICES

Practice 1: Design the street network with multiple connections and relatively direct routes.

Practice 2: Space through-streets no more than a half mile apart, or the equivalent route density in a curvilinear network.

Practice 3: Use traffic calming measures liberally.

Practice 4: Keep speeds on local streets down to 20 mph.

Practice 5: Keep speeds on arterials and collectors down to 35 mph (at least inside communities).

Practice 6: Keep all streets as narrow as possible, and never more than four travel lanes wide.

Practice 7: Align streets to give buildings energy-efficient orientations.

Practice 8: Avoid using traffic signals wherever possible and always space them for good traffic progression.

Practice 9: Provide networks for pedestrians and bicyclists as good as the network for motorists.

Practice 10: Provide pedestrians and bicyclists with shortcuts and alternatives to travel along high-volume streets.

Practice 11: Incorporate transit-oriented design features.

Practice 12: Establish TDM programs at employment centers.

In the design of new communities, the transportation system is often an afterthought, with "bigger is better" as the modus operandi. First, the master planner prepares a land plan and development program based on market opportunities and site constraints. Next, the master planner designs a conceptual street network to serve a largely set land plan and development program. Finally, a traffic engineer is brought in to fine tune the network and "make the traffic work."

The overriding consideration for planner and traffic engineer is that streets operate at or above a given level of service, which means at or above a given average speed.[1] If heavy traffic volumes are projected at individual intersections, the intersections are signalized and outfitted with turn lanes. In later phases of development, as traffic grows, streets are widened, more turn lanes are added, and phases are lengthened at traffic signals.

The result, according to critics, is a transportation system that only an automobile could love. "We are coming to the realization that making the traffic work well is one of the prime contributors to much of what we now see and don't like in our new suburban growth; namely, loss of community, absence of walking atmosphere, boredom, bleakness...."[2]

One goal of these "best practices" is to keep traffic flowing *smoothly* within the community, minimizing traveler delay and other adverse impacts of stop-and-go driving. Slow and steady is the goal, not fast, since high-speed traffic detracts from the sense of community. Another goal is to preserve *options to the automobile* for those who might want or need to exercise them. Diversity is valued here as in other best practices.[3]

Practice 1: Design the street network with multiple connections and relatively direct routes.

Ideally, a large-scale development will have connections to surrounding roads in all directions; a continuous network of internal collectors and subcollectors; multiple entrances to subdivisions; and interconnections between subdivisions. This interconnectedness can be achieved without running traffic through neighborhoods or running street alignments through natural features, provided some creativity is applied to the street network.[4]

U.S. Street Functional Hierarchy

Arterials carry traffic between communities and connect communities to major intrastate and interstate highways.

Collectors convey traffic between arterials and from lower-order streets to arterials. They are the primary routes within residential and commercial areas.

Local streets are of two types. Subcollectors provide frontage for individual lots and carry small amounts of through-traffic between collectors or from access streets to collectors. Traffic volumes on subcollectors typically range from 250 to 1,000 vehicles per day. Access streets provide frontage for individual lots and carry only traffic with an origin or destination on the streets themselves. Traffic volumes on access streets typically range up to 250 vehicles per day.

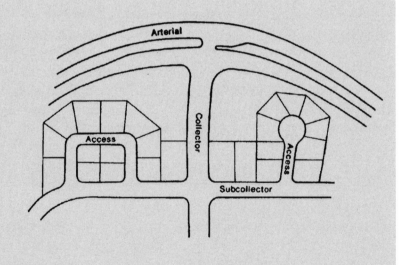

Sources: Adapted from Bucks County Planning Commission, Performance Streets - A Concept and Model Standards for Residential Streets, Doylestown, Pa., 1980, pp. 4-21; and Residential Streets Task Force, Residential Streets, American Society of Civil Engineers/National Association of Home Builders/Urban Land Institute, Washington,D.C., 1990, pp. 25-28.

The traditional urban grid has short blocks, straight streets, and a crosshatched pattern. The typical contemporary suburban street network has large blocks, curving streets, and a branching pattern.

Both network designs have advantages...and disadvantages. Traditional grids disperse traffic rather than concentrating it at a handful of intersections. They offer more direct routes and hence generate fewer vehicle miles of travel (VMT) than do contemporary networks.[5] They encourage walking and biking with their direct routing and their options to travel along high-volume streets.[6] The most pedestrian-oriented cities in the world are those with the densest, web-like street networks.[7]

Grids are also more transit-friendly.[8] They allow transit vehicles to avoid backtracking and frequent turns, and offer transit users relatively direct access to transit stops. Proving what transit advocates have known all along, a recent study found that transit ridership is greatest between tracts that have relatively direct transit connections.[9]

On the other hand, contemporary networks have some obvious advantages over grids. By keeping through-traffic out of neighborhoods, contemporary networks keep accident rates down and property values up.[10] They may also discourage crime, entry and escape being relatively difficult

Traditional Urban Grids

Contemporary Suburban Networks

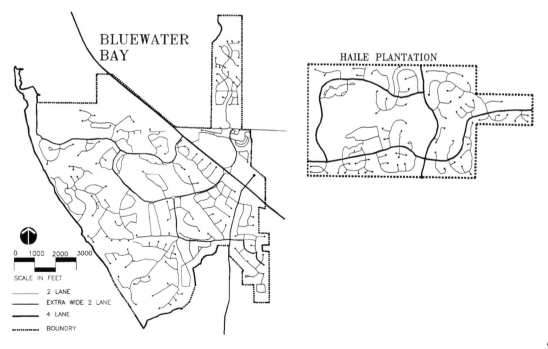

for would-be offenders.[11] Cul-de-sacs, the ultimate in disconnected streets, are quieter and safer for children, encourage more casual interaction among neighbors, and often command a premium in real estate markets.[12]

In addition, contemporary networks, with their curves and dead ends, can go around or stop short of valuable natural areas. Streets can run along ridges or run perpendicular to slopes, thereby minimizing cut-and-fill. Good site planning requires this kind of sensitivity to topography.[13]

We would like the best of both worlds — the mobility of the traditional grid and the safety, security, and topographic sensitivity of the contemporary network. We can have both with hybrid networks. If properly designed, hybrid networks have an order to them that is easily perceived by travelers. Not a simple, mechanistic, and monotonous order like a grid's, but a complex order ("variety within unity" as one source put it) that affords the best possible aesthetics.[14] Short, curved stretches that follow the lay of the land or contribute to good

urban design are okay. So are short loops and cul-de-sacs, as long as they leave the *higher-order street network intact*. By "higher-order street network" we mean arterials, collectors, and any subcollectors that carry *through-traffic*.

The street network of Miami Lakes is a hybrid. It has a "bending" grid of collectors and subcollectors in a wheel-and-spoke pattern; cul-de-sacs, loops, and short straight streets ending in T-intersections all work off the basic grid.

Hybrid Network at Miami Lakes

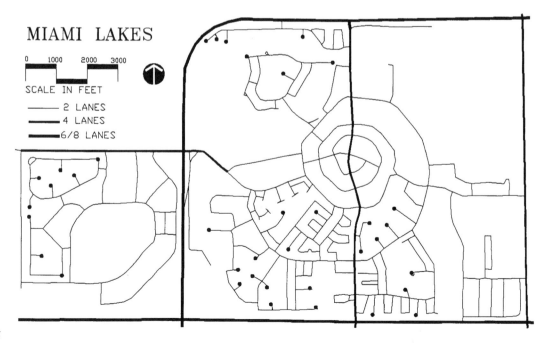

MIAMI LAKES

SCALE IN FEET
— 2 LANES
— 4 LANES
— 6/8 LANES

Miami Lakes' Neighborhood Insulated From Traffic

Network Connectivity Measures

There are various ways to measure the extent to which this best practice is followed. From the literature on networks, a simple measure of connectivity is the number of street links divided by the number of nodes or link ends (including cul-de-sac heads).[15] The more links relative to nodes, the more connectivity.

This index has been computed for several traditional towns and contemporary developments. Note the loss of connectivity in contemporary street networks. Apalachicola and Arcadia (with near-gridirons) have the highest indices. Bluewater Bay and Haile Plantation (designed around cul-de-sacs) have the lowest indices. Miami Lakes, with its hybrid network, is in the middle.

A connectivity index of 1.40, about halfway between the extremes, makes a nice target for network planning purposes. The plan for Rivendell at Palmer Ranch is almost exactly at this target level (see feature box in *Best Land Use Practices*).

Apalachicola	1.69	Bluewater Bay	1.19
Arcadia	1.69	Haile Plantation	1.19
Dade City	1.49	Hunter's Creek	1.23
DeLand	1.55	Miami Lakes	1.38

No one, including the most traditional of the neo-traditional planners, advocates a return to an endless gridiron of parallel streets crossing at right angles.[16] Neo-traditional plans feature interrupted grids of short streets ending at T- or Y-intersections, traffic circles, or town squares. By design, local streets carry some through-traffic, but the truncated nature of local streets means that traffic moves slowly and the heaviest volumes are diverted to higher-order streets.

Some neo-traditional planners flatly reject dead-end streets as "undemocratic." Others make room in their plans for cul-de-sacs or motor courts. Examples include Peter Calthorpe's Laguna West, Peter Brown's Four Mile Creek, and Elizabeth Moule and Stefanos Polyzoides' Playa Vista.[17]

NEO-TRADITIONAL PLANS INCORPORATING CUL-DE-SACS OR COURTS

Laguna West

Playa Vista (portion)

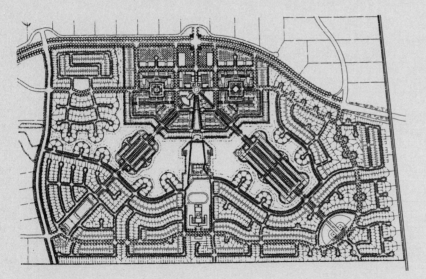

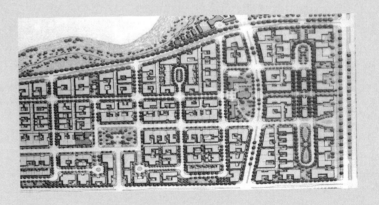

Guarded Gates and Street Closures

In the field of crime prevention through environmental design (CPTED), two distinct perspectives vie for influence.[18] The *defensible space* perspective emphasizes social control. From this perspective, public streets and spaces should be designed to encourage natural surveillance and territorial attitudes; the more people on the street, the better. The *opportunity* perspective emphasizes access control. Public streets and spaces should be designed for difficulty of entry and escape; the fewer potential victims and offenders on the street, the better.

The two models are not mutually exclusive, but where they conflict, developers have a choice. Do you want a more open and integrated layout that generates traffic, or a more closed and segregated layout that discourages traffic (at least from outsiders)?

Even those who favor open communities, including most planners, cannot deny the impetus for and market appeal of closed communities. There is a national epidemic of street closures and a stampede to gated communities.[19] Faced with a veritable crime wave and the need to compete with guarded-gate developments, Miami Lakes is now contemplating street closures and gates in its western section. If it closes off neighborhoods and Business Park West, the community will do so in an exemplary manner. Pedestrian pass-throughs will be maintained at the ends of closed streets; most serious crimes (as opposed to vandalism) involve motor vehicles. The gates will continue to permit public access, though with guards to take down license plate numbers and notify security, if necessary. Miami Lakes has years of successful experience with gated but public streets in its golf course neighborhood.

"Public" Gated Neighborhood at Miami Lakes

Practice 2: Space through-streets no more than a half mile apart, or the equivalent route density in a curvilinear network.

The shift away from gridded streets has been accompanied by a loss of capacity to handle through-traffic. Spaced far apart, arterials and collectors generate long access trips and require multi-lane cross-sections to handle traffic from their catchment areas. If they exist at all, subcollectors no longer connect collectors to one another but instead branch off single collectors, thus serving only local traffic.

Calls for closely spaced through-streets come from three quarters. Those concerned about traffic safety in residential areas, primarily Australian experts, envision access trips of no more than a minute or two at *restrained speeds* before a motorist reaches a higher-order street. If much longer than that, motorists will be tempted to speed through neighborhoods.[20] Transit operators advocate closely spaced arterials and collectors.[21] To keep transit routes within walking distance, such streets must not be spaced too far apart. Finally, neo-traditional planners advocate dense networks of through-streets to disperse traffic and avoid the need for multi-lane streets.[22]

Considering all factors, half-mile spacing of higher-order streets seems a reasonable target for network density. For curvilinear networks, the equivalent network density is 4.0 centerline miles per square mile of land area.

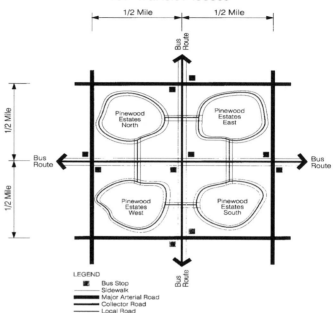

Spacing of Arterials and Collectors for Transit Access

Source: Denver Regional Council of Governments, *Suburban Mobility Design Manual*, Denver, Colo., 1993, p. 26.

The street networks of traditional towns meet or at least approach this network density. Not so the networks of contemporary developments, even the best of them. At build out, most residents will live beyond walking distance of bus stops and shopping centers, and arterials and collectors will need to be four- or even six-laned to handle traffic.

Street Network Densities
(miles of higher-order streets per square mile of land area)

Apalachicola	3.19	Bluewater Bay	2.20
Arcadia	4.15	Haile Plantation	2.64
Dade City	4.14	Hunter's Creek	2.25
DeLand	3.60	Oakbridge	1.49*/3.09**
		Palmer Ranch	2.11*/3.54**

* Without Subcollectors
** With Subcollectors

When subcollector mileage is added in, Oakbridge and Palmer Ranch come closer to the desired network density than do other exemplary developments. Their subcollectors shorten trips in and out of subdivisions and may serve as reliever roads for some through-trips under congested conditions. Network-enhancing subcollectors, a rarity these days, are among the features that made these two developments stand out during the quest for Florida's best.

There is an inherent dilemma in spacing higher-order streets as recommended. It creates more frontage on higher-order streets than can be absorbed by land uses that want to front on higher-order streets. For the most part, residents do not want to live on higher-order streets due to their high traffic volumes and speeds; this is one lesson learned from our survey of traditional towns.[23]

This dilemma is usually resolved through reverse lotting, where subdivisions turn their backs on higher-order streets and are sepa-rated from them by berms or walls. This solves the traffic problem but creates another problem: a sterile street environment with little natural surveillance and poor walkability. Potentially better design solutions leave homes and apartments facing higher-order streets but physically separated from them. Physical separation can be achieved by means of frontage roads or looped local streets that parallel higher-order streets and allow housing to face such streets at a short distance; or "boulevard" designs that use street trees and deep setbacks to buffer housing from traffic.[24]

Network-Enhancing Subcollectors at Palmer Ranch

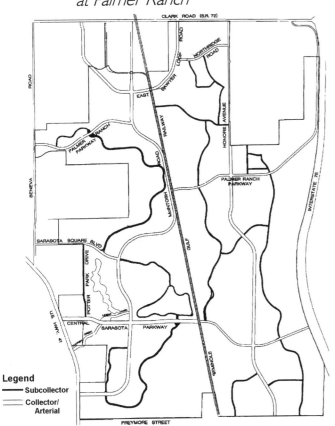

Legend
— Subcollector
= Collector/ Arterial

Alternatives to Reverse Lotting Along Higher-Order Streets

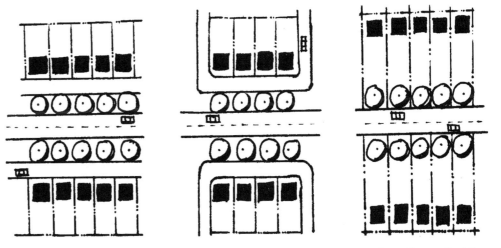

Sources: Adapted from Ontario Ministry of Transportation, *Transit-Supportive Land Use Planning Guidelines*, Toronto, 1992, p. 50; and P. Langdon, "Stroll Down the Boulevard," *Planning*, Vol. 60, November 1994, pp. 16-17.

Practice 3: Use traffic calming measures liberally.

The "livability" of streets declines as the *volume* and *speed* of traffic increase. Residents are more satisfied with the street environment when traffic volumes and speeds are low-to-moderate.[25] They are more likely to walk, bike, and play along such streets. They feel safer. Controlling traffic volume and speed is also the key to pedestrian-oriented commercial streets.[26]

Traffic calming, a term coined in Europe, popularized in Britain and Australia, and recently imported to the U.S., is accomplished through measures that control the volume of traffic, the speed of traffic, or both. While most measures have some effect on both volume and speed, they are usually classified according to their dominant effect. Street closures, restrictive one-way street patterns, diverters at intersections, and turn restrictions are primarily volume control measures. Speed humps/speed tables, traffic circles, sharp bends and chicanes (S-curves), and narrowings at midblock or at intersections are primarily speed control measures.

In the U.S., we rely on volume controls to "calm" traffic on our residential streets. Through-traffic is discouraged by means of cul-de-sacs, loops, and circuitous through-streets (see accompanying feature box). In older urban areas, residential street closures have reached epidemic proportions. These measures may solve one-half of the livability prob-

Cul-de-Sacs, Loops, and Indirect Through-Streets

In contemporary U.S. developments, traffic volumes on local streets are moderated by means of (in order of declining popularity) cul-de-sacs, loops, and circuitous through-streets; all largely eliminate through-traffic. In Britain, the order of priority is reversed. Cul-de-sacs are limited to very small housing clusters, loops are preferred in somewhat larger clusters, and circuitous through-streets are required in still larger clusters.[30] The British rationale applies here as well. Compared to cul-de-sacs, loops eliminate backtracking by service vehicles, provide two ways in and out for emergency vehicles, and shorten access trips by residents. Circuitous through-streets distribute traffic leaving a development between higher-order streets rather than dumping it onto a single street at a single intersection; congestion and access distances are thus reduced. The plan for Rivendell at Palmer Ranch (see feature box in *Best Land Use Practices*) shows how loops can be used to eliminate through-traffic.

British Street Layouts Favored Over Cul-De-Sacs

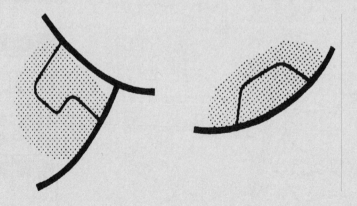

Source: Institution of Highways and Transportation, *Roads and Traffic in Urban Areas*, Her Majesty's Stationary Office, London, 1987, p. 261. Crown copyright is reproduced with the permission of the Controller of HMSO.

lem, holding down traffic volumes, but they do little for the other half, excessive driving speeds.[27] Often, they simply displace the problem to nearby streets.

The Europeans, and recently the British, have placed their emphasis on speed controls.[28] Rather than excluding through-traffic from local streets, they have sought to calm it by slowing it down. They have taken this approach because the alternative—U.S. style traffic calming—adds long detours to access trips and adds congestion to the few remaining through-streets. Some European countries have even extended traffic calming to major thoroughfares in the interest of pedestrian- and transit-friendliness.

For speed control, traffic calming must be designed into a community. The maximum speeds recommended in the best practices that follow, 20 and 35 mph, are *design speeds*, not just posted speed limits. These speeds will surely be exceeded if streets have "gun barrel" designs or even gentle curves with wide cross-sections. Speed zones, "go slow" signs, and lane restriping cannot compensate for flawed roadway engineering.[29] Speed limits must be *self-enforcing*, particularly on local streets.

The Europeans, British, and Australians strive to make every detail of the street and streetscape proclaim, "You are in a protected area—be careful!"[31] Active street-side uses, small building setbacks, street trees at the curb, and other land use and urban design features all help to "program" drivers for slower speeds. On top of that, engineering measures are applied to streets in an integrated, consistent manner. The U.S. may not be ready for European pinch points, raised junctions, *woonerfs*, and other more radical traffic calming measures. But we can certainly make greater use of small setbacks, street trees, short streets, sharp curves, center islands, traffic circles, textured pavements, and speed humps or, better still, flat-topped speed tables.

Woonerf Design

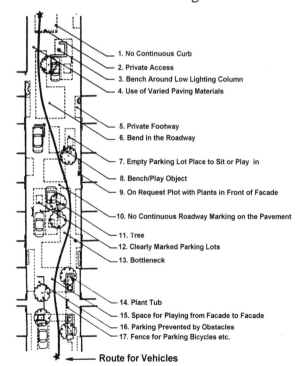

1. No Continuous Curb
2. Private Access
3. Bench Around Low Lighting Column
4. Use of Varied Paving Materials
5. Private Footway
6. Bend in the Roadway
7. Empty Parking Lot Place to Sit or Play in
8. Bench/Play Object
9. On Request Plot with Plants in Front of Facade
10. No Continuous Roadway Marking on the Pavement
11. Tree
12. Clearly Marked Parking Lots
13. Bottleneck
14. Plant Tub
15. Space for Playing from Facade to Facade
16. Parking Prevented by Obstacles
17. Fence for Parking Bicycles etc.

← **Route for Vehicles**

Source: Royal Dutch Touring Club, *Woonerf*, The Hague, Netherlands, 1980, p. 8.

The shorter the uninterrupted length of roadway, the slower the traffic will be. Short stretches ending in T-intersections are particularly effective in reducing speeds and accidents.[32]

Speed Control Devices

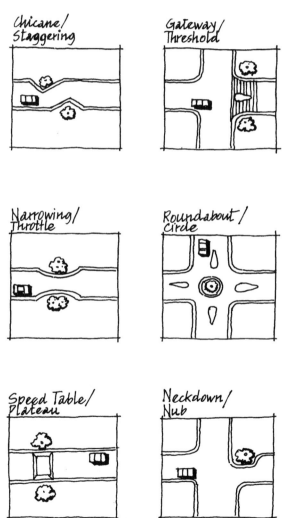

Chicane/Staggering

Gateway/Threshold

Narrowing/Throttle

Roundabout/Circle

Speed Table/Plateau

Neckdown/Nub

Even cul-de-sacs must be kept short if speeding is to be discouraged. National authorities disagree on maximum cul-de-sac lengths, with recommendations ranging from 400 to 1,500 feet.[33] If traffic calming is the object, the lower end of the range is preferable because drivers will spend all their time either accelerating or decelerating and can never get up much speed.

On longer stretches of roadway, it is still possible to calm traffic by dividing the length into shorter sections. Introduced at regular intervals or key junctures, traffic calming devices or *slow points* operate on a simple principle: An abrupt change in either horizontal or vertical alignment causes drivers to naturally slow down. Just how much they slow down depends the type, geometry, and spacing of devices.[34] With the reduction in speed comes a decrease in injury accident rates and an increase in walking, bicycling, and street life.[35] Cities around the U.S. have proven such devices can calm traffic in their older gridded areas.[36]

Design Speeds of Traffic Calming Devices

Device	Design Speed
speed hump (standard Watts design)	15-20 mph
speed table (long flat-topped hump)	25-30 mph
roundabout/circle (25-foot diameter island)	20-25 mph
chicane (90-foot radii)	20-25 mph
chicane with speed table	15-20 mph
narrowing (two-lane)	30-35 mph
narrowing with speed table	20-25 mph
narrowing (single-lane angled)	12-15 mph
raised junction	12-15 mph

Sources: W. Marconi, "Speed Control Measures in Residential Areas," *Traffic Engineering*, Vol. 47, March 1977, pp. 28-30; M.R. Daff and I.D.K. Siggins, "On Road Trials of Some New Types of Slow Points," Vol. 11, 1982, pp. 214-237; J.P. Clement, "Speed Humps and the Thousand Oaks Experience," *ITE Journal*, Vol. 53, January 1983, pp. 35-39; M. Fager, "Environmental Traffic Management in Stockholm," *ITE Journal*, Vol. 54, July 1984, pp. 16-19; D.A. Nicodemus, "Safe and Effective Roadway Humps - The Seminole County Profile," *ITE 1991 Compendium of Technical Papers*, Institute of Transportation Engineers, Washington, D.C., 1991, pp. 102-105; M. Durkin and T. Pheby, "York: Aiming To Be the UK's First Traffic Calmed City," in *Traffic Management and Road Safety*, PTRC Education and Research Services Ltd., London, England, 1992, pp. 73-90; H. Stein et al., "Portland's Successful Experience with Traffic Circles," *ITE 1992 Compendium of Technical Papers*, Institute of Transportation Engineers, Washington, D.C., 1992, pp. 39-44; D. Zaidel, A.S. Hakkert, and A.H. Pistiner, "The Use of Road Humps for Moderating Speeds on Urban Streets," *Accident Analysis and Prevention*, Vol. 24, 1992, pp. 45-56; L. Herrstedt et al., *An Improved Traffic Environment - A Catalogue of Ideas*, Danish Road Directorate, Copenhagen, 1993, p. 47; ITE Technical Council Task Force on Speed Humps, "Guidelines for the Design of Speed Humps," *ITE Journal*, Vol. 63, May 1993, pp. 11-17; and C.E. Walter, "Suburban Residential Traffic Calming," *ITE Journal*, Vol. 65, 1995, pp. 44-48.

Midpoint Speed vs. Distance Between Devices

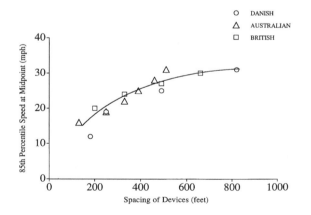

Sources: Main Roads Department, *Guidelines for Local Area Traffic Management*, East Perth, Western Australia, 1990, Table 7.2; J. Noble and A. Smith, *Residential Roads and Footpaths - Layout Considerations - Design Bulletin 32*, Her Majesty's Stationary Office, London, 1992, pp. 24-26; and L. Herrstedt et al., *An Improved Traffic Environment - A Catalogue of Ideas*, Danish Road Directorate, Copenhagen, 1993, p. 59.

Miami Lakes uses angled on-street parking and flared sidewalks, narrow travel lanes, small building setbacks, brick crosswalks, and tree-lined streets to calm traffic in its Town Center. Its residential street network is designed around short segments and T-intersections, and curves have been inserted into its main north-south artery for the sole purpose of slowing traffic. Bluewater Bay has an array of traffic calming devices—traffic circles, center islands, and brick crosswalks—and has reduced the apparent width of its central spine road by striping pavement for bike lanes and leaving mature trees just off the pavement edge. In these two developments, design speeds and speed limits are largely in sync, a rare occurrence in the United States.

Traffic Calmed Environment
in Miami Lakes Town Center

Typical T-Intersection in Miami Lakes

Traffic Circle in Bluewater Bay

TRAFFIC CALMING DEVICES ELSEWHERE IN FLORIDA

Speed Table in Tallahassee

Neckdown in Jacksonville

Chicane in Tampa

Practice 4: Keep speeds on local streets down to 20 mph.

By a wide margin, residents find traffic moving at 20 mph through their neighborhoods "acceptable"; by an equally wide margin, they find traffic at 30 mph, just 10 mph higher, unacceptable.[37] At 20 mph, drivers can anticipate conflicts and have time to stop for pedestrians at crosswalks.[38] Pedestrian-vehicle accidents are less frequent and, when they occur, much less severe.[39] Deep setbacks are not necessary when traffic is slow-moving; houses can be closer to the street, thereby saving land, reducing site development costs, and creating more human-scale streetscapes.[40]

Speed zones of 19 mph (30 kilometers per hour) have become common throughout Europe, always coupled with traffic calming measures; 20 mph speed limits are common on the main streets of traditional towns visited, and one even finds an occasional 15 mph limit. While U.S. authorities differ on this point, one leading street design manual recommends 20 mph design speeds for both access streets and subcollectors.[41] The Florida Department of Transportation (FDOT), in a recent update of its Green Book, allows design speeds as low as 20 mph when local streets have short segments, frequent stop signs, or other speed reduction measures built in (see following table). Thus, in recommending 20 mph design speeds on local streets, we are not out of line with current design philosophy and policy.

Resident Reaction to Speed of Traffic

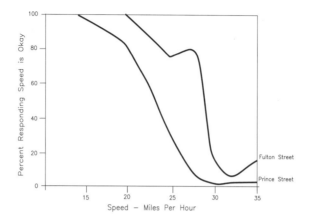

Source: D.T. Smith and D. Appleyard, *Improving the Residential Street Environment—Final Report*, Federal Highway Administration, Washington, D.C., 1981, pp. 116-119.

Chances of a Pedestrian Surviving a Traffic Accident

Vehicle speeds

40 mph — 10% chance of surviving

30 mph — 60% chance of surviving

20 mph — 95% chance of surviving

Source: M. Durkin and T. Pheby, "York: Aiming To Be the UK's First Traffic Calmed City," in *Traffic Management and Road Safety*, PTRC Education and Research Services Ltd., London, England, 1992, pp. 73-90.

Even Less Than 20 mph in Some Traditional Towns

GOOD AND NOT-SO-GOOD RESIDENTIAL STREET DESIGNS

Bluewater Bay

Hunter's Creek

FDOT's Recommended Minimum Design Speeds for Urban Streets
(mph)

	With Speed Restrictions	Without Speed Restrictions
Major Arterial	40	55
Minor Arterial	35	50
Major Collector	35	45
Minor Collector	30	40
Local Street	20	30

Source: Florida Department of Transportation (FDOT), *Manual of Uniform Minimum Standards for Design, Construction, and Maintenance for Streets and Highways (The Green Book)*, Tallahassee, 1994, p. III-6.

Practice 5: Keep speeds on arterials and collectors down to 35 mph (at least inside communities).

High-speed roads have a place in the regional transportation system, but not through the hearts of communities. This is one point on which contemporary and traditional planners agree. Such streets act as barriers to the free movement of pedestrians and cyclists, children and seniors; they have high pedestrian and cyclist fatality rates.[42]

Because they are incompatible with residential uses and demand deep setbacks, high-speed roads create no man's land along roadsides and/or invite commercial strip development. Roads are "abandoned" by people in deference to cars. No amount of landscaping can make them into boulevards in the true sense.

Surprisingly, such streets are not even ideal from the standpoints of highway capacity, vehicle fuel economy, and vehicle exhaust emissions. Maximum traffic flow rates are achieved at uniform speeds of 35 to 40 mph, not at higher speeds where vehicles tend to string out (i.e., vehicle headways increase).[43] Autos are also at their most fuel-efficient and clean-burning at moderate speeds.[44]

Thus, as they run through communities, higher-order streets should be designed for speeds of no more than 35 mph. A 35 mph design speed is at the low end of the acceptable range but does not violate any

Fuel Economy vs. Operating Speed

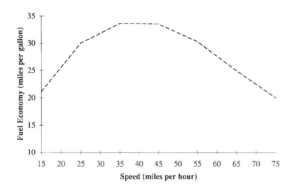

Source: S.C. Davis, *Transportation Energy Data Book: Edition 15*, U.S. Department of Energy, Washington, D.C., 1995, p. 3-54.

national or Florida state standard for urban collectors and minor arterials.[45]

The traditional towns chosen as exemplary follow this best practice; it is one reason why they stand out among the many small towns visited. They have managed to tame traffic as it passes through town by means of one-way pairs, stop signs and traffic signals, on-street parking, curves, street trees, and narrow setbacks.

Contemporary developments have not fared as well. Bluewater Bay and Hunter's Creek fought to reduce speed limits from 55 to 45 mph on state highways running through their communities. But the war was lost long ago when these roads were designed for higher speeds. Motorists still drive at what they correctly perceive as safe speeds, around 55 mph.

State Road 70 Through Downtown Arcadia

State Road 70 Outside Arcadia

No Man's Land Along a Parkway Through Hunter's Creek (even with the speed limit lowered to 45 mph)

68

Practice 6: Keep all streets as narrow as possible, and never more than four travel lanes wide.

"The tendency of many communities to equate wider streets with better streets and to design traffic and parking lanes as if the street were a 'microfreeway' is a highly questionable practice." These words come not from the "livable cities" movement or the "sustainable development" crowd, but instead from the American Society of Civil Engineers (ASCE), National Association of Home Builders (NAHB), and the Urban Land Institute (ULI).[46] There is a growing consensus that streets, particularly local ones, are overdesigned, at substantial cost to society.

Narrow streets are on nearly everyone's list of energy and cost saving ideas.[47] They require less asphalt and energy to begin with, and later have less effect on ambient air temperatures, thus moderating air conditioning demands and physical discomfort for anyone venturing outside in Florida's sub-tropical climate. Narrow street surfaces also save on site development costs, a savings that can be passed on to homebuyers and renters.

Narrow streets calm traffic. Vehicle operating speeds decline somewhat as individual lanes and street sections are narrowed.[48] Beyond lower speeds, drivers seem to behave less aggressively on narrow streets, running fewer traffic signals, for example.[49]

Grade-Separated Highways

Miami Lakes has the Palmetto Expressway dividing the community into east and west sections. Hunter's Creek has the newly opened Orlando beltway (southern leg) dividing north and south. Oakbridge has an expressway alignment running through its southern section. While certainly not ideal from the standpoint of community cohesion, these facilities provide much-needed regional mobility. Being elevated at street crossings, they pose no risk to traffic, pedestrian or vehicular, crossing from one side to the other. In sum, they are not comparable to oversized surface streets and are not at odds with this best practice.

Palmetto Expressway Through Miami Lakes

Pedestrians navigate with ease along and across narrow streets. One study reports higher pedestrian volumes on narrow than wide streets.[50] More elderly users, more bicyclists, more people out walking pets, and more pedestrians crossing back and forth all attest to a level of comfort with traffic on narrow streets that is missing on wide ones.

Why, then, do we continue to design streets with such wide cross-sections? Part of the reason is the lack of adequate route connectivity and density in the contemporary network (see *Transportation Practices 1 and 2*). Beyond that, we always design for the worst case—the occasional service vehicle, emergency vehicle, or parked car on access streets, and the 30th highest hourly traffic volume of the entire year on higher-order streets.[51] Local governments often compound the problem by adopting standards in code that are more conservative than even those recommended by conservative national street design manuals.

Streets, particularly local streets, should instead be designed for the everyday case.[52] We should move to the narrow end of nationally recommended street widths, or narrower still in keeping with the design speeds recommended in *Transportation Practices 4 and 5*. Communities that have opted for narrow

Recommended Residential Street Widths
(paved surface)

	ASCE/NAHB/ULI	Bucks County, PA	Orange County, FL*	Recommended for Florida
Locals	22-24' (access streets)	16-26' (access streets, depending on lot widths)	18' (0-300 average daily traffic volume)	18' (access streets with parking on only one side or in parking bays)
	26-28' (subcollectors)	20-36' (subcollectors, depending on lot widths and on-street parking policies)	20' (301-800 average daily traffic volume) 22' (801-1200 average daily traffic volume)	26' (subcollectors with a striped parking lane on one side)
Collectors	24-36' (minimum applies to streets with no fronting residences)	20-24' (depending on average daily traffic - no provision for on-street parking)	24' (1201-1500 average daily traffic volume) 36' (1501-3500 average daily traffic volume)	28' (with extra-wide curb lanes) 30' (with striped bike lanes on both sides) 34-36' (with striped parking lanes on both sides)

* Values for Orange County are minimum (as opposed to recommended) widths.

Sources: Bucks County Planning Commission, *Performance Streets - A Concept and Model Standards for Residential Streets*, Doylestown, Pa., 1980, pp. 9, 17, and 21; Residential Streets Task Force, *Residential Streets*, American Society of Civil Engineers/National Association of Home Builders/Urban Land Institute, Washington, D.C., 1990, p. 38; and Section 34-171, *Subdivision Regulations*, Orange County, Fla.

streets report that they perform well.[53] Localities around the U.S. are amending their ordinances to permit narrower streets than would have been imaginable a few years ago.[54]

Standards for Bucks County, Pennsylvania, made famous in *Performance Streets*, and for Orange County, Florida, from its code, are offered as sound examples. Also offered are some minimum widths of our own, suggested by design practices of Britain and Australia.[55] These countries have returned to narrow local streets after some experience with wider U.S.-style streets.

Our recommended width of access streets, 18 feet, may seem a bit narrow. If it does, it is only because the norms to which we compare it have become so inflated.[56] The access streets of Radburn, New Jersey, the model development that set the standard for contemporary developments to follow, are 18 feet. So are the access streets of Seaside and Laguna West, models of the new traditionalism. An 18-foot cross-section allows for 9-foot travel lanes, perfect for a design speed of 20 mph.[57] For this width to be workable, residents must be supplied with adequate off-street parking (as they nearly always are under today's subdivision ordinances); and spill-over parking must be restricted to one side of the street or to periodic parking bays (as it seldom is under subdivision ordinances).

The 18-foot width assumes traffic volumes typical of access streets, that is, less than 250 vehicles per day.[58] At such volumes, the probability of two vehicles meeting is less than one in five.[59] Should traffic volumes be much higher, access streets should probably be designed to subcollector standards instead.

At the recommended width, the occasional service or emergency vehicle can comfortably pass a parked car.[60] In the rare instance when two motorists meet across from a parked car,

one can pull over until the other passes. It happens all the time in older neighborhoods and no one seems to mind. If such an arrangement discourages parking on the street in residential areas, it is probably for the best since curb-side parking is a prime contributor to pedestrian accidents (including dart-out accidents involving children).[61] Commercial areas are another matter. There, on-street parking is appropriate in many cases, and recommended street widths for subcollectors or collectors apply.

The recommended widths of collectors provide for continuous two-way traffic operation and 10-foot travel lanes. Ten-foot lanes are appropriate for a design speed of 35 mph. They can accommodate a standard bus or truck (design width of 8.5 feet) and are in keeping

with national standards.[62] Depending on their location, collectors will have extra-wide shared lanes, 5-foot bike lanes, or 7- or 8-foot parking lanes.[63] Ordinarily, they will not have both bike and parking lanes in the same section due to the hazards to bicyclists of cars pulling in and out and car doors opening. Collectors are rarely outfitted with parking lanes these days, but to buffer pedestrians in commercial areas, it would be a good practice to reinstate.

Developers are rediscovering the advantages of narrow streets. Haile Plantation has built several 12-foot access streets into housing clusters, skirting county street standards by calling them "driveways." Hunter's Creek now builds mostly 20-foot residential streets under Orange County's innovative code (see above)

18' Street Accommodating Service and Emergency Vehicles

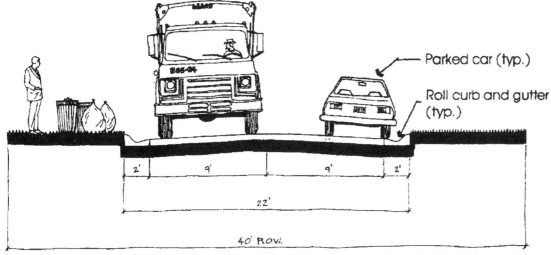

Parked car (typ.)

Roll curb and gutter (typ.)

2'   9'   9'   2'

22'

40' R.O.W.

Source: D. Jensen, *Community Applications of Density, Design and Cost*, National Association of Home Builders, Washington, D.C., 1983, p. 29. Reprinted with permission from Home Builders Press, National Association of Home Builders, 1201 15th St., NW, Washington, DC, 20005; 800-223-2665.

Perfectly Adequate 12' Access Street in Haile Plantation

and has even experimented with 18-foot streets on cul-de-sacs. Oakbridge and Palmer Ranch have sought and been granted variances to build 20-foot residential streets. Bluewater Bay has built 20-foot streets with parking bays.

Higher-order streets through communities should be limited to four lanes, and when built with four, always divided by medians to help pedestrians cross safely with minimum delay (see *Transportation Practice 9*). A parkway will literally split Hunter's Creek in two when it is eventually widened to six lanes. Other "problem" road widenings, guaranteed to render these communities less walkable, are planned for S.W. 104th Street through The Hammocks (four to six lanes), Harden Boulevard through Oakbridge (four to six lanes), and Miami Lakes Drive East (two to four lanes).

Narrow Streets in Traditional Towns

Traditional towns surveyed are generally happy with their older residential streets, some of which are as narrow as 18 or 20 feet from curb-to-curb. They report no citizen complaints, no lawsuits resulting from inadequate road geometrics, and no noticeable difference in accident rates when compared to newer parts of town.

The only concerns recorded in our interviews were minor and situational. In Key West, solid lines of parked cars reduce the effective width of streets, making it difficult for commercial vehicles to maneuver through the historic district. The problem is not the width of streets per se but rather the lack of off-street parking. The width would be no problem in a modern subdivision with adequate off-street parking required by code.[64]

Adequate Street Width (But Lack of Off-Street Parking) in Key West

18' Street with Room to Spare at Hunter's Creek

Parking Bay on a 20' Street at Bluewater Bay

4-Lane Collector with a Median and On-Street Parking at The Hammocks

Practice 7: Align streets to give buildings energy-efficient orientations.

U.S. street design manuals pay little attention to proper building orientation for energy efficiency.[65] This is in contrast to the manuals of our sister countries. One Australian design manual, for example, requires 95 percent of housing units to face within 15 degrees of due north-south; it recommends that collectors be laid out on north-south axes so that local residential streets will mostly lie on east-west axes.[66]

The angle of the sun changes with the seasons. In the summer, when the sun is high at midday, east and west exposures receive about twice as much daily sunlight as do north and south exposures; in the winter, when the sun is lower and more southerly, the reverse is true.[67] Thus, by having buildings' long windowed sides face within a few degrees of true south, Floridians benefit from solar heating in the winter and natural shading in the summer; heating bills can be shaved by up to 50 percent and cooling bills by up to 20 percent.[68] Southern exposure is particularly advantageous when porches, awnings, or other overhangs shade windowed fronts and backs (as they do on so many older homes in traditional towns).

Depending on the direction of breezes in spring, summer, and autumn, the basic north-south orientation may be modified somewhat. For example, in the Miami area with prevailing easterly winds, the optimum orientation is 5 degrees east of south. Orienting a building to catch the wind can be worth a cool 20 percent savings on air-conditioning bills.[69]

Energy-efficient orientation is easy to achieve in a traditional grid; local streets can be laid out predominantly on east-west axes. This places the windowed fronts and backs of buildings on the north and south sides. Where lots are unusually narrow and deep, the sides of buildings may have more window and surface area than do the fronts and backs; there, residential streets should be laid out predominantly on north-south axes.

Energy-efficient orientation is trickier, but still possible, in a contemporary street network. Contemporary networks (with curving through-streets, loops, and cul-de-sacs) need not curve continually in a spaghetti-like pattern. Instead, endless curves can be replaced with short arcs and longer tangents that provide stretches of north-south orientation. Arcs and tangents are not only more energy-efficient, but potentially more efficient from the standpoint of lot yield (producing fewer irregularly shaped lots).[70] And they have qualities important to urban designers such as clarity, simplicity, and focus, all missing from continually curving streets.

Continuous Curves vs. Arcs and Tangents

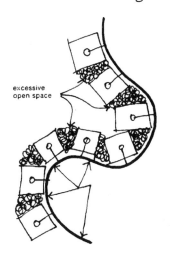

excessive open space

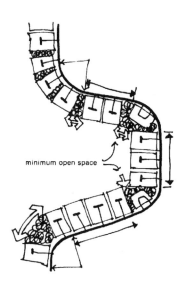

minimum open space

Source: National Association of Home Builders, *Cost Effective Site Planning—Single Family Development*, Washington, D.C., 1986, p. 52. Reprinted with permission from Home Builders Press, National Association of Home Builders, 1201 15th St., NW, Washington, DC, 20005; 800-223-2665.

73

One of the nation's most acclaimed developments, Village Homes in Davis, California, manages to achieve a dominant north-south building orientation and corresponding energy savings within a curvilinear street network; it does so by means of arcs, tangents, and angled lots and homes. Where curves are un-avoidable, homes may be placed at an angle to the street to maintain optimal building orientation. If anything, identically angled houses give more visual order to curving streets than do houses parallel to the street, as explained in the classic, *Man-Made America*.[71]

The Palmer Ranch development order requires that structures be oriented "to reduce solar heat gain by walls and to use the natural cooling effect of wind." This requirement has not always been met at Palmer Ranch, and developers generally, including exemplary ones, could pay more attention to building orientation in their street layouts and lotting.

North-South Orientation in a Curvilinear Network (Village Homes of Davis, Calif.)

Source: M. N. Corbett, *A Better Place To Live—New Designs for Tomorrow's Communities*, Rodale Press, Emmaus, Pa., 1981, p. 101.

Optimal Orientation with Angled Lots and Homes

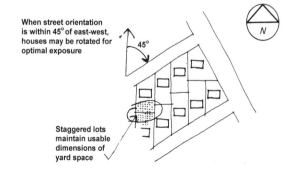

When street orientation is within 45° of east-west, houses may be rotated for optimal exposure

45°

N

Staggered lots maintain usable dimensions of yard space

Source: Adapted from J. Colman, *Streets for Living—A Guide to Better Australian Residential Design Practice*, Australian Road Research Board, Victoria, 1978, p. 47.

Practice 8: Avoid using traffic signals wherever possible and always space them for good traffic progression.

In the U.S., we *rush rush rush* from intersection to intersection, only to *wait wait wait* at traffic signals. This stop-and-go driving is exasperating, fuel-inefficient, and polluting. It is better that traffic move at moderate but sustained speeds.

Over-reliance on signalized intersections is a sign of flawed network design. Either the network has too few routes and too little connectivity, or alternatively, the land plan allows too much development for the network. "In the larger scale developments, when tracts on both sides of major streets are concurrently planned, collector street volumes can be held below signal requirements by providing more intersections."[72] Hence our preference for higher network densities and more interconnections.

The traditional towns surveyed are notable for the absence of traffic signals at all but a handful of intersections. Apalachicola, for example, has only one traffic signal (and a blinking one that) along the entire length of U.S. 98, relying instead on stop signs at the many cross streets. Some of our exemplary new developments also do well in this regard. The Hammocks has only one internal traffic signal (excluding a warning signal at a fire station), and Bluewater Bay and Haile Plantation have none at all.

Where traffic volumes are high enough to warrant traffic signals but not high enough to absolutely require them, 4-way stop signs and roundabouts should be considered instead. While not favored by traffic engineers, 4-way stops are well-liked by residents who value their traffic calming effect and the minimal delays they cause under light traffic conditions. Even from a safety standpoint, the sticking point for traffic engineers, 4-way stops may outperform signals at moderate traffic volumes (say, up to 10,000 vehicles per day on the major street).[73]

U.S. traffic engineers have not favored roundabouts either, but this is largely a case of mistaken identity; modern roundabouts are mistaken for old-fashioned traffic circles (see accompanying feature box). The virtues of roundabouts are beginning to be acknowledged at transportation conferences and in transportation journals. Specifically, they allow traffic from different directions to share space in the intersection, while signals require traffic to take turns. Thus, roundabouts have more capacity and produce shorter delays when traffic flows are somewhat balanced.[74] Properly designed, roundabouts force traffic to slow down as it enters intersections, while traffic goes barreling through signalized intersections on green, yellow, and sometimes even red lights. This gives roundabouts a safety advantage.[75] Roundabouts have an aesthetic advantage, too; their landscaped center islands visually break up expanses of pavement and close vistas. And roundabouts may be less expensive to install and maintain than traffic signals, depending on the size of the center islands.[76]

4-Way Stop Sign Control at Palmer Ranch

High-Capacity Roundabout in Daytona Beach

Roundabouts vs. Traffic Circles

Modern roundabouts are distinct from old-fashioned traffic circles.[77] With a roundabout, approaching traffic must wait for a gap in the traffic flow before entering the intersection, while traffic enters a traffic circle at high speeds and then must merge and weave, a more hazardous operation. Roundabouts also differ from traffic circles in their smaller center islands, greater angles of deflection at entries, and flared approaches (characteristics which moderate land consumption, slow traffic, and increase capacity, respectively). Thus, at a time when traffic circles are *non grata* among traffic engineers and are being from removed from high-accident locations in the Northeast, roundabouts are growing in popularity.

Modern Roundabout Design

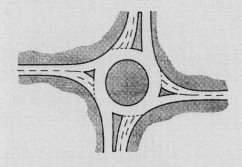

Source: Leif Ourston & Associates, *Roundabout Design, First Draft*, California Department of Transportation, Los Angeles, 1993, p. 1200-4.

In Britain and Australia, roundabouts substitute for traffic signals over a wide range of traffic volumes (see accompanying figure). FDOT now accepts roundabouts on low-volume, two-lane state highways, and local governments throughout Florida are experimenting with roundabouts at higher traffic volumes.[78] Haile Plantation, on the new addition to its site, will install roundabouts at four key intersections.

Where traffic signals cannot be avoided, they should be spaced to allow good progression of traffic from signal to signal. Optimal spacing of signals depends on vehicle operating speeds and signal cycle lengths. At speeds of 35 mph and standard cycle lengths, signals must be at least a third of a mile apart for good progression.[79] Such spacing is consistent with FDOT's standard for state highways, and with its recommended minimums for city and county roads.[80] Whatever combination of speed and cycle length is chosen, signals must be spaced at *uniform intervals* to achieve progressive flow in both directions.

There is a downside to the elimination of traffic signals. Signals create long gaps in the traffic flow, allowing pedestrians and bicyclists to cross more easily at intersections or upstream and downstream of intersections. Note, though, that other *Best Transportation Practices*, particularly those relating to network design and traffic calming, will ease crossings without the artifice of stop-and-go traffic. If true pedestrian safety is the object (safety far beyond that afforded by conventional traffic signals), exclusive pedestrian signals can always be installed at marked crosswalks.[81]

Guidelines for Roundabout Use

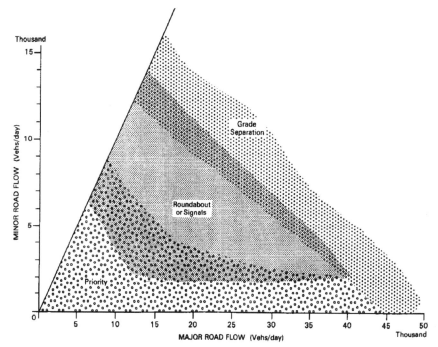

Source: Institution of Highways and Transportation, *Roads and Traffic in Urban Areas*, Her Majesty's Stationary Office, London, 1987, p. 328. Crown copyright is reproduced with the permission of the Controller of HMSO.

Optimal Signal Spacing as a Function of Speed and Cycle Length

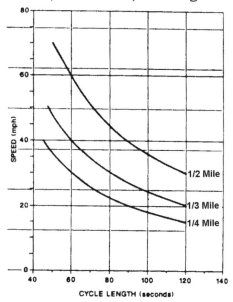

Source: V. G. Stover, P. B. Demosthenes, and E. M. Weesner, "Signalized Intersection Spacing: An Element of Access Management," *ITE 1991 Compendium of Technical Papers*, Institute of Transportation Engineers, Washington, D. C., 1991, pp. 176-181.

Practice 9: Provide networks for pedestrians and bicyclists as good as the network for motorists.

Residents of suburbia may walk or bike for fun within their individual subdivisions. They may walk for other purposes within activity centers reached by automobile. But most would not dream of using these modes for "utilitarian" trips from home to work, home to shopping, etc. And they are loath to let younger children venture outside their immediate subdivisions on foot or bike. Destinations are just too far away, and facilities linking islands of activity are just too spotty.[82]

In design guidelines published separately, suggestions will be offered for making walk/bicycle travel more inviting.[83] In this document, our object is to make travel by these modes safe and hence feasible.[84]

If we expect people to walk at all, we must provide a *network* for them as good as for motorists. This does not require exact parity in miles of roadway vs. miles of sidewalk. Rather it means that the same places must be reachable on foot or bike without jeopardizing life and limb.

Sidewalks are an absolute necessity along all through-streets serving developed areas.[85] Pedestrian accidents are more likely on street sections without sidewalks than those with them, two-and-one-half times more likely according to one study.[86] Sidewalk clearances, vertical curbs, street trees between street and sidewalk, and parked cars all add to the sense of security.

Sidewalks are less essential on quiet residential streets. Many subdivisions in our featured developments lack sidewalks, and families are still seen strolling and riding bikes. Surprisingly, even in traditional towns with their street grids, residents seem comfortable walking on the street in neighborhoods without sidewalks. Through-traffic largely avoids such streets, and local traffic respects the residential character by going slowly.

Yet, the costs of residential sidewalks are not so very great, and the benefits are considerable. In single-family developments, sidewalks, including the land occupied by the sidewalk itself and its planting strip, add about 2 percent to the hard costs of housing.[87] Sidewalks extend the public realm beyond the street itself, encouraging neighborliness and street life.[88] Where there are sidewalks, children play on them. Where there are not, street play is limited.[89] One has to assume that even adults are more comfortable walking on residential streets with sidewalks, and hence are more likely to walk.

BUFFERED SIDEWALKS ALONG COLLECTORS

Haile Boulevard

Miami Lakes Drive East

Thus, we are inclined to err in favor of sidewalks, except at very low densities. Sidewalk guidelines issued by the Federal Highway Administration (FHWA) have become widely accepted.[90] They are endorsed here and reproduced in the accompanying table. Of the exemplary developments, Hunter's Creek, Miami Lakes, and Palmer Ranch come closest to meeting the FHWA guidelines.

Sidewalk Guidelines

Arterials/Collectors	Both Sides
Local Streets	
Commercial Areas	Both Sides
Residential Areas	
More than 4 units per acre	Both Sides
1 to 4 units per acre	One Side
Less than 1 unit per acre	None

Source: R.L. Knoblauch et al., *Investigation of Exposure Based Pedestrian Accident Areas: Crosswalks, Sidewalks, Local Streets and Major Arterials,* Federal Highway Administration, Washington, D.C., 1988, p. 143.

Sidewalks on Both Sides of a Typical Miami Lakes Street

Sidewalk on One Side of a Typical Palmer Ranch Street

Skilled bicyclists prefer to travel on the street system along with automobiles. To accommodate them, striped bike lanes or extra-wide curb lanes are warranted on arterials and collectors. There is some debate about which of the two—the separate bike lane or extra-wide shared lane—is safer for bicyclists.[91] In terms of user acceptance (as opposed to safety), the bike lane seems to have an edge.[92] Regardless of which criterion is used, both bike lanes and extra-wide shared lanes are much preferred to standard-width shared lanes.[93] The State of Florida and many of its cities and counties now build arterials with either bike lanes or extra-wide curb lanes.

Children and casual adult cyclists outnumber highly skilled adult cyclists by more than 20-to-1.[94] The less skilled majority must be separated from high-speed, high-volume traffic or they will not ride. Nearly all examples of "mass bicycle commuting to school" occur where access is possible by separate bike lanes or bike paths or by low-volume residential streets.[95] Places in Florida where the bicycle is a serious mode of travel have miles of bike lanes, bike paths, and/or low-volume side streets paralleling arterials. This is true of Gainesville and Key West, where respectively, 6 percent and 12 percent of commuters bike to work. To encourage more of the same, we endorse and reproduce bikeway guidelines issued recently by FHWA.

After sidewalks, the next most important safety features are marked and lighted crosswalks, and raised medians or refuge islands. Most injuries and fatalities occur as pedestrians attempt to cross streets, and most are at night.[96] Accident rates are significantly lower where marked crosswalks are provided and crossings are lighted.[97] Crosswalks should be provided wherever FHWA guidelines are met (see accompanying figure).

Outside cities, where superblocks are the norm, most pedestrian accidents occur at midblock locations; many pedestrians are simply unwilling to walk to all the way to an intersection.[98] To maintain reasonable spacing, crosswalks should be provided at midblock locations whenever pedestrian traffic is heavy and blocks are more than 600 feet long.[99] Because drivers do not expect to encounter them, midblock crosswalks should be well-marked and outfitted with advance warning signs, warning flashers, and/or pedestrian-activated signals.

Pedestrian accident rates are also lower on streets with raised medians.[100] Raised medians offer refuge to pedestrians crossing wide streets and allow them to focus on one direction of traffic at a time. They are particularly important in the suburbs, where long blocks encourage midblock crossings. Raised medians should be provided on all streets with four or more lanes.

Bike Lane at Bluewater Bay

Guidelines for Crosswalk Installation

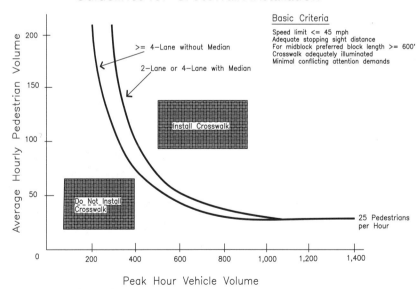

Source: R. L. Knoblauch et al., *Investigation of Exposure Based Pedestrian Accident Areas: Crosswalks, Sidewalks, Local Streets and Major Arterials*, Federal Highway Administration, Washington, D.C., 1988, p. 54.

Practice 10: Provide pedestrians and bicyclists with shortcuts and alternatives to travel along high-volume streets.

Pedestrians and bicyclists travel without benefit of engine-powered, climate-controlled, entertainment-equipped, protective metal shells known as cars. This makes them much more sensitive than motorists to the length of trips and the environment in which they travel.

Pedestrians like to follow lines of least resistance, cutting corners and keeping their routes as direct as possible. They are uncomfortable with heavy automobile traffic; when asked about their likes and dislikes, pedestrians in one survey cited traffic-related conditions as three of their four biggest dislikes—with car exhaust at number 1, dangerous street crossings at number 3, and loud traffic noise at number 4.[101] These dislikes ranked ahead of incomplete sidewalk systems and wind tunnel effects (in Canada, no less).

Back when streets were laid out on grids, pedestrians and bicyclists had access to relatively direct routes and alternatives to travel along high-volume streets (since continuous side streets exist in a grid). These pedestrian-friendly features were lost with the shift to curvilinear, branching street networks. Initially, large-scale developers attempted to compensate by building separate pathway systems for pedestrians and bicyclists, cutting across common property rather than following indirect street alignments.

However, it soon became clear that at suburban densities, these separate systems did not generate enough pedestrian and bicycle traffic for personal security.[102] At least along the street, pedestrians and bicyclists were seen by passing motorists.

How to satisfy pedestrians' competing desires for security, direct routing, and moderate traffic volumes? The best way is through good street network design. Networks can be grid-like without the negatives of the gridiron (see *Transportation Practices 1 and 3*). Miami Lakes, for example, has retained enough street connectivity to permit easy access to the Town Center via back streets.

The next best option—which applies to contemporary developments with superblocks, curvilinear streets, and cul-de-sacs—is to supplement the sidewalk system with pedestrian pass-throughs and passageways following pedestrian desire lines. One source recommends that the ends of cul-de-sacs be connected with pass-throughs, another that blocks more than 800 feet long have midblock passageways.[103] From the literature on defensible space, pass-throughs and passageways are best if short, straight, and well-lighted.[104] Turns that create hiding places should be avoided; users should be able to scan the entire distance for potential threats.[105] Many examples of pedestrian shortcuts are found at The Hammocks and Haile Plantation. Hunter's Creek has provided cul-de-sac pass-throughs along Town Center Boulevard.

Pedestrian Shortcut at The Hammocks

Cul-de-Sac Pass-Throughs at Hunter's Creek

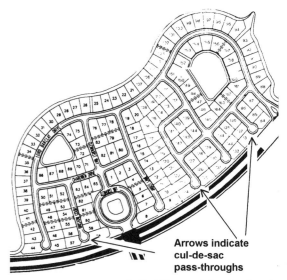

Arrows indicate cul-de-sac pass-throughs

Where longer off-street pathways are provided, they should be designed for connectedness, scenic views, and natural surveillance.[106] Paved pathways along the central spine of The Hammocks are heavily utilized. This is due to the extensive network of pathways (10 miles in total, more than eight miles without street crossings). It is also due to the lake views and the good connections to neighborhoods, schools, recreation centers, and shopping areas. Finally, it is due to the natural surveillance afforded by bordering homes and apartments. A paved trail along a utility easement at Haile Plantation, while used by some children to bike to school, lacks the connections, amenity, surveillance, and hence heavy utilization of The Hammocks' pathways. A paved pathway at Hunter's Creek, connecting neighborhoods to an elementary school, has an intermediate level of amenity and surveillance.

Practice 11: Incorporate transit-oriented design features.

Transit operations have not proven wildly successful in new communities around the United States.[107] Even when the communities are dense enough to support transit service, and most are not, the suburban context in which they find themselves is not conducive to transit use.

Thus, rather than endorsing some particular transit service option, or calling for some form of developer subsidy, we suggest that communities be designed to support transit service when regional transit agencies are ready to provide it. If that day may never arrive, due to a site's remote location or low-density context, a large-scale development probably should not be approved in the first place.

Mode of Travel to Work in New Communities
(% of commuters)

	Carpool	Transit
Columbia, Md.	12%	3%
Coral Springs, Fla.	12	<1
First Colony, Tx.	10	1
Foster City, Calif.	10	4
Miami Lakes, Fla.	9	1
Mission Viejo, Calif.	11	<1
Peachtree City, Ga.	10	<1
Rancho Santa Margarita, Calif.	13	<1
Reston, Va.	13	6
St. Charles, Md.	23	<1
The Woodlands, Tx.	12	4

Source: Journey-to-work data from Summary Tape File 3A, 1990 U.S. Census of Population and Housing.

OFF-STREET PATHWAYS

The Hammocks

Haile Plantation

Hunter's Creek

About 40 transit-oriented development (TOD) manuals are now available across North America.[108] In Florida alone, two transit operators have published TOD guidelines.[109]

Generalizing across the manuals, there is agreement that, at a minimum, medium densities are required to support transit service; a mixture of residential, commercial, and institutional uses is preferable to any single use alone. Our *Land Use Practices 3 and 4*, and *Housing Practice 2*, are in line with TOD manual recommendations.

TOD manuals agree that grid-like street networks are superior to discontinuous, curvilinear networks. Several manuals emphasize the importance, in addition, of collectors spaced not too far apart and penetrating residential areas and activity centers. Our *Transportation Practices 1 and 2* run along these same lines.

TOD manuals call for sidewalks along transit routes, on streets leading to transit routes, and radiating out from transit stops to nearby buildings. Some call for midblock crosswalks, cul-de-sac pass-throughs, diagonal walkways through parking lots, and other pedestrian shortcuts to make access to transit more direct. Our *Transportation Practices 9 and 10* comport with the TOD manuals in this regard.

All that is missing from our best practices are transit facility design standards of the type contained in many TOD manuals. The list includes:

• Minimum lane widths and corner radii on transit streets;

• Guidelines for bus stop spacing and placement at intersections (nearside, farside, or midblock); and

• Specifications for bus benches, shelters, turnout bays, and supporting street furniture.

A pedestrian- and transit-oriented design manual, prepared for the Florida Department of Transportation by the FAU/FIU Joint Center for Environmental and Urban Problems, will cover all of the above. Rather than duplicating that effort, we incorporate the manual by reference.

The best example of transit among the exemplary communities surveyed is at The Hammocks. Its net residential density, 11.5 units per acre, is the highest of featured developments, and its transit trip generators—multifamily housing, a junior high school, and a community shopping center—are all in one place, in or around the Town Center. Transit service penetrates the development, ending in the Town Center itself. Stops have amenities, including bus shelters and benches, and are overlooked by housing for a measure of security. At 2 percent, the mode split for work trips is not high, but it is probably as high as can be expected at an outlying location like The Hammocks.

Transit at The Hammocks Town Center that Is Used

Transit at Miami Lakes that May Be Used

Transit at Hunter's Creek that Will Never Be Used

Practice 12: Establish TDM programs at employment centers.

At the national and state levels, emphasis is shifting from supplying all the street capacity that might be demanded, to managing the demand for peak-hour travel via ridesharing incentives, modified work hours, and telecommuting programs.[110] Such measures fall under the heading of travel demand management, or TDM for short.

Carpooling is common already, at least compared with other alternatives to driving alone.[111] It is the preferred alternative to driving alone when Florida commuters are asked for their second choice.[112] Under Southern California's mandatory trip reduction program, expanded carpooling accounts for nearly all the vehicle trips eliminated to date.[113] In Florida, TDM requirements are appearing with increasing frequency in development orders for large-scale projects, and are a qualifying factor for the Florida Quality Developments Program. Thus, it seems only fitting that these best practices should make TDM a part of exemplary development.

Large employers are the best candidates for TDM programs.[114] They have large pools of employees for ridematching, the ability to stagger shifts, and more financial resources to call upon than do small employers. Peak-hour travel reductions of 20 percent or more are possible at individual employment sites with the right financial and other incentives.[115]

Smaller employers should be enlisted as well. They can offer flexible work hours and part-time telecommuting to their employees; both are as common among small employers as large ones, economies of scale being relatively unimportant for these TDM measures.[116] And small employers can pool their employees and financial resources in cooperative ridesharing programs. There is some evidence that employees at small work sites are just as receptive to ridesharing as are employ-

Peak-Hour Travel Impacts of Modified Work Hours and Telecommuting

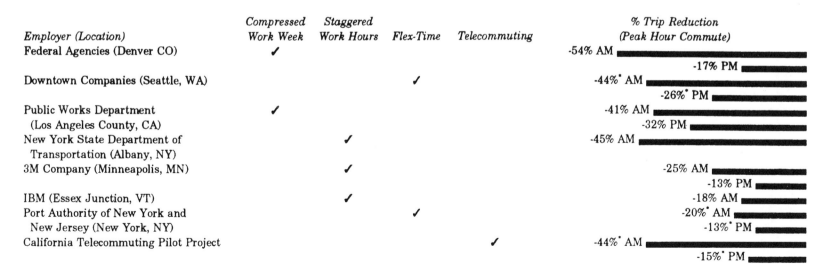

Employer (Location)	Compressed Work Week	Staggered Work Hours	Flex-Time	Telecommuting	% Trip Reduction (Peak Hour Commute)
Federal Agencies (Denver CO)	✓				-54% AM / -17% PM
Downtown Companies (Seattle, WA)			✓		-44%* AM / -26%* PM
Public Works Department (Los Angeles County, CA)	✓				-41% AM / -32% PM
New York State Department of Transportation (Albany, NY)		✓			-45% AM
3M Company (Minneapolis, MN)		✓			-25% AM / -13% PM
IBM (Essex Junction, VT)		✓			-18% AM
Port Authority of New York and New Jersey (New York, NY)			✓		-20%* AM / -13%* PM
California Telecommuting Pilot Project				✓	-44%* AM / -15%* PM

Source: R. Ewing, "TDM, Growth Management, and the Other Four Out of Five Trips," *Transportation Quarterly*, Vol. 47, 1993, pp. 343-366.

ees at large work sites, and with matches across work sites, have just as high ridematching rates.[117]

The pooling of employees and resources is accomplished through Transportation Management Associations (TMAs) or, as they are called lately, Transportation Management Organizations (TMOs). Florida has nine TMAs/TMOs at present, with more to come.[118] These organizations are eligible for seed money and technical assistance from the state.[119] The two business parks at Miami Lakes and the proposed Park of Commerce at Palmer Ranch would be good candidates.[120]

State-of-the-Art in TDM

This best practice may seem like a reach, given the state of TDM practice in Florida. However, TDM programs are becoming quite common nationally, and will be even more so as federal congestion management and air quality requirements take full effect. The emerging state-of-the-art goes beyond employer-based programs to include computerized "instant" carpooling; teleshopping, telebanking, and tele-education via fiber optics; congestion pricing measures with automatic vehicle identification; and advanced traveler information systems. "Green" developments around North America are contemplating a range of high-tech TDM options.

Fiber Optics Comes to Hunter's Creek

[1] See R. Ewing, "Transportation Service Standards—As If People Matter," *Transportation Research Record 1400*, 1993, pp. 10-17.

[2] W. Kulash, "Neotraditional Town Design—Will the Traffic Work?" Session Notes, AICP Workshop on Neotraditional Town Planning, American Institute of Certified Planners, Washington, D.C., 1991.

[3] It has been said that we got ourselves into today's traffic mess by "putting all our transportation eggs in one basket," that basket being the auto-highway system. R.K. Untermann, *Accommodating the Pedestrian—Adapting Towns and Neighborhoods for Walking and Bicycling*, Van Nostrand Reinhold Company, New York, 1984, p. 5.

[4] To our knowledge, this is one of only three recommendations that break with policies or standards of the Florida Department of Transportation (FDOT). FDOT's policy on street network design is: "The general layout of local and collector streets should follow a branching network, rather than a highly interconnected grid network." While not advocating a return to the traditional grid, we advocate more interconnectivity of streets than FDOT's policy suggests. On such other matters as designing networks to minimize traffic signals, limiting the number of driveways on higher-order streets, and using medians to divide multi-lane highways, we are in complete agreement with FDOT. And with respect to design speeds, use of roundabouts, and most other matters, we are in general agreement. Parenthetically, our other differences with FDOT (and they are not big ones) are in our recommended widths of streets (see *Transportation Practice* 6).

[5] F.A. Curtis, L. Neilsen, and A. Bjornsor, "Impact of Residential Street Design on Fuel Consumption," *Journal of Urban Planning and Development*, Vol. 110, 1984, pp. 1-8; M.G. McNally, "Regional Impacts of Neotraditional Neighborhood Development," *ITE 1993 Compendium of Technical Papers*, Institute of Transportation Engineers, Washington, D.C., 1993, pp. 463-467; and M.G. McNally and S. Ryan, "Comparative Assessment of Travel Characteristics for Neotraditional Designs," *Transportation Research Record 1400*, 1993, pp. 67-77.

[6] While less tangible, grids also offer what urban designers refer to as "contextual continuity" and "legibility," which are thought to be important to pedestrians.

[7] Short blocks make trips feel shorter to pedestrians since progress is judged against the milestones of intersections. San Francisco has 300 intersections per square mile, Santa Monica 180, and Irvine 15. The walkability of these places, by all accounts, is in the same rank order. See A.B. Jacobs, "City Streets and Their Contexts," *A Decade Reviewed—Commitment Renewed*, 10th Annual Pedestrian Conference, City of Boulder, Colo., 1989, pp. 41-61.

[8] Alameda-Contra Costa Transit District, *Guide for Including Public Transit in Land Use Planning*, Oakland, Calif., 1983, pp. 17-20; Municipality of Metropolitan Seattle, *Encouraging Public Transportation through Effective Land Use Actions*, Seattle, 1987, p. 44; City of Winnipeg Transit Department, *Incorporating Public Transit Requirements in the Subdivision Design Process*, Winnipeg, 1988 Draft, p. 8; Pace Suburban Bus Service, *Pace Development Guidelines*, Chicago, 1989, p. VI-6; and Ontario Ministry of Transportation, *Transit-Supportive Land Use Planning Guidelines*, Toronto, 1992, pp. 25, 40.

[9] G. Thompson and J. Frank, *Transit Patronage as a Product of Land Use Potential and Connectivity: The Sacramento Case*, Office of Research and Special Programs, U.S. Department of Transportation, Washington, D.C., 1995.

[10] H. Marks, "Subdividing for Traffic Safety," *Traffic Quarterly*, Vol. 11, 1957, pp. 308-325; M.A. Wallen, "Landscaped Structures for Traffic Control," *Traffic Engineering*, Vol. 31, January 1961, pp. 18-22; P.C. Box, "Accident Characteristics of Non-Arterial Streets," *Traffic Digest and Review*, March 1964, pp. 12, 17-19; G.T. Bennett and J. Marland, *Road Accidents in Traditionally Designed Residential Estates*, Supplementary Report 394, Transportation Road Research Laboratory, Crowthorne, England, 1978; D.G. Bagby, "The Effects of Traffic Flow on Residential Property Values," *Journal of the American Planning Association*, Vol. 46, 1980, pp. 88-94; and U. Henning-Hager, "Urban Development and Road Safety," *Accident Analysis and Prevention*, Vol. 18, 1986, pp. 135-145. For general perspectives, see R. Brindle, "Residential Area Planning for Pedestrian Safety," Joint ARRB/DOT Pedestrian Conference, Australian Road Research Board, Victoria, Australia, 1978; and S.O. Gunnarsson, "Urban Traffic Network Design—A Spatial Approach," in *Effecting Change Step-by-Step*, 9th Annual Pedestrian Conference, Boulder, Colo., 1988, pp. 199-218.

[11] C. Bevis and J.B. Nutter, *Changing Street Layouts to Reduce Residential Burglary*, Governor's Commission on Crime Prevention and Control, St. Paul, Minn., 1977; F.J. Fowler, *Reducing Residential Crime and Fear: The Hartford Neighborhood Crime Prevention Program—Executive Summary*, U.S. Department of Justice, Washington, D.C., 1979, pp. 10-11, 26-41; O. Newman, *Community of Interest*, Anchor Press, Garden City, N.Y., 1980, pp. 137-143; S.W. Greenberg, W.M. Rohe, and J.R. Williams, "Safety in Urban Neighborhoods: A Comparison of Physical Characteristics and Informal Territorial Control in High and Low Crime Neighborhoods," *Population and Environment*, Vol. 5, 1982, pp. 141-165; B. Poyner, *Design Against Crime—Beyond Defensible Space*, Butterworths, New York, 1983, pp. 15-27; S.W. Greenberg and W.M. Rohe, "Neighborhood Design and Crime—A Test of Two Perspectives," *Journal of the American Planning Association*, Vol. 50, 1984, pp. 48-61; R.B. Taylor, S.A. Schumaker, and S.D. Gottfredson, "Neighborhood-Level Link Between Physical Features and Local Sentiments: Deterioration, Fear of Crime, and Confidence," *Journal of Architectural and Planning Research*, Vol. 2, 1985, pp. 261-275; P. Stollard, *Crime Prevention Through Housing Design*, E&F N Spon, London, 1991, pp. 68-70; R. Tell, "Fighting Crime: An Architectural Approach," *Journal of Housing*, Vol. 47, 1990, pp. 207-212; T.D. Crowe, *Crime Prevention Through Environmental Design—Applications of Architectural Design and Space Management Concepts*, Butterworth-Heinemann, Boston, 1991, p. 161; and O. Newman, "Defensible Space—A New Physical Planning Tool for Urban Revitalization," *Journal of the American Planning Association*, Vol. 61, 1995, pp. 149-155.

[12] Bennett and Marland, op. cit.; Henning-Hager, op. cit.;

J.B. Lansing, R.W. Marans, and R.B. Zehner, *Planned Residential Environments*, Survey Research Center, University of Michigan, Ann Arbor, 1970, pp. 114-115; C. Zerner, "The Street Hearth of Play," *Landscape*, Vol. 22, 1977, pp. 19-30; and D. Appleyard, *Livable Streets*, University of California Press, Berkeley, 1981, p. 133.

[13] H.M. Rubenstein, *A Guide to Site Planning and Environmental Planning*, John Wiley & Sons, New York, 1987, p. 60; D. Listokin and C. Walker, *The Subdivision and Site Plan Handbook*, Center for Urban Policy Research, Rutgers University, New Brunswick, N.J., 1989, pp. 207-208; and NAHB Research Center, *Proposed Model Land Development Standards and Accompanying Model State Enabling Legislation*, U.S. Department of Housing and Urban Development, Washington, D.C., 1993, p. 8.

[14] C. Tunnard and B. Pushkarev, *Man-Made America—Chaos or Control? An Inquiry into Selected Problems of Design in the Urbanized Landscape*, Harmony Books, New York, 1981, pp. 98-99.

[15] There is no shortage of network performance measures in the literature. See P. Haggett and R.J. Chorley, *Network Analysis in Geography*, St. Martin Press, New York, 1969, pp. 1-35, 57-105, 118-130; E.J. Taaffe and H.L. Gauthier, *Geography of Transportation*, Prentice-Hall, Englewood Cliffs, N.J., 1973, pp. 100-115; H.R. Kirby, "Accessibility Indices for Abstract Road Networks," *Regional Studies*, Vol. 10, 1976, pp. 479-482; W.R. Blunden and J.A. Black, *The Land-Use/Transport System*, Pergamon Press, New York, 1984, pp. 141-144; K.G. Zografos and R.G. Crowley, "Low-Volume Roadway Network Improvements and the Accessibility of Public Facilities in Rural Areas," *Transportation Research Record 1106*, 1987, pp. 26-33; and C.J. Khisty, M.Y. Rahi, and C.S. Hsu, "Morphological Modeling of the City and Its Transportation System: A Preliminary Investigation," *Transportation Research Record 1237*, 1989, pp. 18-28.

[16] ITE Technical Council Committee 5P-8, *Traffic Engineering for Neo-Traditional Neighborhood Design*, Institute of Transportation Engineers, Washington, D.C., 1994.

[17] P.H. Brown, "The Economics of Traditional Neighborhoods: Competing for the Bottom Line with Conventional Subdivisions—A Case Study of Four Mile Creek," *Land Development*, Vol. 6, Fall 1993, pp. 20-24; P. Calthorpe, "New Neighborhoods—Laguna West," *The Next American Metropolis—Ecology, Community, and the American Dream*, Princeton Architectural Press, New York, 1993, pp. 146-149; and P. Katz, "Playa Vista," *The New Urbanism—Toward an Architecture of Community*, McGraw-Hill, New York, 1994, pp. 178-191.

[18] The two perspectives are outlined by Greenberg and Rohe, op. cit. Depicting CPTED philosophical divisions in a slightly different manner are Stollard, op. cit., pp. 14-20; R.A. Gardiner, *Design for Safe Neighborhoods—The Environmental Security Planning and Design Process*, U.S. Department of Justice, Washington, D.C., 1978, pp. 11-17; and B. Hillier, "Against Enclosure," in N. Teymur, T.A. Markus, and T. Woolley (eds.), *Rehumanizing Housing*, Butterworths, London, 1988, pp. 63-88.

[19] D. Dillon, "Fortress America," *Planning*, Vol. 60, June 1994, pp. 8-12; R.M. Elizer and N. Lalani, "Facing Up to the Street Closure Epidemic," *ITE Journal*, Vol. 65, October 1994, pp. 24-28; and E.J. Blakely and M.G. Snyder, *Fortress America: Gated and Walled Communities in the United States*, Lincoln Institute of Land Policy, Cambridge, Mass., 1995, pp. 1-22.

[20] C. Stapleton, *Planning and Road Design for New Residential Sub-Divisions—Guidelines*, Director General of Transport for South Australia, Adelaide, 1988a, p. 29; Model Code Task Force, *Australian Model Code for Residential Development*, Department of Health, Housing and Community Services, Commonwealth of Australia, Canberra, 1990, pp. 48-51; Main Roads Department, *Guidelines for Local Area Traffic Management*, East Perth, Western Australia, 1990, p. 92; and Department of Planning and Housing, *Victorian Code for Residential Development—Subdivision and Single Dwellings*, State Government of Victoria, Melbourne, Australia, 1992, pp. 37-41. Also see Residential Streets Task Force, *Residential Streets*, American Society of Civil Engineers/National Association of Home Builders/Urban Land Institute, Washington, D.C., 1990, p. 27.

[21] Alameda-Contra Costa Transit District, op. cit., p. 20;

Municipality of Metropolitan Seattle, op. cit., p.44; Ontario Ministry of Transportation, op. cit., pp. 45-46; Snohomish County Transportation Authority, *A Guide to Land Use and Public Transportation*, Technology Sharing Program, U.S. Department of Transportation, Washington, D.C., 1989, pp. 7-6 and 7-7; W. Bowes, M. Gravel, and G. Noxon, *Guide to Transit Considerations in the Subdivision Design and Approval Process*, Transportation Association of Canada, Ottawa, Ontario, 1991, p. A-8; and Denver Regional Council of Governments, *Suburban Mobility Design Manual*, Denver, Colo., 1993, p. 26.

[22] Kulash, op. cit.; J.R. Stone and C.A. Johnson, "Neo-Traditional Neighborhoods: A Solution to Traffic Congestion?" in R.E. Paaswell et al. (eds.), *Proceedings of the Site Impact and Assessment Conference*, American Society of Civil Engineers, New York, 1992, pp. 72-76; and M.J. Wells, "Neo-Traditional Neighborhood Developments: You Can Go Home Again," Unpublished paper available from the author, Wells & Associates, Inc., Arlington, Va., 1993.

[23] High turnover of homes on main roads, and succession of residential to commercial uses, are reported in Arcadia and Key West.

[24] Alameda-Contra Costa Transit District, op. cit., p.20; Ontario Ministry of Transportation, op. cit., p. 50; and P. Langdon, "Stroll Down the Boulevard," *Planning*, Vol. 60, November 1994, pp. 16-17.

[25] A discussion of traffic speed vs. livability follows in *Transportation Practice 4*. For more on traffic volume vs. livability, plus the useful concept of "environmental capacity" (maximum acceptable traffic volume), see Appleyard, op. cit., pp. 41-99; C. Buchanan, "Appendix A: The Environmental Capacity of Streets," *Traffic in Towns—A Study of the Long Term Problems of Traffic in Urban Areas*, Her Majesty's Stationery Office, London, 1963, pp. 203-213; H. Marks, "Traffic Capacity," *Traffic Circulation Planning for Communities*, Gruen Associates, Los Angeles, 1974, pp. 223-231; D.T. Smith and D. Appleyard, "Studies of Speed and Volume on Residential Streets," *Improving the Residential Street Environment*, Federal Highway Administration, Washington, D.C., 1981, pp. 113-130; S. Spitz, "How Much Traffic Is Too Much (Traffic)," *ITE Journal*, Vol. 52, May 1982, pp. 44-45; and R. Klaeboe,

"Measuring the Environmental Impact of Road Traffic in Town Areas," in *Environmental Issues*, PTRC Education and Research Services Ltd., London, England, 1992, pp. 81-88. The environmental capacity of a residential street is far less than its physical capacity.

[26] TEST, *Quality Streets—How Traditional Urban Centres Benefit from Traffic-Calming*, London, 1988, pp. 1-20.

[27] J.P. Clement, "Speed Humps and the Thousand Oaks Experience," *ITE Journal*, Vol. 53, January 1983, pp. 35-39.

[28] Their approaches to traffic calming are reviewed in R. Tolley, *Calming Traffic in Residential Areas*, Brefi Press, Brefi, England, 1990; and A. Clarke and M.J. McDornfeld, *Traffic Calming, Auto-Restricted Zones and Other Traffic Management Techniques—Their Effects on Bicycling and Pedestrians*, Case Study No. 19, National Bicycling and Walking Study, Federal Highway Administration, Washington, D.C., 1994. Also see CART, *Traffic Calming*, Sensible Transportation Options for People, Tigard, Ore., 1989, J. Pucher and S. Clorer, "Taming the Automobile in Germany," *Transportation Quarterly*, Vol. 46, 1992, pp. 383-395; A. O'Brien, "Traffic Calming—Ideas Into Practice," *ITE 1993 Compendium of Technical Papers*, Institute of Transportation Engineers, Washington, D.C., 1993, pp. 129-134; and R. Ewing, "Residential Street Design: Do the British and Australians Know Something We Americans Don't?" *Transportation Research Record 1455*, 1994, pp. 42-49.

[29] J.M. Mounce, "Driver Compliance with Stop-Sign Control at Low-Volume Intersections," *Transportation Research Record 808*, 1981, pp. 30-37; D. Meier, "The Policy Adopted in Arlington County, Virginia, for Solving Real and Perceived Speeding Problems on Residential Streets," *ITE 1985 Compendium of Technical Papers*, Institute of Transportation Engineers, Washington, D.C., 1985, pp. 97-101; J.J. Nitzel, F.G. Schattner, and J.P. Mick, "Residential Traffic Control Policies and Measures," *ITE 1988 Compendium of Technical Papers*, Institute of Transportation Engineers, Washington, D.C., 1988, pp. 217-223; and R.F. Beaubien, "Controlling Speeds on Residential Streets," *ITE Journal*, Vol. 59, April 1989, pp. 37-39.

[30] J. Noble and A. Smith, *Residential Roads and Footpaths—Layout Considerations, Design Bulletin 32*, Her Majesty's Stationery Office, London, 1992, p. 22. Also see Institution of Highways and Transportation, *Roads and Traffic in Urban Areas*, Her Majesty's Stationery Office, London, 1987, p. 260.

[31] R. Brindle, "Local Street Speed Management in Australia—Is It 'Traffic Calming'?" *Accident Analysis and Prevention*, Vol. 24, 1992, pp. 29-38. Also see Model Code Task Force, op. cit., pp. 37-66; Noble and Smith, op. cit., 23-31; S. Grava, "Traffic Calming—Can It Be Done in America?" *Transportation Quarterly*, Vol. 47, 1993, pp. 483-505; L. Herrstedt et al., *An Improved Traffic Environment—A Catalogue of Ideas*, Danish Road Directorate, Copenhagen, 1993, pp. 33-64; and K. Halperin and R. Huston, "A Verkehrsberuhigung Design for an American Road," *ITE Journal*, Vol. 64, April 1994, pp. 28-34.

[32] Box, op. cit.; Bennett and Marland, op. cit.; Marks, op. cit., 1957; Wallen, op. cit.; P.R. Staffeld, "Accidents Related to Access Points and Advertising Signs in Study," *Traffic Quarterly*, Vol. 7, 1953, pp. 59-74; N.A. David and J.R. Norman, *Motor Vehicle Accidents in Relation to Geometric and Traffic Features of Highway Intersections*, *Volume II*, Federal Highway Administration, Washington, D.C., 1975, pp. 51-54; and G.F. Hagenauer et al., "Intersections," in *Synthesis of Safety Research Related to Traffic Control and Roadway Elements*, *Volume 1*, Federal Highway Administration, Washington, D.C., 1982, pp. 5-1 through 5-21.

[33] For a review of recommendations from the national literature, and various rationales for limiting the lengths of cul-de-sacs, see Bucks County Planning Commission, *Performance Streets—A Concept and Model Standards for Residential Streets*, Doylestown, Pa., 1980, pp. 12-13. Also see Residential Streets Task Force, op. cit., pp. 54-55; and ITE Technical Council Committee 5A-25A, *Guidelines for Residential Subdivision Street Design—A Recommended Practice*, Institute of Transportation Engineers, Washington, D.C., 1993, p. 9.

[34] Brindle, op. cit.; Herrstedt et al., op. cit.; Main Roads Department, op. cit., pp. 79-82; Noble and Smith, op. cit., pp. 24-26; Smith and Appleyard, op. cit., pp. 97-98; W.

Marconi, "Speed Control Measures in Residential Areas," *Traffic Engineering*, Vol. 47, March 1977, pp. 28-30; M.R. Daff and I.D.K. Siggins, "On Road Trials of Some New Types of Slow Points," Vol. 11, 1982, pp. 214-237; C. Stapleton, *Planning and Road Design for New Residential Subdivisions—Supplement to Guidelines*, Director General of Transport, Adelaide, South Australia, 1988b, pp. 51-54; D. Zaidel, A.S. Hakkert, and A.H. Pistiner, "The Use of Road Humps for Moderating Speeds on Urban Streets," *Accident Analysis and Prevention*, Vol. 24, 1992, pp. 45-56; J. Craus et al., "Geometric Aspects of Traffic Calming in Shared Streets," *ITE 1993 Compendium of Technical Papers*, Institute of Transportation Engineers, Washington, D.C., 1993, pp. 1-5; and M. Klik and A. Faghri, "A Comparative Evaluation of Speed Humps and Deviations," *Transportation Quarterly*, Vol. 47, 1993, pp. 457-469.

[35] Many European traffic calming studies are reviewed in Clarke and Dornfeld, op. cit., pp. 3-24; and Tolley, op. cit. Also see M. Jenks, "Residential Roads Researched: Are Innovative Estates Safer?" *Architects' Journal*, Vol. 177, June 1983, pp. 46-49; M. Fager, "Environmental Traffic Management in Stockholm," *ITE Journal*, Vol. 54, July 1984, pp. 16-19; J.H. Kraay, "Woonerven and Other Experiments in the Netherlands," *Built Environment*, Vol. 12, 1986, pp. 20-29; W.B. Hagan and S.E. Amamoo, "Residential Street Management in South Australia" *ITE Journal*, Vol. 58, March 1988, pp. 35-41; W.S. Homburger et al., *Residential Street Design and Traffic Control*, Prentice Hall, Englewood Cliffs, N.J., 1989, pp. 79-112; B. Eubanks-Ahrens, "A Closer Look at the Users of Woonerven," in A. Vernez Moudon (ed.), *Public Streets for Public Use*, Columbia University Press, New York, 1991, pp. 63-79; S.T. Janssen, "Road Safety in Urban Districts—Final Results of Accident Studies in the Dutch Demonstration Projects of the 1970s," *Traffic Engineering + Control*, Vol. 32, 1991, pp. 292-296; S.D. Challis, "North Earlham Estate, Worwich—The First UK 20 mph Zone," in *Traffic Management and Road Safety*, PTRC Education and Research Services Ltd., London, England, 1992, pp. 61-72; M. Durkin and T. Pheby, "York: Aiming To Be the UK's First Traffic Calmed City," in *Traffic Management and Road Safety*, PTRC Education and Research Services Ltd., London, England, 1992, pp. 73-90; L. Herrstedt, "Traffic Calming Design—A Speed Management Method: Danish Experience on Environmentally Adapted Through Roads,"

Accident Analysis and Prevention, Vol. 24, 1992, pp. 3-16; W. Brilon and H. Blanke, "Extensive Traffic Calming: Results of the Accident Analyses in Six Model Towns," *ITE 1993 Compendium of Technical Papers*, Institute of Transportation Engineers, Washington, D.C., 1993, pp. 119-123; E. Ben-Joseph, "Changing the Residential Street Scene—Adapting the Shared Street (Woonerf) Concept to the Suburban Environment," *Journal of the American Planning Association*, Vol. 61, 1995, pp. 504-515; and C.L. Hoyle, *Traffic Calming*, Planning Advisory Service Report Number 456, 1995.

36 Clarke and Dornfeld, op. cit., pp. 25-39; Hoyle, op. cit.; Meier, op. cit.; S.R. Jepsen, "The American Woonerf, Boulder's Experience," *ITE 1985 Compendium of Technical Papers*, Institute of Transportation Engineers, Washington, D.C., 1985, pp. 102-107; B.D. Kanely and B.E. Ferris, "Traffic Diverters for Residential Traffic Control—The Gainesville Experience," *ITE 1985 Compendium of Technical Papers*, Institute of Transportation Engineers, Washington, D.C., 1985, pp. 72-76; G.S. Rutherford, R.L. McLaughlin, and E. von Borstel, "Traffic Circles for Residential Intersection Control: A Comparison with Yield Signs Based on Seattle's Experience," *Transportation Research Record 1010*, 1985, pp. 65-68; D.A. Nicodemus, "Safe and Effective Roadway Humps—The Seminole County Profile," *ITE 1991 Compendium of Technical Papers*, Institute of Transportation Engineers, Washington, D.C., 1991, pp. 102-105; R.C. Welke, "Guidelines for the Establishment and Maintenance of Realistic Speed Limits on Public Roadways in Montgomery County, Maryland," *ITE 1991 Compendium of Technical Papers*, Institute of Transportation Engineers, Washington, D.C., 1991, pp. 89-96; H. Stein et al., "Portland's Successful Experience with Traffic Circles," *ITE 1992 Compendium of Technical Papers*, Institute of Transportation Engineers, Washington, D.C., 1992, pp. 39-44; W.M. Bretherton and J.E. Womble, "Neighborhood Traffic Management Program," *ITE 1992 Compendium of Technical Papers*, Institute of Transportation Engineers, Washington, D.C., 1992, pp. 398-401; K.L. Gonzalez, "Neighborhood Traffic Control: Bellevue's Approach," *ITE Journal*, Vol. 63, 1993, pp. 43-45; G. Halbert et al., "Implementation of a Residential Traffic Control Program in the City of San Diego," *Environment—Changing Our Transportation Priorities*, Institute of Transportation Engineers, Washington, D.C., 1994, pp. 265-271; and C.E.

Walter, "Suburban Residential Traffic Calming." *ITE Journal*, Vol. 65, 1995, pp. 44-48.

37 Smith and Appleyard, op. cit., pp. 116-119.

38 Not only are stopping distances shorter at low speeds, but drivers are more aware of roadside activity. Drivers at high speeds have a form of tunnel vision, focusing on the road ahead at some distance.

39 Accident studies are cited by R.K. Untermann, "Changing Design Standards for Streets and Roads," in A. Vernez Moudon (ed.), *Public Streets for Public Use*, Columbia University Press, New York, 1991, pp. 256-260. Also see Durkin and Pheby, op. cit.; Noble and Smith, op. cit., p. 12; and N.J. Garber and R. Srinivasan, *Accident Characteristics of Elderly Pedestrians*, Mid-Atlantic Universities Transportation Center, University Park, Pa., 1990, pp. 35-37; and J.H. Kraay, M.P. Mathijssen, and F.C. Wegman, *Towards Safer Residential Areas*, Institute of Road Safety Research SWOV/Ministry of Transport, Leidschendam, Switzerland, undated, p. 33.

40 Small setbacks accentuate the impacts of traffic, deep ones soften them. Appleyard, op. cit., p. 140. If traffic is slow-moving, the impacts are so moderate anyway that small setbacks should suffice.

41 Residential Streets Task Force, op. cit., p. 43.

42 Garber and Srinivasan, op. cit.; R.J. Bush, *Statewide Pedestrian Study, Phase 3 Report—Correlation and Evaluation of Pedestrian Accident Data*, Federal Highway Administration, Washington, D.C., 1986, pp. 16 and 34; and W.W. Hunter, W.E. Pein, and J.C. Stutts, "Bicycle/Motor Vehicle Crash Types: The Early 1990s," Paper presented at the 74th Annual Meeting, Transportation Research Board, Washington, D.C., 1995.

43 V.G. Stover, "Signalized Intersection Spacing: An Element of Access Management," *ITE 1991 Compendium of Technical Papers*, Institute of Transportation Engineers, Washington, D.C., 1991, pp. 176-181. That traffic flow is maximized at 35 to 40 mph is a bit of conventional wisdom. Actually, studies have pegged the flow-maximizing speed at anywhere from 9 to 45 mph,

depending in part on the type of highway. See the literature review in K.A. Small, *Urban Transportation Economics*, Harwood Academic Publishers, Chur, Switzerland, 1992, pp. 61-69.

44 D.S. Parker and T.C. Stedman, *Energy Efficient Transportation for Florida*, Florida Solar Energy Center, Cape Canaveral, 1991, p. 3; and S.C. Davis, *Transportation Energy Data Book: Edition 15*, U.S. Department of Energy, Washington, D.C., 1995, p. 3-54. EPA's most recent version of the MOBILE emissions factor model, MOBILE 5a, shows volatile organic compound emissions and carbon monoxide emissions (on a grams/mile basis) dropping with increases in average operating speeds up to 20 mph, leveling off, and then rising again above 55 mph. Nitrogen oxide emissions (again, on a grams/mile basis) decline up to about 10 mph, level off, and then begin to rise rapidly above 45 mph.

45 ITE Technical Council Committee 5A-25A, op. cit., p. 13; ITE Committee 6Y-19, *Planning Urban Arterial and Freeway Systems—A Recommended Practice*, Institute of Transportation Engineers, Washington, D.C., 1988, p. 7; American Association of State Highway and Transportation Officials (AASHTO), *A Policy on Geometric Design of Highways and Streets*, Washington, D.C., 1990, pp. 68, 480, and 524; and Florida Department of Transportation (FDOT), *Manual of Uniform Minimum Standards for Design, Construction, and Maintenance for Streets and Highways (The Green Book)*, Tallahassee, 1994, p. III-6.

46 Residential Streets Task Force, op. cit., p. 37.

47 C.C. Harwood, *Using Land to Save Energy*, Ballinger Publishing Co., Cambridge, Mass., 1977, pp. 98-99; W. Sanders and D. Mosena, *Changing Development Standards for Affordable Housing*, PAS Report Number 371, American Planning Association, Chicago, 1982, pp. 8-9; D. Jensen, *Community Applications of Density, Design, and Cost*, National Association of Home Builders, Washington, D.C., 1983, pp. 25-28; NAHB National Research Center, *Affordable Residential Land Development: A Guide for Local Government and Developers*, U.S. Department of Housing and Urban Development, Washington, D.C., 1987, pp. 43-53; E.L. Fisher, *Affordable Housing: Development Guidelines for State and Local Government*, U.S. Department of Housing and Urban Development, Washington, D.C., 1991, p. 40;

and S.M. White, *Affordable Housing—Proactive and Reactive Planning Strategies*, PAS Report Number 441, American Planning Association, Chicago, 1992, p. 44.

[48] How much effect lane and street widths have on running speeds is debatable, but the weight of evidence indicates that they have some effect. Clark, op. cit.; Smith and Appleyard, op. cit., p. 125; O.T. Farouki and W.J. Nixon, "The Effect of Width of Suburban Roads on the Mean Free Speed of Cars," *Traffic Engineering and Control*, Vol. 17, 1976, pp. 518-519; C.L. Heimbach, P.D. Cribbins, and M.S. Chang, "Some Partial Consequences of Reduced Traffic Lane Widths on Urban Arterials," *Transportation Research Record 923*, 1983, pp. 69-72; H.S. Lum, "The Use of Road Markings to Narrow Lanes for Controlling Speed in Residential Areas," *ITE Journal*, Vol. 54, June 1984, pp. 50-53; J.E. Clark, "High Speeds and Volumes on Residential Streets: An Analysis of Physical Street Characteristics as Causes in Sacramento, California," *ITE 1985 Compendium of Technical Papers*, Institute of Transportation Engineers, Washington, D.C., 1985, pp. 93-96; D.W. Harwood, *Effective Utilization of Street Width on Urban Arterials*, Appendix A, National Cooperative Highway Research Program Report 330, Transportation Research Board, Washington, D.C., 1990, pp. 127-137; and S.A. Ardekani, J.C. Williams, and C.S. Bhat, "The Influence of Urban Network Features on the Quality of Traffic Service," *Transportation Research Record 1358*, 1992, pp. 6-12.

[49] R.K. Untermann, "Street Design—Reassessing the Function, Safety and Comfort of Streets for Pedestrians," in *The Road Less Traveled: Getting There by Other Means*, 11th International Pedestrian Conference, City of Boulder, Colo., 1990, pp. 19-26.

[50] Ibid.

[51] See Ewing, op. cit., 1994; and R. Ewing, "Roadway Levels of Service in an Era of Growth Management," *Transportation Research Record 1364*, 1992, pp. 63-70.

[52] For concurring opinions from three countries, see Noble and Smith, op. cit., p. 63; Residential Streets Task Force, op. cit., p. 49; and AUSTROADS, *Guide to Traffic Engineering Practice—Local Area Traffic Management*, Sydney, Australia, 1988, p. 19.

[53] D. Bassert, "Street Standards Survey Finds Narrower Streets Perform Well," *Land Development*, Vol. 1, December 1988, pp. 6-7.

[54] L. Paretchan, "Skinny Streets for Residential Neighborhoods," in *Alternative Transportation: Planning, Design, Issues, Solutions*, 14th International Pedestrian Conference, City of Boulder, Colo., 1993, pp. 41-44; and J.M. Fernandez, "Boulder Brings Back the Neighborhood Street," *Planning*, Vol. 60, June 1994, pp. 21-26.

[55] Ewing, op. cit., 1994.

[56] For the history of street standards, and a between-the-lines critique of contemporary standards, see M. Southworth and E. Ben-Joseph, "Street Standards and the Shaping of Suburbia," *Journal of the American Planning Association*, Vol. 61, 1995, pp. 65-81.

[57] Admittedly, our recommended 9-foot lane width on local streets falls short of the Florida Department of Transportation's standard of 10 feet. We would only note that FDOT provides for certain exceptions to its standard and that, by FDOT's own declaration, its standards need be applied only "to the extent that *economic and environmental considerations* and existing development will allow" (emphasis added). See Florida Department of Transportation (FDOT), op. cit., p. III-28 and unnumbered introductory page.

[58] Bucks County Planning Commission, op. cit., p. 7; and Residential Streets Task Force, op. cit., p. 28.

[59] On residential streets, a daily volume of 250 vehicles corresponds to an afternoon peak-hour volume of about 18 vehicles. Of the 18, 12 are typically coming home and 6 are going out. If the average distance traveled along an access street is 500 feet (which is higher than recommended in *Transportation Practice 3* but may be more realistic), and the average speed is 10 mph (which would include time spent backing out of driveways, accelerating, and decelerating), the time spent on the access street will average just over 30 seconds. It can be shown that the 12 vehicles coming and 6 vehicles going stand a 1 in 5 chance of meeting one another under such circumstances. The traffic parameters used in this calculation are derived from Institute of Transportation Engineers (ITE), *Trip Generation*, Washington, D.C., 1991, pp. 257 and 265.

[60] Passenger cars and trucks have "design vehicle" widths of 7 and 8.5 feet, respectively. An 18-foot section, even with parking on one side, leaves a 2-3 foot clearance for emergency vehicles. A perennial sticking point, opposition to narrow streets by local fire officials, can be best addressed as follows. First, several jurisdictions considering neo-traditional developments have performed mock demonstrations proving that narrow streets and tight corners still allow access by emergency vehicles. Second, literally hundreds of older communities around the United States, plus communities in Britain, Australia, and Europe, have streets as narrow as recommended here and seem to function just fine. Third, fire departments have proven resourceful in those rare instances when access to property is blocked, cutting across lawns, pushing vehicles out of the way, etc. Fourth, our recommended 18-foot width applies only to streets with little development and traffic on them. Longer streets with more traffic should, as indicated in the text, be built to subcollector standards and/or designed as loops or circuitous through-streets that provide access from two directions. Ewing, op. cit., 1994; Jensen, op. cit., p. 28; and E. Lerner-Lam et al., "Neo-Traditional Neighborhood Design and Its Implications for Traffic Engineering," *ITE Journal*, Vol. 62, January 1992, pp. 17-25.

[61] See the literature review in D.E. Cleveland, M.J. Huber, and M.J. Rosenbaum, "On-Street Parking," in *Synthesis of Safety Research Related to Traffic Control and Roadway Elements, Volume 1*, Federal Highway Administration, Washington, D.C., 1982, pp. 9-1 through 9-16. Also see Henning-Hager, op. cit.; J.B. Humphreys et al., *Safety Aspects of Curb Parking—Final Technical Report*, Federal Highway Administration, Washington, D.C., 1978, pp. 33-121; and G. Sokolow, "Should the Transportation Profession Encourage On-Street Parking in Our Neighborhoods?" Unpublished paper available from the author, Florida Department of Transportation, Tallahassee, 1991. In residential areas, on-street parking is seen as more of a threat than a protection from traffic. Appleyard, op. cit., p. 141.

62 American Association of State Highway and Transportation Officials (AASHTO), op. cit., p. 482; and Residential Streets Task Force, op. cit., p. 38. The Florida Department of Transportation prescribes slightly wider (11') lanes on collectors and arterials. We agree that wider lanes are required on high-speed arterials, but not on collectors designed for moderate speeds. See D.W. Harwood, op. cit.; Heimbach et al., op. cit.; and Roy Jorgensen Associates, *Cost and Safety Effectiveness of Highway Design Elements*, National Cooperative Highway Research Report 197, Washington, D.C., 1978, p. 76.

63 Fourteen-foot shared curb lanes and 5-foot bike lanes are suitable for road design speeds of 35 mph or less, per *Transportation Practice 5*. See D.T. Smith, *Safety and Locational Criteria for Bicycle Facilities—Final Report*, Federal Highway Administration, Washington, D.C., 1975, pp. 19-20; Florida Department of Transportation (FDOT), *Bicycle Facilities Planning & Design Manual*, Tallahassee, Fla., 1982, pp. 5-10 through 5-12; S.R. McHenry and M.J. Wallace, *Evaluation of Wide Curb Lanes as Shared Lane Bicycle Facilities*, Maryland Department of Transportation, Baltimore, 1985, pp. 62-63; American Association of State Highway and Transportation Officials (AASHTO), *Guide for the Development of Bicycle Facilities*, Washington, D.C., 1991, pp. 14-18; J. Forester, *Bicycle Transportation: A Handbook for Cycling Transportation Engineers*, MIT Press, Cambridge, Mass., 1994, p. 236; and W.C. Wilkinson et al., *Selecting Roadway Design Treatments to Accommodate Bicycles*, Federal Highway Administration, Washington, D.C., 1994, p. 19. Eight-foot parking lanes are required on urban collector streets through commercial areas; 7-foot parking lanes are sufficient in residential areas. American Association of State Highway and Transportation Officials (AASHTO), op. cit., 1990, pp. 411-415 and 482-483.

64 One other problem with narrow streets was cited during our interviews. In Arcadia, semi-tractor trailers have trouble negotiating corners in the old industrial area just south of downtown. This problem, too, is situational. The industrial area is too close to downtown and sits within a neighborhood. Otherwise, it would be possible to spare everyone the aggravation by establishing a truck route to the industrial area and banning semis from narrow residential streets.

65 Only one of the three generally accepted U.S. residential street design manuals even mentions energy conservation, and then only in a passing reference to solar access. Residential Streets Task Force, op. cit., p. 32.

66 Stapleton, op. cit., 1988a, pp. 30, 43.

67 R.K. Vieira, K.G. Sheinkopf, and J.K. Sonne, *Energy-Efficient Florida Home Building*, Florida Solar Energy Center, Cape Canaveral, Fla., 1988, pp. 3-2 and 3-5. Building orientation, siting, and spacing for energy efficiency is discussed most completely in G.Z. Brown, *Sun, Wind, and Light—Architectural Design Strategies*, John Wiley & Sons, New York, 1985.

68 Vieira et al., op. cit., pp. 3-1 and 3-2.

69 Vieira et al., op. cit., pp. 3-1 and 3-7.

70 National Association of Home Builders (NAHB), *Cost Effective Site Planning—Single Family Development*, Washington, D.C., 1986, p. 52.

71 Tunnard and Pushkarev, op. cit., pp. 98-105. Works touting the overall design and street layout of Village Homes, a 70-acre development that could be reproduced almost anywhere but remains one-of-a-kind, include: D. Erley and M. Jaffe, *Site Planning for Solar Access—A Guidebook for Residential Developers and Site Planners*, U.S. Department of Housing and Urban Development, Washington, 1980, pp. 69-81; J. Zanetto, "Master Planning," in E.G. McPherson (ed.), *Energy-Conserving Site Design*, American Society of Landscape Architects, Washington, D.C., 1984, pp. 87-114; S. Weissman and J. Corbett, *Land Use Strategies for More Livable Places*, The Local Government Commission, Sacramento, Calif., 1992, p. 70; C.L. Girling and K.I. Helphand, *Yard - Street - Park—The Design of Suburban Open Space*, John Wiley & Sons, New York, 1994, pp. 155-158; and J.T. Lyle, *Regenerative Design for Sustainable Development*, John Wiley & Sons, New York, 1994, pp. 12 and 126.

72 ITE Technical Council Committee 5A-25A, op. cit., p. 14.

73 D. Syrek, "Accident Rates at Intersections," *Traffic Engineering*, Vol. 25, 1962, pp. 312-316; G.M. Ebbecke and J.J. Schuster, "Areawide Impact of Traffic Control Devices," *Transportation Research Record 644*, 1977, pp. 54-57; and H.H. Bissell and L.G. Neudorff, "Criteria for Removing Traffic Signals," *ITE 1980 Compendium of Technical Papers*, Institute of Transportation Engineers, Washington, D.C., 1980, pp. 56-66. Also see W.M. Bretherton, "Signal Warrants—Are They Doing the Job?" *ITE 1991 Compendium of Technical Papers*, Institute of Transportation Engineers, Washington, D.C., 1991, pp. 163-167; and J.N. LaPlante and C.R. Kropidlowski, "Stop Sign Warrants: Time for Change," *ITE Journal*, Vol. 62, 1992, pp. 25-29.

74 K. Todd, "Modern Rotaries: A Transportation System Management Alternative," *Transportation Research Record 737*, 1979, pp. 61-72; S. Sabanayagam, "Capacity Analysis of Unsignalized Traffic Circles," *ITE 1990 Compendium of Technical Papers*, Institute of Transportation Engineers, Washington, D.C., 1990, pp. 298-302; M.J. Wallwork, "Roundabouts for the U.S.A.," *ITE 1991 Compendium of Technical Papers*, Institute of Transportation Engineers, Washington, D.C., 1991, pp. 608-611; W.F. Savage and K. Al-Sahili, "Traffic Circles—A Viable Form of Intersection Control?" *ITE Journal*, Vol. 64, September 1994, pp. 40-45; E.J. Myers, "Modern Roundabouts for Maryland," *ITE Journal*, Vol. 64, October 1994, pp. 18-22; and L. Ourston, "Nonconforming Traffic Circle Becomes Modern Roundabout," *ITE 1994 Compendium of Technical Papers*, Institute of Transportation Engineers, Washington, D.C., 1994, pp. 275-278.

75 British and Australian accident studies are reviewed in A. O'Brien and E. Richardson, "Use of Roundabouts in Australia," *ITE 1985 Compendium of Technical Papers*, Institute of Transportation Engineers, Washington, D.C., 1985, pp. 180-187. Several European studies are reviewed in Savage and Al-Sahili, op. cit.; and L. Ourston, "A Synthesis of Roundabout Safety Research, with Recent Increases in Numbers of Roundabouts in a Few Countries," Unpublished manuscript available from the author, Leif Ourston & Associates, Santa Barbara, Calif., 1993. Also see Myers, op. cit.; M.A. Rahman and T. Hicks, "A Critical Look at Roundabouts," *ITE 1994 Compendium of Technical Papers*, Institute of Transportation Engineers, Washington, D.C., 1994, pp. 260-264; and A. Flannery and T.K. Datta,

"Modern Roundabouts and Traffic Crash Experience in the United States," Paper presented at the 75th Annual Meeting, Transportation Research Board, Washington, D.C., 1996.

[76] The City of Gainesville priced two traffic control options — a roundabout vs. an upgraded traffic signal system — for the intersection of S.E. 4th Avenue and 7th Street. The roundabout had the edge in both capital and operating cost categories, and was chosen over the upgraded signal.

Capital Costs:

Cost to Install Roundabout	$ 3,100
Cost to Upgrade Traffic Signal	11,700
Capital Cost Savings with Roundabout	8,600

Annual Operating Costs:

Maintenance and Electricity for Traffic Signal	1,100
Landscape Maintenance for Roundabout Center Island	500
Operating Cost Savings with Roundabout	600

[77] For an introduction to roundabout design and an overview of U.S. experience, see L. Ourston, "Wide Nodes and Narrow Roads," Paper presented at the 72nd Annual Meeting, Transportation Research Board, Washington, D.C., 1993.

[78] See Florida Department of Transportation (FDOT), op. cit., 1994, p. III-45; and FDOT memorandum of October 11, 1993, "Modern Roundabout Design/DOT Applications." Localities with new roundabouts include Bradenton Beach, Boca Raton, Gainesville, Ft. Walton Beach, Naples, Tallahassee, Tampa, and West Palm Beach.

[79] See V.G. Stover and F.J. Koepke, Transportation and Land Development, Institute of Transportation Engineers, Washington, D.C., 1988, pp. 94-97; and V.G. Stover, P.B. Demosthenes, and E.M. Weesner, "Signalized Intersection Spacing: An Element of Access Management," ITE 1991 Compendium of Technical Papers, Institute of Transportation Engineers, Washington, D.C., 1991, pp. 176-181.

[80] Systems Planning Office, Chapter 14-97—State Highway System Access Management Classification System and Standards, Florida Department of Transportation, Tallahassee, 1990; K.M. Williams et al., Model Land Development Regulations That Support Access Management for Florida Cities and Counties, Florida Department of Transportation, Tallahassee, 1994, p. 2-11; and Florida Department of Transportation (FDOT), Access Management on the State Highway System, Tallahassee, undated, pp. 3-4.

[81] Pedestrian signals do little for pedestrians where vehicle turning movements are allowed at the same time across the paths of pedestrians. However, where protected pedestrian crossings are provided via exclusive signals (traffic is held on all approaches while pedestrians cross), accident rates are significantly lower. C.V. Zegeer, K.S. Opiela, and M.J. Cynecki, "Effect of Pedestrian Signals and Signal Timing on Pedestrian Accidents," Transportation Research Record 847, 1982, pp. 62-72; and C.V. Zegeer, K.S. Opiela, and M.J. Cynecki, Pedestrian Signalization Alternatives—Final Report, Turner-Fairbank Highway Research Center, McLean, Va., 1985, pp. 33-43.

[82] A survey of Florida residents found that while 95 percent of them feel safe riding bicycles within their single-family detached home subdivisions, only 16 percent feel safe outside. R.K. Vieira and D.S. Parker, Energy Use in Attached and Detached Residential Developments, Florida Solar Energy Center, Cape Canaveral, Fla., 1991, pp. 35-36.

[83] A pedestrian- and transit-oriented design manual, prepared for the Florida Department of Transportation by FAU/FIU Joint Center for Environmental and Urban Problems, is due out in 1996.

[84] In a recent pedestrian survey, "security" and "safety" were rated far more important than "convenience," "attractiveness," "system continuity," and other attributes of pedestrian facilities. C.J. Khisty, "Evaluation of Pedestrian Facilities: Beyond the Level-of-Service Concept," Transportation Research Record 1438, 1994, pp. 45-50. Similar results were obtained in a recent survey of bicyclists. C.L. Antonakos, "Environmental and Travel Preferences of Cyclists," Transportation Research Record 1438, 1994, pp. 25-33.

[85] Everyone from highway officials to pedestrian advocates would agree with this recommendation. Higher-order streets, by definition, carry through-traffic. Regardless of posted speed limits, through-traffic tends to travel at higher speeds than does local traffic (locals having to face their neighbors). Our own Transportation Practice 5 recommends a design speed of 35 mph for collectors and arterials running through a development, well beyond the speed at which pedestrians and vehicles happily co-exist.

[86] H.N. Tobey, E.M. Shunamen, and R.L. Knoblauch, Pedestrian Trip Making Characteristics and Exposure Measures, Federal Highway Administration, Washington, D.C., 1983, pp. 74-75. Also see R.L. Knoblauch et al., Investigation of Exposure Based Pedestrian Accident Areas: Crosswalks, Sidewalks, Local Streets and Major Arterials, Federal Highway Administration, Washington, D.C., 1988, pp. 126-133.

[87] This figure is based on typical site plans and engineering cost estimates in National Association of Home Builders (NAHB), op. cit., pp. 56-103. Sidewalks are about 3 percent of site development costs, and require about 5 percent of the land area of sites (assuming a 4-foot sidewalk with a 3-foot planting strip). If site development and land costs each average 25 percent of total housing costs, sidewalks add 2 percent to the total (3% x 25% + 5% x 25%).

[88] In her classic, The Death and Life of Great American Cities, Jane Jacobs devotes three chapters to the value of city sidewalks for street security, neighborly contact, and assimilation of children into adult society. Sidewalks perform these valuable functions thanks to their status as the most public of public places, where casual contact can occur comfortably between old and young, rich and poor, resident and stranger. By comparison, even public parks are relatively private places where social contact tends to be more formal, users act territorially, and antisocial behavior occurs for lack of natural surveillance (the kind of natural surveillance from which sidewalks benefit). Obviously, the importance of sidewalks is much reduced in suburban neighborhoods, where neighbors are from the same socioeconomic class, travel is mainly by automobile, and the need for community is met (albeit incompletely) through private interactions at home, work, and play. This best practice endorses sidewalks in the hope/belief that at

least a modicum of public life might thereby be generated in contexts other than great cities.

89 To accommodate play of young children, vehicles can pass no more than about once every 5 minutes at speeds of no more than 10 mph. Street play is thus practical only on the occasional short cul-de-sac. See Zerner, op. cit; and R.C. Moore, "Streets as Playgrounds," in A. Vernez Moudon (ed.), *Public Streets for Public Use*, Columbia University Press, New York, 1991, pp. 45-62.

90 These guidelines were promoted most recently by C.V. Zegeer, J.C. Stutts, and W.W. Hunter, *Safety Effectiveness of Highway Design Features, Volume VI: Pedestrians and Bicyclists*, Federal Highway Administration, Washington, D.C., 1992, pp. 10-12; and F. Ranck, "Chapter 2. Sidewalks and Paths," in *Design of Pedestrian Facilities*, Institute of Transportation Engineers, Washington, D.C., November 1993 draft, pp. 2-1 through 2-6.

91 Forester, op. cit., pp. 127-144.

92 A comparison of cities with high and low levels of bicycle commuting found that the former have six times as many *bike lane miles per arterial road mile* as the latter. S.A. Goldsmith, *Reasons Why Bicycling and Walking Are and Are Not Being Used More Extensively as Travel Modes*, Federal Highway Administration, Washington, D.C., 1992, pp. 39-42 and 54-56. Also see C.L. Antonakos, op. cit.; and W.W. Hunter and H.F. Huang, "User Counts on Bicycle Lanes and Multi-Use Trails in the United States," Paper presented at the 74th Annual Meeting, Transportation Research Board, Washington, D.C., 1995.

93 McHenry and Wallace, op. cit., pp. 39-63; D.T. Smith, op. cit., pp. 24-29 and 56-72; D.F. Lott and D.Y. Lott, "Effect of Bike Lanes on Ten Classes of Bicycle-Automobile Accidents in Davis, California," *Journal of Safety Research*, Vol. 8, 1976, pp. 171-179; B. Kroll and M.R. Ramey, "Effects of Bike Lanes on Driver and Bicyclist Behavior," *Transportation Engineering Journal*, Vol. 103, 1977, pp. 243-256; Bikeways Oregon, Inc., "On-Street Bicycle Lanes," *Bicycles in Cities: The Eugene Experience*, Eugene, Ore., 1981; B. Kroll and R. Sommer, "Bicyclists' Response to Urban Bikeways," in H.S. Levinson and R.A. Weant (eds.), *Urban Transportation—Perspectives and Prospects*, Eno

Transportation Foundation, Landsdowne, Va., 1982, pp. 245-252; S.I. Badgett, D.A. Niemeier, and G.S. Rutherford, "Bicycle Commuting Deterrents and Incentives: A Survey of Selected Companies in the Greater Seattle Area," Paper presented at the 73rd Annual Meeting, Transportation Research Board, Washington, D.C., 1994; and A. Sorton and T. Walsh, "Bicycle Stress Level as a Tool to Evaluate Urban and Suburban Bicycle Compatibility," *Transportation Research Record 1438*, 1994, pp. 17-24.

94 The Bicycle Federation of America estimates that fewer than 5 percent of all bicyclists qualify as experienced or highly skilled. Wilkinson et al., op. cit., p. 1.

95 M.D. Everett and J. Spencer, "Empirical Evidence on Determinants of Mass Bicycle Commuting in the United States: A Cross-Community Analysis," *Transportation Research Record 912*, 1983, pp. 28-37.

96 National Safety Council, *Accident Facts*, Chicago, 1993, pp. 55, 69.

97 Knoblauch et al., op. cit., pp. 9-16; R.N. Schwab et al., "Roadway Lighting," in *Synthesis of Safety Research Related to Traffic Control and Roadway Elements, Volume 2*, Federal Highway Administration, Washington, D.C., 1982, pp. 12-1 through 12-17; and C.V. Zegeer, *Synthesis of Safety Research: Pedestrians*, Federal Highway Administration, Washington, D.C., 1991, pp. 38-50.

98 Garber and Srinivasan, op. cit., pp. 17-18; and National Safety Council, op. cit., p. 69.

99 This crosswalk guideline is promoted by both the Federal Highway Administration and the Florida Department of Transportation. See Knoblauch et al., op. cit., p. 54; and Post, Buckley, Schuh & Jernigan and J. Fruin, *Recommended Design Standards for the Florida Pedestrian Design Standards Development Study*, Florida Department of Transportation, Tallahassee, 1988, p. 32. It is a conservative guideline. Richard Untermann, a leading expert on pedestrianization, recommends crosswalks every 100 feet on pedestrian streets. Untermann, op. cit., 1990. The benefits of midblock crosswalks are twofold: cars tend to slow down as they approach crosswalks, and pedestrians tend not to cross between parked cars when they have the option of midblock

crosswalks. W.G. Berger, *Urban Pedestrian Accident Countermeasures Experimental Evaluation, Volume 1— Behavioral Evaluation Studies*, National Highway Safety Administration and Federal Highway Administration, Washington, D.C., 1975, pp. 3-25 through 3-32.

100 For a review of literature and the most comprehensive evaluation of median safety impacts to date, see B.L. Bowman and R.L. Vecellio, "An Assessment of Current Practice in the Selection and Design of Urban Medians to Benefit Pedestrians," Paper presented at the 73rd Annual Meeting, Transportation Research Board, Washington, D.C., 1994; and B.L. Bowman and R.L. Vecellio, "The Effect of Urban/ Suburban Median Types on Both Vehicular and Pedestrian Safety," Paper presented at the 73rd Annual Meeting, Transportation Research Board, Washington, D.C., 1994.

101 W.A. Hawthorne, "No Sales Job Here: Ontarians Want to Walk But Are Prevented by Anti-Pedestrian Policies," in *The Road Less Traveled: Getting There By Other Means*, 11th International Pedestrian Conference, City of Boulder, Colo., 1990, pp. 219-229.

102 S.A. Smith et al., *Planning and Implementing Pedestrian Facilities in Suburban and Developing Rural Areas*, National Cooperative Highway Research Program Report 294A, Transportation Research Board, Washington, D.C., 1987, p. 33.

103 Smith et al., op. cit., p. 25; and R.K. Untermann, "Can We Pedestrianize the Suburbs?" in A. Vernez Moudon (ed.), *Public Streets for Public Use*, Columbia University Press, New York, 1991, pp. 123-131. For a discussion of shortcuts generally, see Untermann, op. cit, 1984, pp. 189-193.

104 Stollard, op. cit., p. 44.

105 O. Newman, *Defensible Space—Crime Prevention Through Urban Design*, Collier Books, New York, 1972, p. 82.

106 RTKL Associates, Inc., *Feasibility Analysis and Design Concepts and Criteria for Community-wide Separated Pedestrian Networks*, Federal Highway Administration, Washington, D.C., 1975.

107 J.R. Kelly, "Planned and Unplanned New Town

Impacts: Applying a Method," *Environment and Behavior*, Vol. 7, 1975, pp. 330-357; R.J. Burby and S.F. Weiss, *New Communities U.S.A*, Lexington Books, Lexington, Mass., 1976, p. 337; and R. Cervero, *Transit-Supportive Development in the United States: Experiences and Prospects*, Technology Sharing Program, U.S. Department of Transportation, Washington, D.C., 1993, pp. 178-179.

[108] Some are *urban design manuals* with a transit orientation. Others are *transit facility design manuals* with an urban design orientation. The former emphasize the needs of transit users accessing the system, the latter the needs of the transit operator running the system. Robert Cervero uncovered 26 sets of established design guidelines through his nationwide survey of transit agencies; 12 agencies were preparing guidelines at the time of his survey. We became aware of 14 additional sets through a less comprehensive literature search. Cervero, op. cit.; 1993, pp. 27-40; and D. Everett, T. Herrero, and R. Ewing, *Transit-Oriented Development Guidelines—Review of Literature*, Background paper prepared for the Florida Department of Transportation, Tallahassee, 1995.

[109] The two transit operators are HART in Tampa and LYNX in Orlando.

[110] Recent "state-of-the-art" reports on TDM include Cambridge Systematics, *Effects of Demand Management and Land Use on Traffic Congestion: Literature Review*, Federal Highway Administration, Washington, D.C., 1991; E. Ferguson, C. Ross, and M. Meyer, *Transportation Management Associations in the United States*, Office of Technology Sharing, U.S. Department of Transportation, Washington, D.C., 1992; COMSIS Corporation, *Implementing Effective Travel Demand Management Measures: Inventory of Measures and Synthesis of Experience*, Technology Sharing Program, U.S. Department of Transportation, Washington, D.C., 1993; and EG&G/Dynatrend, *Transportation Implications of Telecommuting*, Office of the Secretary, U.S. Department of Transportation, Washington, D.C., 1993.

[111] This is true for work trips, and even more so, nonwork trips. See R. Ewing, "Getting Around a Traditional City, A Suburban PUD, and Everything In-Between," *Transportation Research Record 1466*, 1994, pp. 53-62. Also

see A.E. Pisarski, *Travel Behavior Issues in the 90s*, Federal Highway Administration, Washington, D.C., 1992, p. 32; and A.E. Pisarski, *New Perspectives in Commuting*, Federal Highway Administration, Washington, D.C., 1992, pp. 11-14. While it remains more common than other alternative modes, like other alternatives, carpooling is on the decline. See D.T. Hartgen and K.C. Bullard, "What Has Happened to Carpooling: Trends in North Carolina, 1980 to 1990," *Transportation Research Record 1390*, 1993, pp. 50-59; and E. Ferguson, "Recent Declines in Carpooling," in *Nationwide Personal Transportation Survey—Travel Mode Special Reports*, April 1994 draft, pp. 61-130.

[112] If required by an employer to commute one day a week by some mode other than driving alone, 59 percent of surveyed Florida commuters would carpool, 21 percent would use transit, and 5 percent each would walk or bike. Florida Institute for Marketing Alternative Transportation, *Florida Commuter Attitudes: Survey Results*, Florida Department of Transportation, Tallahassee, 1993.

[113] R. Young and R. Luo, "Five-Year Results of Employee Commute Options in Southern California," Paper presented at the 74th Annual Meeting, Transportation Research Board, Washington, D.C., 1995.

[114] K. Bhatt and T. Higgins, *An Assessment of Travel Demand Management Approaches at Suburban Activity Centers*, Technology Sharing Program, U.S. Department of Transportation, Washington, D.C., 1989, p. 27; COMSIS Corporation, *Evaluation of Travel Demand Management Measures to Relieve Congestion*, Technology Sharing Program, U.S. Department of Transportation, Washington, D.C., 1990, p. 26; and E.T. Ferguson, "Evaluation of Employer-Sponsored Ridesharing Programs in Southern California," *Transportation Research Record 1280*, 1990, pp. 59-72.

[115] R. Ewing, "TDM, Growth Management, and the Other Four Out of Five Trips," *Transportation Quarterly*, Vol. 47, 1993, pp. 343-366.

[116] EG&G/Dynatrend, op. cit., pp. 17-19; E.J. Hines, "Estimating Users and Impacts of a Regional Alternative Work Schedule Program," *Transportation Research Record 845*, 1982, pp. 1-8; R. Cervero and B. Griesenbeck, "Factors

Influencing Commuting Choices in Suburban Labor Markets: A Case Analysis of Pleasanton, California," *Transportation Research A*, Vol. 22A, 1988, pp. 151-161; C. Collier and T. Christiansen, "The State of the Commute in Southern California," *Transportation Research Record 1338*, 1992, pp. 73-81; and C. Collier and T. Christiansen, "State of the Commute in Southern California, 1992," *Transportation Research Record 1390*, 1993, pp. 74-77.

[117] W.R. Hershey and A.J. Hekimian, "Measuring the Effectiveness of Personalized Ridesharing Assistance," *Transportation Research Record 914*, 1983, pp. 14-21; T. Christiansen, L. Gordon, and R. Young, "Transportation Demand Management at Small Employer Sites, *Transportation Research Record 1390*, 1993, pp. 66-73; and B.G. Hamwi and J.P. Braaksma, "Propensity for Ridesharing: Some Key Factors," Paper presented at the 73rd Annual Meeting, Transportation Research Board, Washington, D.C., 1994.

[118] The nine are: in the Orlando area, University-Alafaya Corridor Transportation Authority and Downtown Orlando TMA; in the Tampa area, Westshore and Downtown Tampa TMAs; in the Miami area, the Civic Center TMO and South Beach TMA; in Tallahassee, the Capital City TMA; the Downtown Ft. Lauderdale TMA; and the West Palm Beach TMA.

[119] Technical assistance is supplied through the TMA Clearinghouse, housed at the Center for Urban Transportation Research, University of South Florida — also through regional commuter services agencies and the Florida Institute for Marketing Alternative Transportation at Florida State University. For descriptions of state-funded programs, see Center for Urban Transportation Research, *Commute Alternatives Program Director's Manual*, Florida Department of Transportation, Tallahassee, 1993, pp. IV-13 through IV-15.

[120] Miami Lakes has about 10,000 employees between its two parks. The Palmer Park of Commerce is slated to have 5,700 employees. By comparison, TMAs in California average 7,041 member employees and those outside California average only 2,980 employees (excluding a handful of areawide TMAs). Ferguson et al., op. cit., p. 65.

V. BEST ENVIRONMENTAL PRACTICES

Practice 1: Use a systems approach to environmental planning.

Practice 2: Channel development into areas that are already disturbed.

Practice 3: Preserve patches of high-quality habitat, as large and circular as possible, feathered at the edges, and connected by wildlife corridors.

Practice 4: Design around significant wetlands.

Practice 5: Establish upland buffers around all retained wetlands and natural water bodies.

Practice 6: Preserve significant uplands, too.

Practice 7: Restore and enhance environmental functions damaged by prior site activities.

Practice 8: Minimize runoff by clustering development on the least porous soils and using infiltration devices and permeable pavements.

Practice 9: Detain runoff with open, natural drainage systems.

Practice 10: Design man-made lakes and stormwater ponds for maximum habitat value.

Practice 11: Use reclaimed water and integrated pest management on large landscaped areas.

Practice 12: Use and require the use of Xeriscape landscaping.

Natural amenities—woodlands, hedgerows, slopes, rock outcroppings, and water—cost nothing in their pure state and are beloved by residents.[1] Wild places (natural areas with nothing done to them at all) are a particular favorite with children.[2] Greenbelts and other open spaces, if designed for physical and visual access, can enhance property values of nearby developable lands.[3]

The woods at Haile Plantation, the wetlands at Palmer Ranch, and the nature preserves at Bluewater Bay are among the most memorable features of these developments. Such features do not occupy much land area *in toto*, yet seem ubiquitous as you travel through these communities. Four of our seven exemplary developments—Bluewater Bay, Hunter's Creek, Palmer

Ranch, and most recently, Haile Plantation—have competed for and won the Florida Association of Realtors' prestigious Environmental Award (ENVY for short). These developments, as well as Oakbridge, use environmental themes, quite successfully it would appear, in their marketing campaigns.

Hunter's Creek Logo

By designing with nature, developers can help themselves at the same time they further the State Comprehensive Plan goals of *habitat protection*, *stormwater management*, *water conservation*, and *aquifer protection*. They can also contribute to a cross-cutting goal—preserving and restoring diversity, *biological diversity* in this case.

The following best practices go hand-in-hand with *Land Use Practice 4*, which calls for clustering of development. The exemplary developments featured here have plenty of room to build, while still preserving significant natural areas, mitigating environmental impacts on-site, and relying on natural drainage. This flexibility to respond to environmental opportunities and constraints is one of the chief advantages of large developments over their smaller competitors that build on every square inch.[4]

Environmental Requirements of the Florida Quality Developments (FQD) Program

In one respect—environmental protection—Florida already has a set of *best development practices*. Projects that would otherwise be processed as Developments of Regional Impact (DRIs) can qualify for expedited review (and the title "Florida Quality Development") by meeting certain additional requirements contained in the Florida Administrative Code.

The basic difference between DRIs and FQDs is in the environmental area, not in housing, transportation, or other state growth management concerns. Developers are required to preserve—through donations or conservation easements—wetlands and water bodies; areas important to endangered or threatened animal species; and areas known to contain endangered plant species.

The FQD Program also awards points (toward a required total of 15) for preservation of:

- upland habitats for species of special concern (SSC),
- high groundwater recharge areas, and
- acquisition areas for the Conservation and Resource Lands (CARL) Program.

Additional points are awarded for reuse of treated effluent, use of water saving devices, and use of Xeriscape landscaping.

Our *Best Environmental Practices* are really not so different from the requirements of the FQD Program, but for the attempt to be more specific about what constitutes quality development.

Practice 1: Use a systems approach to environmental planning.

This is an overarching recommendation. Other best practices complement and embellish it.

Planning and regulatory emphasis is shifting from the individual development site to the basin or ecosystem. The shift is prompted by the realization that functional systems are the appropriate units of environmental analysis and management. Wildlife must be managed as a "community" of interrelated species; actions that affect one species affect others.[5] Stormwater is best managed on a watershed basis to coordinate the timing of stormwater releases and achieve economies of scale.[6] Wetlands, streams, and other interconnected water bodies must be managed jointly to meet the life cycle needs of aquatic species that use them all.[7] Integrated pest management is effective only if pests, beneficial organisms, and turfgrasses are managed as an ecosystem.[8]

On the west side of Palmer Ranch, environmental issues were addressed on a project-by-project basis within the framework of a general master plan. When it came time to develop the east side, the developer and regulatory agencies agreed that environmental resources could be better protected if planning were system-wide. Palmer Ranch's surface water management plan for the east side considers the entire South Creek watershed. The open space plan emphasizes connections to off-site habitat and preservation of corridors rather than isolated patches. Comparing the extent of wetlands and uplands preserved on the two sides, the systems approach seems to have worked better than the piecemeal approach.

Open Space Corridors Preserved on East and West Sides of Palmer Ranch

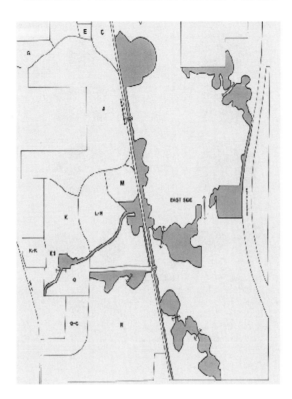

Practice 2: Channel development into areas that are already disturbed.

This is another overarching recommendation. Even the most environmentally sound development in the wrong place is not environmentally sound. Starting with a pristine site, Bluewater Bay could not have developed without significant loss of ecological functions. In this sense, the best sites for development are those already degraded, such as The Hammocks and Miami

Lakes, both farms originally, or Oakbridge, a reclaimed phosphate mine and landfill. In such places, there are no natural systems to fragment and no ecological functions to lose.

Where a site contains relatively pristine areas, they should be preserved intact while other sections are developed. The southeast quadrant of Oakbridge has the only significant natural areas left after years of mining. The wooded portions will be preserved, providing a visual buffer and offering passive recreation. Critical habitat owned by Palmer Ranch, just north of Oscar Scherer State Recreational Area, has been preserved through public acquisition rather than developed into a golf course community, as originally planned.

OAKBRIDGE SITE

Before   *After*

Practice 3: Preserve patches of high-quality habitat, as large and circular as possible, feathered at the edges, and connected by wildlife corridors.

A debate once raged among biologists over the value of a single large preserve versus numerous small preserves of equal area. The controversy was put to rest when leading biologists from opposing sides finally agreed that "bigness" and "multiplicity" are both essential for regional biodiversity.[9] Preserves large enough for wide-ranging species must be assembled by government, through land acquisition and mitigation banking programs.[10] A matrix of smaller preserves, suitable for the many other species with lesser needs, can be pieced together with the help of land developers.[11]

Patches preserved in an urbanizing landscape should be as large as possible. In general, the bigger the patch, the more species will colonize it.[12] More important than the sheer numbers, most species at risk require good-sized patches or specialized habitat or both.

Where land is limited, preserves should be as nearly circular as possible to minimize edge effects.[13] Edges engender competition from generalist species, predation, human disturbance, etc.[14] The edges themselves should be "feathered" wherever possible; predation rates are lower where edges are gradual and undulating rather than hard and straight.[15]

How much habitat is enough? Estimates

Habitat Planning Guidelines

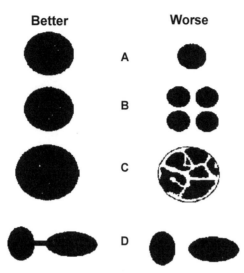

Source: Adapted from J. M. Diamond, "The Island Dilemma: Lessons of Modern Biogeographic Studies for the Design of Natural Reserves," *Biological Conservation*, Vol. 7, 1975, pp. 129-146; and M. E. Soule, "Land Use Planning and Wildlife Maintenance—Guidelines for Conserving Wildlife in an Urban Landscape," *Journal of the American Planning Association*, Vol. 57, 1991, pp. 313-323.

"Soft" vs. "Hard" Edges

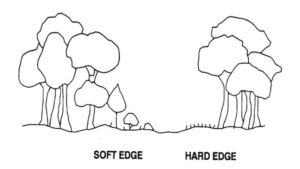

Source: L. W. Adams, *Urban Wildlife Habitats—A Landscaped Perspective*, University of Minnesota Press, Minneapolis, 1994, p. 108.

Patch Size and Species Diversity

A Florida study investigated the relationship between bird species richness and patch size for 12 mesic hardwood hammocks.[18] Patch size accounted for 79% of the variation in species richness. The number of species doubled with every seven-fold increase in patch area. The largest patch, 75 acres, served as breeding territory for 22 of the 45 species endemic to the mesic hardwood forests of north Florida.

Bird Species Richness vs. Patch Area (North Central Florida)

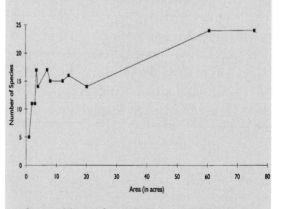

Source: Adapted from L.D. Harris and R.D. Wallace, "Breeding Bird Species in Florida Forest Fragments," *Proceedings of the Thirty Eighth Annual Conference of the Southeastern Association of Fish and Wildlife Agencies*, Montgomery, Ala., 1984, pp. 87-96.

of edge widths vary from 50 to 200 meters.[16] Taking 100 meters as an average, a circular preserve will begin to offer interior habitat when it reaches 8 acres in size (just over 100 meters in radius); it will offer as much interior as edge habitat when it reaches 90 acres. Given the right kind of habitat, patches of 15 to 75 acres have been found to support many interior bird species, a host of smaller mammals, and most reptiles and amphibians.[17]

Isolated patches, even large ones, may not sustain many species of concern over long periods. The young must disperse to avoid competition with their parents and inbreeding among themselves, and entire populations may have to temporarily evacuate patches in the face of flooding, fire, etc. While controversial, the weight of evidence and opinion supports wildlife corridors as useful "land bridges" between "habitat islands" and as dwelling habitats in their own right.[19] The strong preference is for natural landscape connections that have long been used as movement corridors (as opposed to man-made connections along hedgerows, drainage ditches, rail lines, etc.).

The distinction is sometimes made between *strip* and *line* corridors. Strip corridors are wide enough to maintain interior conditions in their centers, whereas line corridors are essentially all edge habitat. Since some interior species will not even migrate through unsuitable habitat, strip corridors are more valuable than lines.[20] By one assessment, strips must be at least 100 meters wide, and preferably much wider, to support significant wildlife movement.[21]

Riparian strips along rivers and streams are the most productive of all corridors.[22]

They are used by nearly 70 percent of all vertebrate species in some significant way during their life cycles.[23] The presence of water supports fish and other aquatic organisms that form the bases for terrestrial food chains. Moist shaded conditions offer refuge to many terrestrial species during times of drought and high temperature.

To provide movement corridors for diverse species, riparian strips should incorporate the entire floodplains of rivers and streams, both banks, and a continuous band of upland forest, at least on one side.[24] After reviewing a host of studies, one source recommends strips at least 60 meters wide on both sides of wide streams, and a total of 60 meters divided between the two sides of narrow streams that can be easily crossed by wildlife.[25]

Beaver Dam in a 22-Acre Preserve at Bluewater Bay

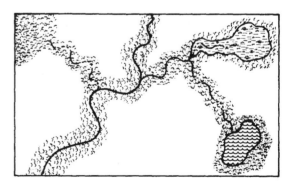

Riparian Strips Serving as Wildlife Corridors

Source: T. King, R. Stout, and T. Gilbert, *Habitat Reclamation Guidelines*, Florida Game and Fresh Water Fish Commission, Bartow, 1985, p. 27.

Several exemplary developments have wooded buffers that provide visual screening and climatic relief but could not support wildlife movement. Hunter's Creek is a clear exception, with the Shingle Creek corridor of wetlands and upland buffers running down its western side. Palmer Ranch is a possible exception. As development proceeds on the east side, four wildlife corridors are being preserved, the longest and widest along an abandoned rail line. This corridor will be 100-feet wide at a minimum, and expand to take in wetlands and a bald eagle protection zone. Palmer Ranch is considered a test case for Sarasota County's policy of preserving wildlife corridors in developing areas.

Practice 4: Design around significant wetlands.

Florida lost almost half of its wetlands back when they were still just "swamps." This was before anyone realized their value for wildlife, pollution control, and flood storage.[26] The loss continues to this day, despite a national policy of *no net loss* of wetlands. In Florida, 2,000 wetland tracts were destroyed in 1989 alone, often with little or no attempt at replacement.[27]

CONSERVATION AREA ALONG SHINGLE CREEK AT HUNTER'S CREEK

Master Plan
(with Shingle Creek on west side)

Nature Trail
at Edge of Conservation Area

Stormwater Pond
at Edge of Conservation Area
(Wood Storks in foreground)

❖ *Best Environmental Practices* ❖

Increase in Pollutant Load with Loss of Wetland Area

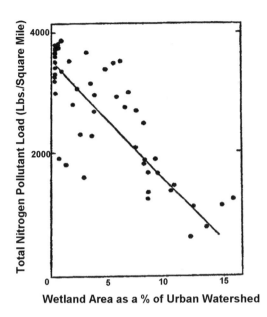

Source: Adapted from G. L. Oberts, "Impact of Wetlands on Watershed Water Quality," in B. Richardson (ed.), *Selected Proceedings of the Midwest Conference on Wetland Values and Management*, Freshwater Foundation, Gray Freshwater Center, 2500 Shadywood Road, Navarre, MN 55331, 1981, pp. 213-226. © Minnesota Water Planning Board.

When wetlands are destroyed, their natural functions are supposedly replaced through mitigation—enhancement, restoration, or creation of other wetlands. But evaluation studies suggest that as a group, mitigation projects fall short of achieving no net loss of wetland functions. In many cases, no mitigation is required or attempted, or the attempt fails to yield a functional wetland.[28] In other cases, replacement wetlands are of a different type or are in a different location removed from the point of impact.[29]

After reviewing the record of mitigation projects, Florida's chief environmental agency concluded: "The primary focus...must be on avoiding and minimizing the effects of permitted activities on wetlands."[30] Preservation remains the preferred option, preferred to any form of destruction with mitigation, under federal regulations and Florida's own wetlands law.

"Regionally significant" wetlands deserve protection and generally get it under existing rules and regulations. Included in this category are all wetlands connected to waters of the state, all isolated wetlands of at least five acres, and all wetlands providing habitat for protected species, regardless of the wetlands' size.[31]

"Locally significant" wetlands also deserve protection, but they (in contrast to larger wetlands) tend to be overlooked by regulators, environmental consultants, and just about everyone else. They add to *landscape diversity* of upland areas and may be the only sources of water available.[32] As part of a wetland mosaic, they serve as stepping stones between larger wetlands (just as patches of preserved forest serve as stepping stones for upland species).[33] Often located at the headwaters of streams, small wetlands attentuate flood peaks and protect streams from polluted runoff.[34] They are particularly vital for stormwater management in flat landscapes like Florida's.[35]

Even ephemeral wetlands may be significant. Their dry periods leave them free of fish and other predators, allowing amphibian reproduction and thus affecting entire food chains.[36] As they draw down or dry out, such wetlands offer rich feeding areas for many bird species.[37]

Given the same site and development program, development can stand back from wetlands or encroach into them. It all depends on the alignment of roads and the layout of buildings. Impacts to significant wetlands should be limited to road crossing points, and then only if *no alternative route* exists. When road crossings are unavoidable, they should be at the point of minimum impact, ordinarily the narrowest point.

More and Less Sensitive Site Plans

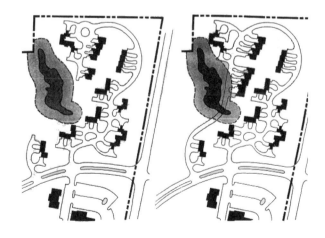

Source: K. Callahan et al., *An Inland Wetland Commissioner's Guide to Site Plan Review*, Connecticut Department of Environmental Protection, Hartford, 1992, p. 46.

While Bluewater Bay filled many acres of wetlands early in its development, as public interest in wetlands has grown, so has the developer's interest in preserving them. A recreation center built recently on the far side of a slough is accessed by a boardwalk, thus avoiding the wetland impacts of an access road. Palmer Ranch has done an ever-better job of preserving wetlands as development has progressed. Future development on the east side will leave 98 percent of the wetland acreage undisturbed; the routes of major roadways were chosen to minimize impacts. Hunter's Creek had to cross Shingle Creek to gain access to the western portion of its site. By crossing at the narrowest point, wetland impacts were limited to just over one acre.

Boardwalk through a Preserved Wetland at Bluewater Bay

Recreation Center at the End of the Boardwalk

Wetlands Preserved by Featured Developments

	Original Wetland Acreage	% Preserved or Restored
Bluewater Bay	298	53%
Hunter's Creek	881	74%
Palmer Ranch		
West Side	173	83%
East Side	495	98%

Wetland Evaluation Methods

There are many techniques for assessing wetland values.[38] The best known are the U.S. Fish and Wildlife Service's Habitat Evaluation Procedure (HEP) and the U.S. Army Corps of Engineers' Wetland Evaluation Technique (WET). HEP was used in the design of a conservation area along Shingle Creek through Hunter's Creek; while sacrificing smaller isolated wetlands, the developer was able to demonstrate that a corridor of preserved and created wetlands, and adjacent uplands, offered much greater habitat value than would preservation of isolated wetlands by themselves.

Due to limitations of HEP and WET, at least two Florida counties have developed wetland evaluation methods of their own.[39] Broward County's *wetland benefit index* and Seminole County's *wetland significance checklist* assign points for habitat diversity, hydrological intactness, connectedness to water bodies, quality of adjacent uplands, and other factors unique to each scoring scheme. On the basis of a wetland's total score, more or less protection is afforded by county government.

Practice 5: Establish upland buffers around retained wetlands and natural water bodies.

If wetlands and natural water bodies are valuable enough to preserve in the first place, they are valuable enough to protect with natural upland buffers. Wetlands, lakes, and streams, plus the uplands that border them, are interdependent. Upland buffers protect wetlands and natural water bodies from erosion, nutrient overload, and loss of many species that require more than one habitat to meet their feeding, nesting, and shelter needs; upland buffers contribute woody debris, control water temperatures, supply food, and provide cover for fish in adjacent waters.[40]

How wide must upland buffers be to protect wetlands and natural water bodies? Many states require buffers of 50 feet or more next to wetlands, lakes, and/or streams.[41] The technical literature supports buffers of this width (or much wider in some cases).[42] A plethora of different buffer requirements have been adopted in Florida to protect wetlands and water bodies, with required widths ranging from 15 to 550 feet.[43]

Upland buffers once proposed by the East Central Florida Regional Planning Council (ECFRPC) are probably as well-reasoned and well-documented as any in the literature. ECFRPC's buffers were much assailed at the time, but the technical basis for them was never seriously challenged. They do not appear overreaching when applied to large sites with a "normal" mix of uplands and wetlands. Hunter's Creek has established upland buffers at least 50 feet wide along the entire length of Shingle Creek. If other regionally significant wetlands (30- to 80-acre wetlands) had been similarly buffered, following ECFRPC guidelines, 75 percent of the total land area would still have been available for development (versus 78 percent without buffers).

Upland Buffer on a Lake at Bluewater Bay

ECFRPC Buffers Applied to Hunter's Creek

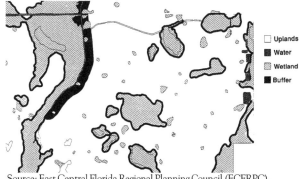

Source: East Central Florida Regional Planning Council (ECFRPC), *Proposed Wetland Buffer Criteria Draft #7—Analysis of Proposed Buffer Impact on Previously Approved DRI Projects*, Winter Park, Fla., 1991.

Practice 6: Preserve significant uplands, too.

Wetlands are legally protected to some degree. Uplands are not unless they can be shown to be home to protected species. Hardwood hammocks are ideal building sites, being high, well-drained, shaded, and beautiful. Scrub and long-leaf pine forests, while not as pretty, are also high, well-drained, and therefore good for building. These and certain other upland communities have become imperiled because they have so much monetary value in other uses.[44] In need of protection are all upland communities rated as rare or endangered by the Florida Natural Areas Inventory (FNAI) or equivalent regional inventories.[45]

Even exemplary developments have not always preserved imperiled uplands to the extent suggested by this best practice.[46] Two partial exceptions are Haile Plantation and Palmer Ranch. Haile Plantation saved approximately 120 acres of xeric habitat, less than originally planned but still substantial. Palmer Ranch is preserving at least 75 percent of the mesic hammock/hardwood habitat on the east side of its site. In effect, relatively abundant pine flatwoods are being turned over to development while rare upland habitat is held back.

Nature Trail through Preserved Xeric Habitat at Haile Plantation

*Perching Site
in an Enlarged Eagle Protection Zone
at Palmer Ranch*

For biodiversity at the regional scale, saving rare upland habitat is necessary but not sufficient. All habitats are part of larger regional ecosystems, and unique associations of habitats, some rare and some not, are the essence of biodiversity at this scale.

For biodiversity at the local scale, nodes of diversity should be preserved wherever they occur. They may be areas of unusually high species diversity or concentrations of endemic species.[47] They may be as small as a single "champion" tree or as large as an entire basin.[48]

"Node of Biodiversity"—One of Florida's Oldest Trees at Bluewater Bay

Practice 7: Restore and enhance environmental functions damaged by prior site activities.

Preserving some natural areas, per *Environmental Practices 3 through 6*, still leaves a net loss of environmental functions. What was once 100 percent natural or at least undeveloped may now be 50 percent to 80 percent developed.

Fortunately, habitat *quality* can substitute to some extent for habitat *quantity*. Where sites are degraded to begin with by prior farming, grazing, logging or mining activities, or by neighboring urban development, it is possible to compensate for this loss by *restoring* and/or *enhancing* the natural areas that remain after development.[49]

Wetlands can be restored by removing the levees, drains, or fills that altered them in first place; restoring severed connections to other water bodies; reintroducing native wetland plants; removing nuisance species; and, if necessary, using levees and water control structures to restore hydroperiods.[50] Streams can be restored by backfilling dredged sections; stabilizing banks; revegetating the riparian zone; and diverting or treating polluted inflows.[51] Lakes can be restored by removing nutrient-rich sediments; reducing phosphorous levels by chemical means; harvesting aquatic plants; aerating waters that are oxygen-poor; and again, diverting or treating polluted inflows.[52] Upland patches and corridors can be restored by recreating original site topography and drainage

channels; importing top soil and litter for their seed stock and beneficial soil organisms; planting groundcovers, shrubs, and trees native to the site; and removing weeds and weed seed stock.[53]

Techniques for Solving Lake Pollution Problems

	Problem		
Technique	Eutro-phication	Silta-tion	Exotic Species
Alum Treatment	X		
Biocontrol			X
Drawdown	X	X	
Bioharvesting	X		X
Aeration	X		
Dredging	X	X	

Source: Adapted from Committee on Restoration of Aquatic Ecosystems, "Lakes," In *Restoration of Aquatic Ecosystems—Science, Technology, and Public Policy*, National Academy Press, Washington, D.C., 1992, p. 114.

Restoring systems to a functioning state is one thing. Enhancing them is another. Enhancement strategies depend, of course, on what functions and values are being enhanced, and if habitat is one, what species are being targeted. Habitat for many animals is enhanced by adding complexity, that is, by adding new vegetative layers, introducing new plant species, manipulating water levels, or supplying artificial nesting structures, watering places, spawning areas, and cover.[54] A tree canopy may be opened and a shrub layer or groundcover planted underneath; weirs, deflectors, boulders, or logs may be introduced to create pools and riffle

areas in a stream; littoral zones on ponds may be recontoured to different depths to support different aquatic plants; and brush piles, snags, roosts, platforms, and/or nest boxes may be added.

Habitat Enhancement for Wildlife Enhancement

Source: Adapted from B. W. Anderson and R. D. Ohmart, "Revegetating the Riparian Floodplain for Wildlife," in *Strategies for Protection and Management of Floodplain Wetlands and Other Riparian Ecosystems*, U.S. Department of Agriculture, Washington, D.C., pp. 318-331.

Habitat *complexity* is not to be confused with habitat *patchiness*.[55] The former is all to the good, while the latter (as emphasized in *Environmental Practice 3*) is a mixed blessing. At any given patch size, greater habitat complexity leads to greater diversity and/or abundance of wildlife; it does so by increasing the number of potential niches and variety of resources available.[56] As a fringe benefit, woodlands of varying height and species composition not only receive higher habitat ratings from biologists but also higher aesthetic ratings from residents.[57]

Environmental restoration and enhancement have been practiced to varying degrees at exemplary developments. Oakbridge has reclaimed an abandoned phosphate mine and landfill; this is restoration on a grand scale, for nature as well as man. Haile Plantation left its wooded buffers in their natural state, except where existing vegetation was sparse; there, a program of seeding and planting restored and enhanced the buffers. Palmer Ranch restored Catfish Creek, long confined to a drainage canal, to its natural state. By replacing a narrow ditch with a wide, slow-moving slough, Palmer Ranch has reduced pollutant loads dumped into Sarasota Bay by 50 percent.

Restored Slough at Palmer Ranch (Replacing a Drainage Canal)

Effect of Restored Slough on Pollutant Loads (with Treatment Provided by Slough)

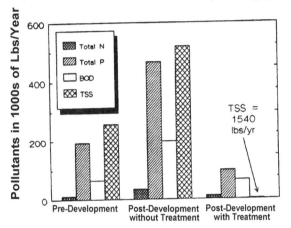

BIRDLIFE (WHERE THERE ONCE WAS NONE) AT OAKBRIDGE

Great Blue Heron

Sandhill Cranes

Limpkin

Practice 8: Minimize runoff by clustering development on the least porous soils and using infiltration devices and permeable pavements.

When land is developed, a large volume of stormwater that once seeped into the ground or nourished vegetation is deflected by rooftops, roads, parking lots, and other impervious surfaces; it ends up as runoff, picking up urban pollutants as it goes. By one recent estimate, conversion of woodlands to high-density residential and commercial uses causes an eleven- to nineteen-fold increase in direct storm runoff, with a corresponding 11-100 percent loss of natural groundwater recharge.[58]

This change in hydrology creates four related problems. *Peak discharges*, *pollutant loads*, and *volumes* of runoff leaving a site all increase, as compared to pre-development levels. The higher peak discharges contribute to erosion and flooding downstream. Pollutant loads in urban runoff kill aquatic life, detract from aesthetics of receiving waters, and may contaminate drinking water supplies. Greater volumes of runoff may adversely affect aquatic life; they necessarily result in a one-to-one loss of groundwater recharge capability. By reducing groundwater recharge, land development also reduces *base flows* in nearby rivers and streams.[59] This is why so many urban streams run low during dry periods and then experience flash flooding when it rains. Low base flows limit the ability of rivers and streams to support aquatic life and to assimilate pollutants in runoff.

To mitigate these adverse impacts of development, *best management practices* (BMPs) are widely prescribed.[60] BMPs fall into two principal categories, BMPs for stormwater *infiltration* and BMPs for stormwater *detention*.[61] Particular BMPs cannot be used everywhere; there are technical limitations relating to the size of the watershed, soil type, and intensity of development; and there are cost-effectiveness considerations that may disqualify a particular BMP from a particular application (see accompanying figures).[62] Still, on sites where one BMP will not work, another is likely to work well. For large-scale developments at suburban densities, there is always some role for BMPs.

Pollutant (Total Suspended Solids) Removal Efficiencies of BMPs

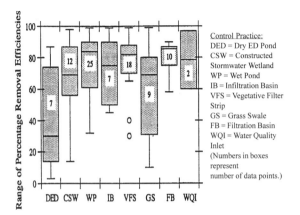

Source: U.S. Environmental Protection Agency (EPA), *Guidance Specifying Management Measures for Sources of Nonpoint Pollution in Coastal Waters*, Washington, D.C., 1993, p. 4-35.

Applicability of Best Management Practices (BMPs)

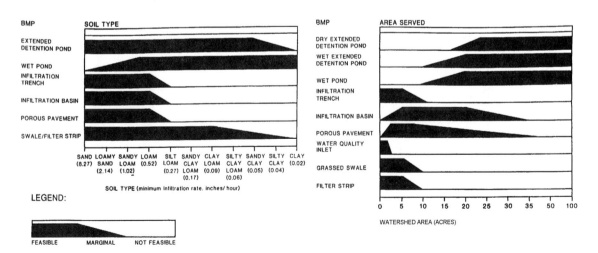

Source: E. H. Livingston and E. McCarron, *Stormwater Management: A Guide for Floridians*, Florida Department of Environment Regulation, Tallahassee, undated, p. 32.

Stormwater detention is much more common than stormwater infiltration, in part because infiltration devices can fail (become clogged) unless properly designed and maintained. Yet, experts are beginning to favor infiltration as the only complete approach to stormwater management. Where soils and water table elevations permit, infiltration can maintain the water balance in a basin and mitigate all four adverse stormwater-related impacts of development.[63] Further, infiltration may require less land than detention and may even have a cost advantage.[64]

On large sites with a variety of soils, infiltration can be maximized by clustering development on the least porous soils. In this way soils that allowed infiltration prior to development continue to allow it, while soils that were impervious to begin with remain so, though now covered with buildings and pavement. The Woodlands outside Houston, Texas, perhaps the most environmentally innovative new community of its era, was master planned in this manner and managed to avoid flooding when neighboring subdivisions were awash.[65]

As it happens, most of the imperiled upland habitats in Florida (scrub and sandhill, in particular) sit on well-drained soils; they are at risk precisely because their soils are well-drained, making them ideal building sites. Thus, this practice and *Environmental Practice* 6 (calling for preservation of rare uplands) go hand-in-hand.

Infiltration rates can be further boosted by means of infiltration basins, infiltration trenches, swales with check dams, and/or permeable pavements.[66] Haile Plantation has preserved and sometimes enhanced (through excavation) natural depressions to create a system of infiltration basins; the existing 23 basins largely eliminate any runoff from the site. Bluewater Bay has small parks that double as infiltration basins. Miami Lakes has infiltration trenches throughout the development, having been pre-

Edge of a Large Infiltration Basin at Haile Plantation

Small Infiltration Basin That Doubles as a Pocket Park at Bluewater Bay

Runoff Before and After Development (with Different Approaches to Mitigation)

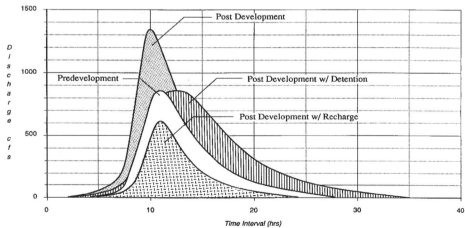

Source: Cahill Associates, *Stormwater Management Systems-Porous Pavement System with Underground Recharge Beds-Engineering Design Report*, West Chester, Pa., 1993, p. 20.

cluded by regulation from dumping stormwater into its manmade lakes.

Permeable pavements have tremendous (and largely untapped) potential for stormwater management. They eliminate runoff at the source and therefore require no extra land. With a 20 percent void structure, they can pass three to five gallons per minute for each square foot (assuming a gravel recharge bed underneath).[67] This is a higher infiltration rate than attainable with natural groundcovers.

Both porous asphalt and porous concrete are strong enough for use in walkways, parking lots, and low-volume roads.[68] Porous materials are used in major roadways, too, though typically only in the surface layer for skid resistance or the base for rapid water removal and extended pavement life.[69] Open-celled (turf) pavers can

be used in overflow parking areas and emergency access drives.[70]

Considered strictly as a surface material, porous pavements cost about 10 percent more than conventional pavements; open-celled pavers are more expensive still. But as part of a stormwater system, porous pavements' ability to substitute for storm drains can make them 12-38 percent less expensive than conventional pavements.[71]

Fear of clogging—that is, pore spaces becoming filled with finer particles, preventing stormwater from penetrating—is the most common reason engineers shy away from permeable pavements. While real, the fear is out of proportion to the problem: "...most researchers have found that proper design, installation and maintenance can prevent any loss of porosity over time."[72] All sediment-laden runoff should be di-

rected away from porous pavement, and filter fabric should be placed on the floor and sides of the recharge bed to prevent fine soils from migrating into the bed.[73] Porous asphalt should be cleaned periodically with pavement vacuuming equipment.[74] The cost of vacuuming is no greater than, and may be less than, the costs of maintaining detention ponds and other conventional stormwater management facilities.

Where infiltration is precluded by slowly percolating soils or high water tables, water harvesting may be an alternative.[75] The simplest harvesting method is to direct runoff into planted areas without formal storage or treatment; system efficiency can be improved at additional expense by adding storage basins and irrigation pumps and pipes. At Bluewater Bay, a stormwater pond serves as a storage basin for water used to irrigate the golf course.

Runoff from Various Surfaces

Coefficient of Runoff

------------------------------ % Slope ------------------------------

Castellated Paver			Lattice Paver			Lawn with Clay Soil			Asphalt
2%	4%	7%	2%	4%	7%	2%	4%	7%	(No Slope)

Source: Adapted from G. E. Day, "Investigation of Concrete Grid Pavements," in W.L. Downing (ed.), *Proceedings of the National Conference on Urban Erosion and Sediment Control: Institutions & Technology*, Great Lakes National Program Office, U.S. Environmental Protection Agency (EPA), Chicago, 1980, pp. 127-136.

Open-Celled Paving at Miami Lakes

Practice 9: Detain runoff with open, natural drainage systems.

Infiltration is the first line of defense in stormwater management. Ideally, at least the "first flush" (first inch) of stormwater will be retained and recharged. This alone will largely solve the stormwater pollution and water balance problems created by land development.[76]

However, to handle the big storms, secondary drainage systems are required (regardless of what primary systems are used). *Open* systems are preferable to *closed* ones. A closed system removes stormwater from a site as fast as possible with curbs and gutters, catch basins, underground pipes, culverts, and/or lined channels. An open system, on the other hand, detains stormwater for short periods in swales and filter strips, and for much longer periods in ponds and wetlands.

Two of the four stormwater-related impacts of development are mitigated by open systems. Extended detention both lowers peak discharge rates and gives physical, chemical, and biological processes time to work on pollutants. Swales and filter strips remove some pollutants; wet ponds, if properly sized and stocked with aquatic plants, remove more pollutants; and wetlands, if not overloaded beyond their absorption capacities, remove still more pollutants.[77] Simple additions such as sediment basins, multiple inflow points, energy dissipators, and skimmers can boost removal efficiencies.

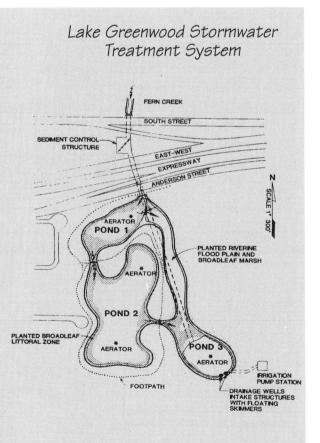

Pollutant Removal Efficiencies

The Lake Greenwood Stormwater Treatment System in the Orlando area consists of a sediment catch basin, three wet ponds with planted littoral zones, and a created marsh. During larger storm events of 1993-94, pollutant levels were measured for stormwater flowing into, through, and out of the system. Average percent reductions in concentrations of major pollutants were:

Pollutant	Removal Efficiency
Total solids	91%
Total lead	81
Total zinc	59
Total phosphorus	85
Total nitrogen	64

Source: K. McCann and L. Olson, *Greenwood Urban Wetland Treatment Effectiveness*, Florida Department of Environmental Protection, Tallahassee, 1994, pp. 17 and 28.

Lake Greenwood Stormwater Treatment System

Lake Outlet with Skimmer at Hunter's Creek

Open drainage has other advantages. If designed properly, open drainage can provide valuable habitat (see *Environmental Practice 10*). It can save money relative to storm sewer systems—hundreds of dollars per dwelling unit.[78] And wet ponds, and perhaps wetlands, have amenity value that can be captured in the price of bordering lands.[79]

The more "natural" the drainage system, the more valuable it will be for wildlife and water quality. In *both* respects, heavily vegetated swales are superior to grassy swales, wet ponds superior to dry ponds, and a combination of marsh and open water superior to open water alone.[80] The Center for Wetlands at the University of Florida recommends that swales be made into first-order streams (complete with riparian vegetation) and that stormwater ponds be made into wetlands (shallow enough for emergent plants to cover most of the surface).

Bluewater Bay runs its drainage through a series of natural swales, wet ponds, and wetlands before discharging it into Choctawhatchee Bay. Hunter's Creek, Oakbridge, and Palmer Ranch have "treatment trains" similar to Bluewater Bay's. In all these developments, open drainage is used wherever soils, water table elevations, and densities permit.

Vegetated Swale at Palmer Ranch

Wetland Used for Stormwater Polishing at Bluewater Bay

HIGH- AND LOW-VALUED STORMWATER PONDS AT HUNTER'S CREEK

Wet Pond

Dry Pond

Role of Wetlands
in Stormwater Management

Under state law, isolated wetlands may be incorporated into stormwater systems as long as their environmental functions are protected. Ditched and drained wetlands may be used where their functions will be restored.

To protect and restore wetland functions, discharges to wetlands ordinarily must first pass through spreader swales and/or pre-treatment ponds to extract pollutants, attenuate flows, and distribute flows more evenly over flow paths.[81] Alternatively, wetlands may be placed "off-line" (off the major flow path), leaving higher-volume flows to be treated by other means.[82]

Palmer Ranch uses stormwater ponds to hydrate wetlands and uses wetlands to attenuate and polish stormwater. The wetlands are protected from the "first flush" of polluted stormwater by placing them on-line in series after ponds, or alternatively, off-line in parallel with ponds but separated by berms that only allow overflows into the wetlands.

Bermed Wetland at Palmer Ranch

Practice 10: Design man-made lakes and stormwater ponds for maximum habitat value.

Lakes and ponds designed for recreation or stormwater management can perform double-duty as wildlife habitat. In general, the more complex the lake/pond environment, the richer the species mix will be. The following design features all add to the complexity of lake/pond environments. Most contribute as well to the value of created and restored wetlands.[83]

Depths. Shallow ponds (averaging 2-3 feet in depth) are more heavily used by wetland birds than are deep ones.[84] At the same time, ponds need some deep areas to serve as refuges for fish and foraging areas for diving birds. Considered ideal for waterbirds is a hemimarsh, that is, marsh and open water in a ratio of about 1:1.[85] A mix of shallow and deep water is also ideal for pollutant removal.[86]

Species Diversity at Peak in a Hemimarsh

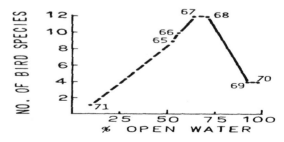

Source: M. W. Weller and L. H. Fredrickson, "Avian Ecology of a Managed Glacial Marsh," in D. A. Lancaster and J. R. Johnson (eds.), *The Living Bird—Twelfth Annual of the Cornell Laboratory of Ornithology 1973*, Cornell University, Ithaca, N.Y., 1973, p. 286.

Littoral Shelves. Littoral shelves outfitted with aquatic plants support populations of insects, amphibians, fish, and the wading birds and mammals that feed upon them. The shallowness of littoral shelves promotes mixing of water and natural aeration of bottom sediment; the presence of aquatic vegetation and associated algae allows nutrient uptake and metals absorption.[87] As an additional benefit, littoral shelves reduce the risk of drowning accidents.

Specifications for Stormwater Ponds

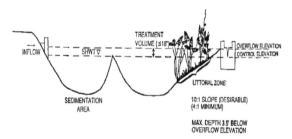

Source: Southwest Florida Water Management District (SFWMD), *Management and Storage of Surface Waters—Permit Information Manual*, Brooksville, 1993, p. D-23.

Shoreline. Vegetation preserved or newly planted along sections of shoreline adds to habitat value. Shoreline trees and shrubs provide cover for wildlife and waterbirds, and nesting and perching sites. Shoreline vegetation also controls erosion and pretreats runoff. A mix of open and densely vegetated shoreline sections is preferable to either alone since wildlife and waterbirds need some open "loafing" areas, too. One source recommends that vegetation be retained along 80 percent of the shoreline.[88]

Shape. Irregular shapes are preferred. Sinuous shorelines provide more space for vegetation in littoral shelves and offer visual isolation conducive to wildlife breeding.[89] As a bonus, they create waterfront development opportunities, add visual interest to water bodies, and produce a less engineered look. If inlets and outlets are placed at opposite ends, long/narrow/irregular ponds will detain stormwater longer than simple shaped ponds, thereby increasing sedimentation and nutrient removal.

Sandbars, Mudflats, and Islands. Sandbars, mudflats, and islands all add to the landscape complexity of lakes and ponds.[90] Sandbars and mudflats provide feeding areas for wading birds and resting and loafing areas for waterfowl. They emerge naturally in shallow ponds with gradually sloped sides; the sides are under water during periods of heavy rainfall and exposed during dry periods, thus keeping permanent vegetation from becoming established. Islands surrounded by open water offer protection for low-nesting waterfowl and wading birds. To prevent erosion and provide nesting cover, islands should be vegetated. If located between inlets and outlets, islands will increase stormwater detention time and, with it, pollutant removal.

Placement. A final feature of lakes and ponds relates more to their location than their design. Placed between residential development and nature preserves, lakes and ponds can protect wildlife from domestic cats and dogs. These pets (and strays) represent a particular threat to wildlife because they often roam freely, are at population levels far higher than nature could sustain, and hunt even when well-fed at home; they are devastating to ground feeding and nesting species.[91]

Newer exemplary developments have followed this best practice in spirit, if not always in every detail. Man-made lakes and ponds have littoral shelves that are often, though not always, vegetated with native species. Some vegetation has been preserved or planted along the shorelines of larger lakes. The shorelines are nearly always irregularly shaped. A few man-made lakes at Bluewater Bay and Palmer Ranch have been designed with environmental islands. A couple lakes at Palmer Ranch have been placed between neighborhoods and nature preserves to act as barriers to domestic cats and dogs.

Mile-Long Lake Buffering
Wildlife Corridor at Palmer Ranch

Bluewater Bay

Palmer Ranch

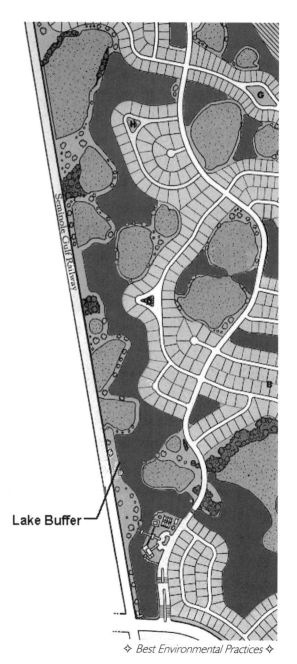

Lake Buffer

Littoral Shelves on Lakes in Exemplary Developments

According to the experts, littoral shelves should underlie at least 25% of the total surface area of lakes and ponds, be no more than two to three feet deep, and slope no more than a foot for every six to 10 feet of distance from the shore.[92]

The following table provides specifications for shelves on lakes and ponds in selected developments. They can be compared with the specifications above to see how they measure up.

	% of Surface Area	Maximum Depth	Slope
The Hammocks	none specified	5' below normal water level	5:1
Hunter's Creek	none specified	10' below low water level	5:1
Oakbridge	35%	4-6' below high water level	4:1
Palmer Ranch	35%	2' below normal water level	4:1

Practice 11: Use reclaimed water and integrated pest management on large landscaped areas.

Master-planned suburban communities are known for their vast, manicured areas of turfgrass. Such areas are not limited to golf courses. They are everywhere—in the planted medians and bermed borders of parkways; the grounds of campus-style business parks; and the large-lawn subdivisions.

Expansive turf areas have been criticized on two fronts. Urban designers pan them as lifeless. "While suburban developments often have a variety of pleasant features–attractive landscaping, tidiness, compatible colors–they still fail miserably at the task of being interesting."[93]

Environmentalists have even more fundamental concerns relating to the water, fertilizer, and pesticide demands of turf. To address these concerns, this best practice calls for use of reclaimed water and integrated pest management on large areas of turf; *Environmental Practice 12* calls for native vegetation in areas that do not absolutely demand turf.

Wastewater can be safely used for urban landscaping if it receives secondary treatment plus filtration and high-level disinfection.[94] Using wastewater solves two problems—scarcity of freshwater and abundance of wastewater. Freshwater is conserved for human consumption; unwanted wastewater is disposed of over land rather than dumped into bays, rivers, and other surface waters that have trouble assimilating it. In addition, less fertilizer may be required on landscaped areas since treated wastewater already contains nutrients; this results in cost savings to landscapers. With landscaped common areas accounting for 30 percent to 45 percent of total water use in master-planned communities, savings on freshwater and fertilizers can outweigh the costs of upgraded treatment facilities, dual storage facilities, and dual water lines for wastewater delivery.[95]

Economics of Water Reuse at Palmer Ranch

Palmer Ranch was required (in its master development order) to build a wastewater treatment plant. The developer had to decide how to dispose of the effluent. As it turned out, treating effluent to the required standard for discharge into Sarasota Bay would have cost as much as treating it to an urban landscaping standard and building the associated wastewater storage and transmission system. Thus, in 1985, an economic decision was made to build such a system and use wastewater on Palmer Ranch's golf courses and landscaped parkways.

When it came time to develop the east side of Palmer Ranch, the developer was discouraged by regional agencies from drilling new wells for landscape irrigation. While drinking water from the county's water utility could have been used for landscaping, at $4.50 per thousand gallons, it would have cost homeowners an additional $360 per year (on average) for irrigation. Thus, in 1992, another economic decision was made, this time to expand the water reuse program to include new neighborhoods. This was a first in Sarasota County. Dual water lines are being installed at a cost of about $500 per lot. Once lines are in place, wastewater will be supplied to homeowners free-of-charge. The wastewater utility saves money because expanded wastewater storage and transmission facilities cost less than drilling another deep well. Homeowners save money, too, after recouping the initial cost of the dual water lines.

This arrangement works well financially, due, in part, to the proximity of the wastewater treatment plant to the receiving neighborhoods. As domestic reuse becomes more commonplace, and two water lines rather than one must be extended to every residential property, economics will favor a return to smaller wastewater treatment plants closer to reuse sites (after a 20-year trend toward ever-larger regional plants). Fortunately, the technology of package plants and small regional plants has improved to the point where they may produce higher-quality effluent than super-regional plants saddled with industrial wastes as part of their waste streams.[96] Florida administrative rules allow plants with capacities as low as 100,000 gallons per day to supply wastewater for urban reuse.

Integrated pest management (IPM) controls pests by introducing and maintaining their natural enemies, cultivating disease- and insect-resistant grasses, and following cultural practices that keep grasses healthy.[99] When pesticides are used, it is only tempo- rarily, usually in spot applications, to get a particular outbreak under control. An experimental program in Florida reported a 90 percent reduction in pesticide use with IPM; there was no loss of turf quality.[100] Conversion to IPM by a master planned community in Maryland resulted in a 22 percent cost savings (the savings on pesticides more than offsetting higher labor costs associated with vigilent monitoring of pest populations).[101] In the Maryland case, a great majority of residents perceived an improvement in the appearance of community landscaping with IPM.

With IPM, pesticides are chosen for their effectiveness in controlling pests, their limited threat to other organisms, and their low potential to leach into the groundwater or run off the surface. Toward this end, researchers at the University of Florida have developed a pesticide selection procedure that matches soil properties to available pesticides; soils in most counties have been mapped and rated by the U.S. Soil Conservation Service. So it is simply a matter of looking up the pesticides that will do the job most effectively at particular application sites.[102]

When Haile Plantation decided to build a golf course, there were concerns about possible contamination and/or drawdown of the regional aquifer. The developer responded by adopting an IPM plan and agreeing to irrigate the golf course with wastewater from a regional treatment facility. To improve the economics, dual water lines are being installed in developing neighborhoods around the golf course and in the emerging village center. Only reclaimed water will be used for landscape irrigation in these areas.

In its decision to use reclaimed water, Haile Plantation has joined two other exemplary developments—Hunter's Creek and Palmer Ranch. Both rely on reclaimed water for golf course irrigation, and Palmer Ranch uses it on landscaped parkways as well. In its decision to use integrated pest management, Haile Plantation may be joined by Palmer Ranch. Use of organic fertilizers and biological pest management are planned for common areas of the Rivendell development.

Landscape Irrigation with Reclaimed Water at Palmer Ranch

Environmentally Sound Golf Courses?

In a recent survey, golf course designers nearly everywhere reported difficulty getting projects approved due to environmental concerns.[107] These concerns include loss of habitat, groundwater depletion, and water pollution from fertilizers and pesticides. Yet, golf courses are being built in record numbers and, if anything, are of growing importance as a residential marketing factor. Thus, it is in everyone's interest that they be designed and managed with environmental sensitivity.

Good examples of environmental sensitivity are found among our exemplary developments. The golf course at Haile Plantation has narrow fairways that wrap around tree stands; gopher tortoise habitat is preserved on the sides of fairways; and the major water feature is lined to prevent contamination of an unusually high water table. Oakbridge's course has transformed an environmental disaster into a sanctuary for wading birds, gopher tortoises, and alligators. The course at Hunter's Creek is registered in the Cooperative Sanctuary Program of the New York Audubon Society and the United States Golf Association; certification for the course is being sought in the areas of environmental planning, water conservation, and water enhancement. Some of Florida's premiere wetland restoration/creation projects are incorporated into a golf course at Palmer Ranch.

Golf Course Wrapped Around Tree Stands at Haile Plantation

Golf Course Wrapped Around a Wetland at Palmer Ranch

Practice 12: Use and require the use of Xeriscape landscaping.

Conventional turf landscapes are somewhat adapted to cool temperate climates, but not to Florida, with its sandy soils, sub-tropical climate, periods of drought, and large pest populations. Particularly in Florida's many critical water supply problem areas, Xeriscape is a best practice.

The term Xeriscape may conjure up images of cactus-and-rock landscaping in desert regions. But it actually refers to any landscape treatment that conserves water by following certain principles (see feature box).[108]

Xeriscape can cut water use in planned unit developments by 50-60 percent; fertilizer use and landscape maintenance are reduced by like amounts.[109] A homeowner can recoup the higher initial cost of a water-conserving landscape in three years through savings on irrigation and maintenance; the payback period for a business is estimated at nine years.[110] The financial advantage of Xeriscape is even greater where sites have good native vegetation to begin with. There, the developer can benefit from native plants that would cost hundreds of dollars at a nursery.

Xeriscape has other advantages. For stormwater management, many locally-adapted plants have large leaf surfaces and deep and fibrous root systems that reduce runoff and raise infiltration rates.[111] For aesthetics, many of these plants are quite distinctive in appearance, ensuring that even if everything else looks alike in suburbia, a Xeriscape landscape will vary from place to place. "Much of the urban landscape...has been subjected to a universal design standard that denies a sense of place. The ecological diversity of the native landscape is replaced by horticulture."[112] Homeowners appreciate variety and distinctiveness in their landscaping. One visual preference survey found that lawns with up to 50 percent native groundcover are perceived as more attractive and less work (as well as much more "natural") than are conventional turf lawns.[113]

With Xeriscape, plants are chosen for their adaptability to local conditions. Naturally, native plants are well-adapted (being "native," after all). Many require little or no irrigation, fertilizers, pesticides, etc. Some nonnative plants are just as good, or may be better where development has altered the microclimate of a site. Several guidebooks are available to assist in the selection of plants for different regions.[114]

Turf is used where it serves a specific purpose, such as erosion control or recreation, rather than as fill-in material. Large turfed areas are planted with low-water-using turfgrasses such as bermudagrass and zoysiagrass.[115]

Plants with similar irrigation requirements are grouped together into hydrozones. Irrigation systems can then be tailored to different zones rather than operated uniformly.[116] It is recommended that high water use zones (turfgrasses and plants that require supplemental watering year-round) be limited to 50 percent of total landscaped area, and that drip, bubbler, or subsurface irrigation be used on trees, shrubs, and ornamentals.[117]

Seven Principles of Xeriscape Landscaping

- Design landscapes for minimum maintenance.
- Analyze and improve soil conditions.
- Use locally adapted plants.
- Irrigate efficiently.
- Use turf only where it is needed.
- Use mulches to retain soil moisture.
- Maintain landscapes properly.

Source: Adapted from C.L. Ellefson, T.L. Stephens, and D. Welsh, *Xeriscape Gardening: Water Conservation for the American Landscape*, Macmillan Publishing Company, New York, 1992.

Four Hydrozone Plan for a Single-Family Home

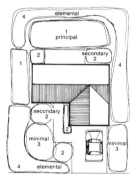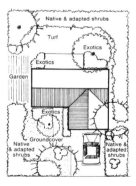

Source: R. L. Thayer and T. Richman, "Water-Conserving Landscape Design," in E.G. McPherson (ed.), *Energy-Conserving Landscape Design*," American Society of Landscape Architects, Washington, D.C., 1984, pp. 185-213.

These principles apply to common areas and common facilities, and may be extended through covenants or design guidelines to individual homesites and commercial properties. Haile Plantation has preserved or planted native vegetation on all homesites landscaped by the developer's own contractors (as opposed to outside builders). Palmer Ranch is beginning to experiment with Xeriscape.

Other good examples of Xeriscape dot the state. Expect to see more of the same as other developers discover that a palette of native and adapted plants is more economical and visually pleasing than is endless turfgrass.

Xeriscape in Florida

In 1991, Florida passed the nation's first Xeriscape law. The law requires local governments to enact Xeriscape ordinances if the benefits are determined to outweigh the costs. As an inducement, regional water management districts must create incentive programs.

Toward this end, the three largest water management districts have collaborated on a model Xeriscape code.[118] As local governments renew their water use permits (consumptive use permits), they are required by the South Florida Water Management District, and encouraged by the other two districts, to adopt ordinances at least as strict as the districts' model code.

TREND TOWARD XERISCAPE IN FLORIDA

Haile Plantation

Palmer Ranch

Seaside

Pelican Landings

1 M. Fried, "Residential Attachment: Sources of Residential and Community Satisfaction," *Journal of Social Issues*, Vol. 38, 1982, pp. 107-119; T.R. Herzog, S. Kaplan, and R. Kaplan, "The Prediction of Preference for Unfamiliar Urban Places," *Population and Environment*, Vol. 5, 1982, pp. 43-59; L.W. Adams, L.E. Dove, and D.L. Leedy, "Public Attitudes Toward Urban Wetlands for Stormwater Control and Wildlife Enhancement," *Wildlife Society Bulletin*, Vol. 12, 1984, pp. 299-303; R.S. Ulrich, "Human Responses to Vegetation and Landscapes," *Landscape and Urban Planning*, Vol. 13, 1986, pp. 29-44; J.F. Talbot, L.V. Bardwell, and R. Kaplan, "The Functions of Urban Nature: Uses and Values of Different Types of Urban Nature Settings," *The Journal of Architectural and Planning Research*, Vol. 4, 1987, pp. 47-63; T.R. Herzog, "A Cognitive Analysis of Preference for Urban Nature," *Journal of Environmental Psychology*, Vol. 9, 1989, pp. 27-43; R. Kaplan and S. Kaplan, *The Experience of Nature - A Psychological Perspective*, Cambridge University Press, New York, 1989, pp. 150-163; and J.L. Nasar, "The Evaluative Image of the City," *Journal of the American Planning Association*, Vol. 56, 1990, pp. 41-53.

2 R. Hart, *Children's Experience of Place*, Irvington Publishers, New York, 1979, p. 334; L. Schicker, "Design Criteria for Children and Wildlife in Residential Developments," in L.W. Adams and D.L. Leedy (eds.), *Integrating Man and Nature in the Metropolitan Environment*, National Institute for Urban Wildlife, Columbia, Md., 1987, pp. 99-105; and L. Schicker, "Children and Wildlife in Residential Developments," *Urban Land*, Vol. 47, 1988, pp. 2-5.

3 R.C. Smardon, "Perception and Aesthetics of the Urban Environment: Review of the Role of Vegetation," *Landscape and Urban Planning*, Vol. 15, 1988, pp. 85-106. Also see M.R. Correll, J.H. Lillydahl, and L.D. Singell, "The Effects of Greenbelts on Residential Property Values: Some Findings on the Political Economy of Open Space," *Land Economics*, Vol. 54, 1978, pp. 207-217; B. Didato, "The Paths Less Traveled—A Wrapup on the Nation's Greenways," *Planning*, Vol. 56, 1990, pp. 6-10; National Park Service, "Real Property Values," *Economic Impacts of Protecting Rivers, Trails, and Greenway Corridors*, San

Francisco, 1990, pp. 1-1 through 1-18; and D.A. King, J.L. White, and W.W. Shaw, "Influence of Urban Wildlife Habitats on the Value of Residential Properties," in L.W. Adams and D.L. Leedy (eds.), *Wildlife Conservation in Metropolitan Environments*, National Institute for Urban Wildlife, Columbia, Md., 1991, pp. 165-169.

4 R. Ewing, *Developing Successful New Communities*, Urban Land Institute, Washington, D.C., 1991, p. 15.

5 S.A. Temple, "Ecological Principles of Wildlife Management," in J.B. Hale, L.B. Best, and R.L. Clawson (eds.), *Management of Nongame Wildlife in the Midwest: A Developing Art*, BookCrafters, Chelsea, Mich., 1986, pp. 11-21.

6 APWA Research Foundation, *Urban Stormwater Management*, American Public Works Association (APWA), Chicago, 1981, p. 143; and J.P. Hartigan, "Watershed-Wide Approach Significantly Reduces Local Stormwater Management Costs," *Public Works*, December 1983, pp. 34-37.

7 J.R. Clark, "Regional Aspects of Wetlands Restoration and Enhancement in the Urban Waterfront Environment," in J.A. Kusler and M.E. Kentula (eds.), *Wetland Creation and Restoration—The Status of the Science*, Island Press, Washington, D.C., 1990, pp. 497-515.

8 W. Olkowski et al., "Ecosystem Management: A Framework for Urban Pest Control," *BioScience*, Vol. 26, 1976, pp. 384-389; and D.R. Bottrell, *Integrated Pest Management*, Council on Environmental Quality, Washington, D.C., 1979, pp. 19-21.

9 M.E. Soule and D. Simberloff, "What Do Genetics and Ecology Tell Us About the Design of Nature Reserves?" *Biological Conservation*, Vol. 35, 1986, pp. 19-40.

10 J. Cox et al., *Closing the Gaps in Florida's Wildlife Habitat Conservation System—Recommendations to Meet Minimum Conservation Goals for Declining Wildlife Species and Rare

Plant and Animal Communities*, Florida Game and Fresh Water Fish Commission, Tallahassee, 1994, pp. 19-145.

11 R.F. Noss, "A Regional Landscape Approach to Maintain Diversity," *BioScience*, Vol. 33, 1983, pp. 700-706; R.S. Kautz, "Criteria for Evaluating Impacts of Development on Wildlife Habitats," *Proceedings of the Annual Conference of the Southeastern Association of Fish and Wildlife Agencies*, Vol. 38, 1984, pp. 121-136; J.T. Lyle, "A General Approach to Landscape Design for Wildlife Habitat," in L.W. Adams and D.L. Leedy (eds.), *Integrating Man and Nature in the Metropolitan Environment*, National Institute for Urban Wildlife, Columbia, Md., 1987, pp. 87-91; J.F. Lynch, "Responses of Breeding Bird Communities to Forest Fragmentation," in D.A. Saunders et al. (eds.), *Nature Conservation: The Role of Remnants of Native Vegetation*, Surrey Beatty and Sons, Chipping Norton, New South Wales, Australia, 1987, pp. 123-140; and L.W. Adams and L.E. Dove, *Wildlife Reserves and Corridors in the Urban Environment—A Guide to Ecological Landscape Planning and Resource Conservation*, National Institute for Urban Wildlife, Columbia, Md., 1989.

12 Early studies of species-area relationships are reviewed in E.F. Connor and E.D. McCoy, "The Statistics and Biology of the Species-Area Relationship," *The American Naturalist*, Vol. 113, 1979, pp. 791-833. For more recent studies, see B.M. Gottfried, "Small Mammal Populations in Woodlot Islands," *The American Midland Naturalist*, Vol. 102, 1979, pp. 105-112; M.B. Usher, "Changes in the Species-Area Relations of Higher Plants on Nature Reserves," *Journal of Applied Ecology*, Vol. 16, 1979, pp. 213-215; A.J. Higgs and M.B. Usher, "Should Nature Reserves Be Large or Small," *Nature*, Vol. 285, 1980, pp. 568-569; D.J. Kitchener, A. Chapman, and B.G. Muir, "The Conservation Value for Mammals of Reserves in the Australian Wheatbelt," *Biological Conservation*, Vol. 18, 1980, pp. 179-207; T.E. Martin, "Diversity and Abundance of Spring Migratory Birds Using Habitat Islands on the Great Plains," *Condor*, Vol. 82, 1980, pp. 430-439; C.S. Robbins, "Effect of Forest Fragmentation on Breeding Bird Populations in the Piedmont of the Mid-Atlantic Region," *Atlantic Naturalist*, Vol. 33, 1980, pp. 31-36; S.H. Anderson and C.S. Robbins,

"Habitat Size and Bird Community Management," *Transactions of the 46th North American Wildlife and Natural Resources Conference*, Wildlife Management Institute, Washington, D.C., 1981, pp. 511-520; P.E. Matthiae and F. Stearns, "Mammals in Forest Islands in Southeastern Wisconsin," in R.L. Burgess and D.M. Sharpe (eds.), *Forest Island Dynamics in Man-Dominated Landscapes*, Springer-Verlag, New York, 1981, pp. 55-66; R.F. Whitcomb et al., "Effects of Forest Fragmentation on Avifauna of the Eastern Deciduous Forest," in R.L. Burgess and D.M. Sharpe (eds.), *Forest Island Dynamics in Man-Dominated Landscapes*, Springer-Verlag, New York, 1981, pp. 125-205; W.F. Humphreys and D.J. Kitchener, "The Effect of Habitat Utilization on Species-Area Curves: Implications for Optimal Reserve Area," *Journal of Biogeography*, Vol. 9, 1982, pp. 391-396; O. Jarvinen, "Conservation of Endangered Plant Populations: Single Large or Several Small Reserves?" *Oikos*, Vol. 38, 1982, pp. 301-307; D.J. Kitchener, "Predictors of Vertebrate Species Richness in Nature Reserves in the Western Australian Wheatbelt," *Australian Wildlife Research*, Vol. 9, 1982, pp. 1-7; B. Ambuel and S.A. Temple, "Area-Dependent Changes in Bird Communities and Vegetation of Southern Wisconsin Forests," *Ecology*, Vol. 64, 1983, pp. 1057-1068; J.G. Blake, "Trophic Structure of Bird Communities in Forest Patches in East-Central Illinois," *Wilson Bulletin*, Vol. 95, 1983, pp. 416-430; M.E.J. Woolhouse, "The Theory and Practice of the Species-Area Effect, Applied to the Breeding Birds of British Woods," *Biological Conservation*, Vol. 27, 1983, pp. 315-332; J.G. Blake and J.R. Karr, "Species Composition of Bird Communities and the Conservation Benefit of Large Versus Small Forests," *Biological Conservation*, Vol. 30, 1984, pp. 173-187; L.D. Harris and C.R. Vickers, "Some Faunal Community Characteristics of Cypress Ponds and the Changes Induced by Perturbations," in K.C. Ewel and H.T. Odum (eds.), *Cypress Swamps*, University of Florida Press, Gainesville, Fla., 1984, pp. 171-185; D.R. Helliwell, "The Conservation Value of Areas of Different Size: Worcestershire Ponds," *Journal of Environmental Management*, Vol. 17, 1983, pp. 179-184; R.W. Howe, "Local Dynamics of Bird Assemblages in Small Forest Habitat Islands in Australia and North America," *Ecology*, Vol. 65, 1984, pp. 1585-1601; J.F. Lynch and D.F. Whigham, "Effects of Forest Fragmentation on Breeding Bird Communities in Maryland, USA," *Biological Conservation*, Vol. 28, 1984, pp. 287-324; D. Simberloff and N. Gotelli,

"Effects of Insularisation on Plant Species Richness in the Prairie-Forest Ecotone," *Biological Conservation*, Vol. 29, 1984, pp. 27-46; R.W. Rafe, M.B. Usher, and R.G. Jefferson, "Birds on Reserves: The Influence of Area and Habitat on Species Richness," *Journal of Applied Ecology*, Vol. 22, 1985, pp. 327-335; G.L. Williams, "Classifying Wetlands According to Relative Wildlife Value: Application to Water Impoundments," in *Water Impoundments for Wildlife: A Habitat Management Workshop*, North Central Forest Experiment Station, Forest Service, U.S. Department of Agriculture, St. Paul, Minn., 1985, pp. 110-119; J.G. Blake, "Species-Area Relationship of Migrants in Isolated Woodlots in East-Central Illinois," *Wilson Bulletin*, Vol. 98, 1986, pp. 291-296; W.J. Boecklen, "Effects of Habitat Heterogeneity on the Species-Area Relationships of Forest Birds," *Journal of Biogeography*, Vol. 13, 1986, pp. 59-68; M. Brown and J.J. Dinsmore, "Implications of Marsh Size and Isolation for Marsh Bird Management," *Journal of Wildlife Management*, Vol. 50, 1986, pp. 392-397; K.E. Freemark and H.G. Merriam, "Importance of Area and Habitat Heterogeneity to Bird Assemblages in Temperate Forest Fragments," *Biological Conservation*, Vol. 36, 1986, 115-141; C.H. McLellan et al., "Effects of Forest Fragmentation on New- and Old-World Bird Communities: Empirical Observations and Theoretical Implications," in J. Verner, M.L. Morrison, and C.J. Ralph (eds.), *Wildlife 2000—Modeling Habitat Relationships of Terrestrial Vertebrates*, University of Wisconsin Press, Madison, 1986, pp. 305-313; K.V. Rosenberg and M.G. Raphael, "Effects of Forest Fragmentation on Vertebrates in Douglas-Fir Forests," in J. Verner, M.L. Morrison, and C.J. Ralph (eds.), *Wildlife 2000 - Modeling Habitat Relationships of Terrestrial Vertebrates*, University of Wisconsin Press, Madison, 1986, pp. 263-272; R.A. Askins, M.J. Philbrick, and D.S. Sugeno, "Relationship Between the Regional Abundance of Forest and the Composition of Forest Bird Communities," *Biological Conservation*, Vol. 39, 1987, pp. 129-152; A.F. Bennett, "Conservation of Mammals within a Fragmented Forest Environment: The Contributions of Insular Biogeography and Autecology," in D.A. Saunders et al. (eds.), *Nature Conservation: The Role of Remnants of Native Vegetation*, Surrey Beatty & Sons, Chipping Norton, New South Wales, Australia, 1987, pp. 41-52; J.G. Blake and J.R. Karr, "Breeding Birds of Isolated Woodlots: Area and Habitat Relationships," *Ecology*, Vol. 68, 1987, pp. 1724-1734; C.R. Dickman, "Habitat Fragmentation and

Vertebrate Species Richness in an Urban Environment," *Journal of Applied Ecology*, Vol. 24, 1987, pp. 337-351; R.H. Loyn, "Effects of Patch Area and Habitat on Bird Abundances, Species Numbers and Tree Health in Fragmented Victorian Forests," in D.A. Saunders et al. (eds.), *Nature Conservation: The Role of Remnants of Native Vegetation*, Surrey Beatty & Sons, Chipping Norton, New South Wales, Australia, 1987, pp. 65-77; N.G. Tilghman, "Characteristics of Urban Woodlands Affecting Breeding Bird Diversity and Abundance," *Landscape and Urban Planning*, Vol. 14, 1987, pp. 481-495; M.B. Usher, "Effects of Fragmentation on Communities and Populations: A Review with Applications to Wildlife Conservation," in D.A. Saunders et al. (eds.), *Nature Conservation: The Role of Remnants of Native Vegetation*, Surrey Beatty & Sons, Chipping Norton, New South Wales, Australia, 1987, pp. 103-121; T.E. Martin, "Habitat and Area Effects on Forest Bird Assemblages: Is Nest Predation an Influence?" *Ecology*, Vol. 69, 1988, pp. 74-84; M.E. Soule et al., "Reconstructed Dynamics of Rapid Extinctions of Chaparral-Requiring Birds in Urban Habitat Islands," *Conservation Biology*, Vol. 2, 1988, pp. 75-92; S.A. Temple, "When Is a Bird's Habitat Not Habitat," *Passenger Pigeon*, Vol. 50, 1988, pp. 37-41; C.S. Robbins, D.K. Dawson, and B.A. Dowell, "Habitat Area Requirements of Breeding Forest Birds of the Middle Atlantic States," *Wildlife Monographs*, No. 103, 1989, pp. 1-34; and M.E. Soule, "Land Use Planning and Wildlife Maintenance—Guidelines for Conserving Wildlife in an Urban Landscape," *Journal of the American Planning Association*, Vol. 57, 1991, pp. 313-323.

[13] J.M. Diamond, "The Island Dilemma: Lessons of Modern Biogeographic Studies for the Design of Natural Reserves," *Biological Conservation*, Vol. 7, 1975, pp. 129-146; S.T.A. Pickett and J.N. Thompson, "Patch Dynamics and the Design of Nature Reserves," *Biological Conservation*, Vol. 13, 1978, pp. 27-37; C.R. Margules, A.J. Higgs, and R.W. Rafe, "Modern Biogeographic Theory: Are There Any Lessons for Nature Reserve Design?" *Biological Conservation*, Vol. 24, 1982, pp. 115-128; R.T.T. Forman and M. Godron, *Landscape Ecology*, John Wiley & Sons, New York, 1986, pp. 110-111; D.S. Wilcove, C.H. McLellan, and A.P. Dobson, "Habitat Fragmentation in the Temperate Zone," in M.E. Soule (ed.), *Conservation Biology: The Science of Scarcity and Diversity*, Sinauer Associates, Sunderland, Mass., 1986, pp. 237-256; J.G.

Gosselink and L.C. Lee, *Cumulative Impact Assessment in Bottomland Hardwood Forests*, Office of Wetland Protection, U.S. Environmental Protection Agency (EPA), Washington, D.C., 1987, pp. 30-31; and L.W. Adams, *Urban Wildlife Habitats—A Landscape Perspective*, University of Minnesota Press, Minneapolis, 1994, pp. 73-77.

[14] J.E. Gates and L.W. Gysel, "Avian Nest Dispersion and Fledgling Success in Field-Forest Ecotones," *Ecology*, Vol. 59, 1978, pp. 871-883; M.C. Brittingham and S.A. Temple, "Have Cowbirds Caused Forest Songbirds to Decline?" *BioScience*, Vol. 33, 1983, pp. 31-35; R.L. Kroodsma, "Effect of Edge on Breeding Forest Bird Species," *Wilson Bulletin*, Vol. 96, 1984, pp. 426-436; D.S. Wilcove, "Nest Predation in Forest Tracts and the Decline of Migratory Songbirds," *Ecology*, Vol. 66, 1985, pp. 1211-1214; S.A. Temple, "Predicting Impacts of Habitat Fragmentation on Forest Birds: A Comparison of Two Models," in J. Verner, M.L. Morrison, and C.J. Ralph (eds.), *Wildlife 2000—Modeling Habitat Relationships of Terrestrial Vertebrates*, University of Wisconsin Press, Madison, 1986, pp. 301-304; S.A. Temple, "Predation on Turtle Nests Increases Near Ecological Edges," *Copeia*, No. 1, 1987, pp. 250-252; H. Andren and P. Angelstam, "Elevated Predation Rates as an Edge Effect in Habitat Islands: Experimental Evidence," *Ecology*, Vol. 69, 1988, pp. 544-547; S.K. Robinson, "Reappraisal of the Costs and Benefits of Habitat Heterogeneity for Nongame Wildlife," *Transactions of the 53rd North American Wildlife and Natural Resources Conference*, Wildlife Management Institute, Washington, D.C., 1988, pp. 145-155; M.F. Small and M.L. Hunter, "Forest Fragmentation and Avian Nest Predation in Forested Landscapes," *Oecologia*, Vol. 76, 1988, pp. 62-64; S.A. Temple and J.R. Cary, "Modelling Dynamics of Habitat-Interior Bird Populations in Fragmented Landscapes," *Conservation Biology*, Vol. 2, 1988, pp. 340-347; R.H. Yahner and D.P. Scott, "Effects of Forest Fragmentation on Depredation of Artificial Nests," *Journal of Wildlife Management*, Vol. 52, 1988, pp. 158-161; and C.S. Robbins, "Managing Suburban Forest Fragments for Birds," in D.J. Decker et al. (eds.), *Challenges in the Conservation of Biological Resources: A Practitioner's Guide*, Westview Press, Boulder, Colo., 1991, pp. 253-264.

[15] J.T. Ratti and K.P. Reese, "Preliminary Test of the Ecological Trap Hypothesis," *Journal of Wildlife Management*, Vol. 52, 1988, pp. 484-491. Also see Adams, op. cit., pp.

108-109; Forman and Godron, op. cit., p. 105; J.R. Bider, "Animal Activity in Uncontrolled Terrestrial Communities as Determined by the Sand Transect Technique," *Ecological Monographs*, Vol. 38, 1968, pp. 269-308; and M.L. Morrison, B.G. Marcot, and R.W. Mannan, *Wildlife-Habitat Relationships—Concepts and Applications*, University of Wisconsin Press, Madison, 1992, p. 87. In fairness, one experimental study casts doubt on the value of feathered edges as a deterrent to predation. R.H. Yahner, T.E. Morrell, and J.S. Rachael, "Effects of Edge Contrast on Depredation of Artificial Avian Nests," *Journal of Wildlife Management*, Vol. 53, 1989, pp. 1135-1138.

[16] Andren and Angelstam, op. cit.; Gates and Gysel, op. cit.; Kroodsma, op. cit.; Robbins, op. cit., 1991; Temple, op. cit., 1986; Temple, op. cit., 1987; and Temple and Cary, op. cit. Where the edge ends and interior begins is not always so clear-cut in practice; it is different for plants and animals, and for animals, depends on what animal-related functions are considered. See J.E. Gates and J.A. Mosher, "A Functional Approach to Estimating Habitat Edge Width for Birds," *American Midland Naturalist*, Vol. 105, 1981, pp. 189-192; J.W. Ranney, M.C. Bruner, and J.B. Levenson, "The Importance of Edge in the Structure and Dynamics of Forest Islands," in R.L. Burgess and D.M. Sharpe (eds.), *Forest Island Dynamics in Man-Dominated Landscapes*, Springer-Verlag, New York, 1981, pp. 67-95; and R.H. Yahner, "Changes in Wildlife Communities Near Edges," *Conservation Biological*, Vol. 2, 1988, pp. 333-339.

[17] Bennett, op. cit.; Brown and Dinsmore, op. cit.; Dickman, op. cit.; Harris and Vickers, op. cit.; Kitchener et al., op. cit.; Loyn, op. cit.; Lynch and Whigham, op. cit.; Robbins, op. cit.; Rosenberg and Raphael, op. cit.; Temple, op. cit., 1988; Tilghman, op. cit.; Williams, op. cit.; R.T.T. Forman, A.E. Galli, and C.F. Leck, "Forest Size and Avian Diversity in New Jersey Woodlots with Some Land Use Implications," *Oecologia*, Vol. 26, 1976, pp. 1-8; and T.E. O'Meara, "Habitat-Island Effects on the Avian Community in Cypress Ponds," *Proceedings of the Annual Conference of the Southeastern Association of Fish and Wildlife Agencies*, Vol. 38, 1984, pp. 97-110.

[18] L.D. Harris and R.D. Wallace, "Breeding Bird Species in Florida Forest Fragments," *Proceedings of the Thirty Eighth Annual Conference of the Southeastern Association of Fish

and Wildlife Agencies*, Montgomery, Ala., 1984, pp. 87-96.

[19] The value of corridors has been hotly debated, with Floridians out front in the national debate. See D. Simberloff and J. Cox, "Consequences and Costs of Conservation Corridors," *Conservation Biology*, Vol. 1, 1987, pp. 63-71; R.F. Noss, "Corridors in Real Landscapes: A Reply to Simberloff and Cox," *Conservation Biology*, Vol. 1, 1987, pp. 159-164; L.D. Harris and P.B. Gallagher, "New Initiatives for Wildlife Conservation: The Need for Movement Corridors," in G. Mackintosh (ed.), *Preserving Communities and Corridors*, Defenders of Wildlife, Washington, D.C., 1989, pp. 11-34; L.D. Harris and K. Atkins, "Faunal Movement Corridors in Florida," in W.E. Hudson (ed.), *Landscape Linkages and Biodiversity*, Island Press, Washington, D.C., 1991, pp. 117-134; L.D. Harris and J. Scheck, "From Implications to Applications: The Dispersal Corridor Principle Applied to the Conservation of Biological Diversity," in D.A. Saunders and R.J. Hobbs (eds.), *Nature Conservation 2: The Role of Corridors*, Surrey Beatty & Sons, Chipping Norton, New South Wales, Australia, 1991, pp. 189-220; D. Simberloff et al., "Movement Corridors: Conservation Bargains or Poor Investments?" *Conservation Biology*, Vol. 6, 1992, pp. 493-504; and R.F. Noss, "Wildlife Corridors," in D. Smith and P. Hellmund (eds.), *Ecology of Greenways*, University of Minnesota Press, Minneapolis, 1993, pp. 43-68. Also see Adams and Dove, op. cit.; Forman and Godron, op. cit.; Soule, op. cit.; Soule et al., op. cit.; L.E. Stevens et al., "The Importance of Riparian Habitat to Migrating Birds," in *Importance, Preservation and Management of Riparian Habitat: A Symposium*, Forest Service, U.S. Department of Agriculture, Washington, D.C., 1977, pp. 156-164; J.F. Wegner and G. Merriam, "Movements by Birds and Small Mammals Between a Wood and Adjoining Farmland Habitats," *Journal of Applied Ecology*, Vol. 16, 1979, pp. 349-357; R.T.T. Forman and J. Baudry, "Hedgerows and Hedgerow Network in Landscape Ecology," *Environmental Management*, Vol. 8, 1984, pp. 495-510; G. Merriam, "Connectivity: A Fundamental Ecological Characteristic of Landscape Pattern," in J. Brandt and P. Agger (eds.), *Methodology in Landscape Ecological Research and Planning*, Roskilde University Centre, Roskilde, Denmark, 1984, pp. 5-15; L. Fahrig and G. Merriam, "Habitat Patch Connectivity and Population Survival," *Ecology*, Vol. 66, 1985, pp. 1762-1768; M.T. Henderson, G. Merriam, and J.

Wegner, "Patchy Environments and Species Survival: Chipmunks in an Agricultural Mosaic," *Biological Conservation*, Vol. 31, 1985, pp. 95-105; J. Szacki, "Ecological Corridor as a Factor Determining the Structure and Organization of a Bank Vole Population," *Acta Theriologica*, Vol. 32, 1987, pp. 31-44; G. Mackintosh (ed.), *Preserving Communities and Corridors*, Defenders of Wildlife, Washington, D.C., 1989; A.F. Bennett, "Habitat Corridors and the Conservation of Small Mammals in a Fragmented Forest Environment," *Landscape Ecology*, Vol. 4, 1990, pp. 109-122; K. Henein and G. Merriam, "The Elements of Connectivity Where Corridor Quality Is Variable," *Landscape Ecology*, Vol. 4, 1990, pp. 157-170; G. Merriam and A. Lanoue, "Corridor Use by Small Mammals: Field Measurements for Three Experimental Types of *Peromyscus Leucopus*," *Landscape Ecology*, Vol. 4, 1990, pp. 123-131; W.E. Hudson (ed.), *Landscape Linkages and Biodiversity*, Island Press, Washington, D.C., 1991; G. Merriam, "Corridors and Connectivity: Animal Populations in Heterogeneous Environments," in D.A. Saunders and R.J. Hobbs (eds.), *Nature Conservation 2: The Role of Corridors*, Surrey Beatty & Sons, Chipping Norton, New South Wales, Australia, 1991, pp. 133-142; D.A. Saunders and C.P. de Rebeira, "Values of Corridors to Avian Populations in a Fragmented Landscape," in D.A. Saunders and R.J. Hobbs (eds.), *Nature Conservation 2: The Role of Corridors*, Surrey Beatty & Sons, Chipping Norton, New South Wales, Australia, 1991, pp. 221-240; D.A. Saunders, R.J. Hobbs, and C.R. Margules, "Biological Consequences of Ecosystem Fragmentation: A Review," *Conservation Biology*, Vol. 5, 1991, pp. 18-32; and N.F. Payne and F.C. Bryant, "Corridors and Riparian Areas," *Techniques for Wildlife Habitat Management of Uplands*, McGraw-Hill, New York, 1994, pp. 191-222.

[20] R.T.T. Forman and M. Godron, "Patches and Structural Components for a Landscape Ecology," *BioScience*, Vol. 31, 1981, pp. 733-740.

[21] R.S. Kautz, "Criteria for Evaluating Impacts of Development on Wildlife Habitats," *Proceedings of the Annual Conference of the Southeastern Association of Fish and Wildlife Agencies*, Vol. 38, 1984, pp. 121-136. Corridors must be much wider than 100 meters — perhaps by a factor of five or more — to eliminate all edge effects, accommodate large mammals, and/or facilitate the dispersal of entire populations. Noss, op. cit., 1993; and R.L. Harrison, "Toward a Theory of Inter-Refuge Corridor Design," *Conservation Biology*, Vol. 6, 1992, pp. 293-295.

[22] J.W. Thomas, C. Maser, and J.E. Rodiek, "Riparian Zones," in J.W. Thomas (ed.), *Wildlife Habitats in Managed Forests—The Blue Mountains of Oregon and Washington*, Forest Service, U.S. Department of Agriculture, Washington, D.C., 1979, pp. 40-47; M.M. Brinson et al., *Riparian Ecosystems: Their Ecology and Status*, Eastern Energy and Land Use Team, U.S. Fish and Wildlife Service, Kearneysville, West Virginia, 1981, pp. 69-101; L.D. Harris, *The Fragmented Forest*, University of Chicago Press, Chicago, 1984, pp. 141-144; and M.L. Hunter, *Wildlife, Forests, and Forestry—Principles of Managing Forests, and Forestry*, Prentice-Hall, Englewood Cliffs, N.J., 1990, pp. 139-153.

[23] R.J. Naiman, H. Decamps, and M. Pollock, "The Role of Riparian Corridors in Maintaining Regional Biodiversity," *Ecological Applications*, Vol. 3, 1993, pp. 209-212.

[24] Forman and Godron, op. cit., pp. 146-153.

[25] R.J. Howard and J.A. Allen, "Streamside Habitats in Southern Forested Wetlands: Their Role and Implications for Management," in D.D. Hook and R. Lea (eds.), *The Forested Wetlands of the Southern United States*, Southeastern Forest Experimental Station, Forest Service, U.S. Department of Agriculture, Asheville, N.C., 1989, pp. 97-106. Also see references on stream and river buffer widths in *Environmental Practice 5*.

[26] Wetland functions and values are reviewed by J.H. Sather and R.D. Smith, *An Overview of Major Wetland Functions and Values*, Fish and Wildlife Service, U.S. Department of the Interior, Washington, D.C., 1984; D.A. Hammer, "Wetlands: Functions and Values," *Creating Freshwater Wetlands*, Lewis Publishers, Boca Raton, Fla., 1992, pp. 69-103; and W.J. Mitsch and J.G. Gosselink, *Wetlands*, Van Nostrand Reinhold, New York, 1993, pp. 507-540.

[27] L.A. Lord, *Guide to Florida Environmental Issues and Information*, Florida Conservation Foundation, Winter Park, 1993, p. 154.

[28] R.J. Reimold and S.A. Cobler, *Wetlands Mitigation Effectiveness*, U.S. Environmental Protection Agency (EPA), Region 1, Boston, 1986; K.L. Erwin, *An Evaluation of Wetland Mitigation in the South Florida Water Management District, Volume 1*, South Florida Water Management District, West Palm Beach, 1991; Florida Department of Environmental Regulation (DER), *Report on the Effectiveness of Permitted Mitigation*, Tallahassee, 1991; and Department of Resource Management, *Status Report on the Assessment of Wetland Creation for Mitigation in the SJRWMD*, St. Johns River Water Management District, Palatka, Fla., 1992. Also see articles by Broome, Clewell and Lea, Fonseca, Hollands, Lewis, and Shisler in J.A. Kusler and M.E. Kentula (eds.), *Wetland Creation and Restoration—The Status of the Science*, Island Press, Washington, D.C., 1990.

[29] Even when overall wetland acreage is maintained, net losses may still occur in wetland **type**, **location**, and **timing** (the last of these, if wetlands are destroyed before full-functioning wetlands are available to replace them). See K. Kunz, M. Rylko, and E. Somers, "An Assessment of Wetland Mitigation Practices in Washington State," *National Wetlands Newsletter*, May-June 1988, pp. 2-4; J.A. Kusler, "No Net Loss and the Role of Wetlands Restoration/Creation in a Regulatory Context," in J.A. Kusler, S. Daly, and G. Brooks (eds.), *Proceedings of the National Wetland Symposium—Urban Wetlands*, Association of Wetland Managers, Berne, N.Y., 1988, pp. 378-389; C.R. Owen, *Effectiveness of Compensatory Wetland Mitigation in Wisconsin*, Wisconsin Wetlands Association, Madison, 1990, pp. 9-15; N.M. Jarman et al., "Evaluation of Created Freshwater Wetlands in Massachusetts," *Restoration & Management Notes*, Vol. 9, 1991, pp. 26-31; A. Crabtree et al., *Evaluation of Wetland Mitigation Measures, Volume 1: Final Report*, Office of Engineering and Highway Operations, Federal Highway Administration, McLean, Va., 1992, pp. 26-171; and M.E. Kentula et al., "Trends and Patterns in Section 404 Permitting Requiring Compensatory Mitigation in Oregon and Washington, USA," *Environmental Management*, Vol. 16, 1992, pp. 109-119.

[30] Florida Department of Environmental Regulation (DER), op. cit., p. 23.

[31] This definition is borrowed from the East Central Florida Regional Planning Council (ECFRPC). Regulatory agencies have established similar criteria for judging which wetlands deserve special protection. In most cases, while agencies insist that large, connected wetlands be avoided, they permit other wetlands to be filled, with mitigation in some cases and without in others.

[32] Harris and Vickers, op. cit.

[33] J.P. Gibbs, "Importance of Small Wetlands for the Persistence of Local Populations of Wetland-Associated Animals," *Wetlands*, Vol. 13, 1993, pp. 25-31.

[34] H.T. Odum, "Role of Wetland Ecosystems in the Landscape of Florida," in D.O. Logofet and N.K. Luckyanov (compilers), *Ecosystem Dynamics in Freshwater Wetlands and Shallow Water Bodies, Volume 2*, Centre for International Projects GKNT, Moscow, Russia, 1982, pp. 33-72; and D.F. Whigham, C. Chitterling, and B. Palmer, "Impacts of Freshwater Wetlands on Water Quality: A Landscape Perspective," *Environmental Management*, Vol. 12, 1988, pp. 663-671.

[35] M.T. Brown and M.F. Sullivan, "The Value of Wetlands in Low Relief Landscapes," in D.D. Hook et al. (eds.), *The Ecology and Management of Wetlands, Volume 1*, Timber Press, Portland, Ore., 1988, pp. 133-145.

[36] W.R. Heyer, R.W. McDiarmid, and D.L. Weigmann, "Tadpoles, Predation, and Pond Habitats in the Tropics," *Biotropica*, Vol. 7, 1975, pp. 100-111; P.E. Moler and R. Franz, "Wildlife Values of Small, Isolated Wetlands in the Southeastern Coastal Plain," in R.R. Odum, K.A. Riddleberger, and J.C. Ozier (eds.), *Proceedings of the Third Southeast Nongame and Endangered Wildlife Symposium*, Georgia Department of Natural Resources, Atlanta, 1988, pp. 234-241; C.K. Dodd and B.G. Charest, "The Herpetofaunal Community of Temporary Ponds in North Florida Sandhills: Species Composition, Temporal Use, and Management Implications," in *Management of Amphibians, Reptiles, and Small Mammals in North America*, Rocky Mountain Station, Forest Service, U.S. Department of Agriculture, Ft. Collins, Colo., 1988, pp. 87-97; J.H.K. Pechmann et al., "Influence of Wetland Hydroperiod on Diversity and Abundance of Metamorphosing Juvenile

Amphibians," *Wetlands Ecology and Management*, Vol. 1, 1988, pp. 3-11; and L.V. LaClaire and R. Franz, "Importance of Isolated Wetlands in Urban Landscapes," *Proceedings of the Second Lake Management Symposium*, Oviedo, Fla., 1990, pp. 9-15.

[37] J.A. Kushlan, "Feeding Ecology and Prey Selection in the White Ibis," *Condor*, Vol. 81, 1979, pp. 376-389; L.H. Walkinshaw, "Nesting of the Florida Sandhill Crane in Central Florida," in J.C. Lewis (ed.), *Proceedings of the 1981 Crane Workshop*, National Audubon Society, Tavernier, Fla., 1981, pp. 53-62; and S.R. Beissinger and J.E. Takekawa, "Habitat Use By and Dispersal of Snail Kites in Florida During Drought Conditions," *Florida Field Naturalist*, Vol. 11, 1983, pp. 89-106.

[38] S.H. Anderson and K.J. Gutzwiller, "Habitat Evaluation Methods," in T.A. Bookhout (ed.), *Research and Management Techniques for Wildlife and Habitats*, The Wildlife Society, Bethesda, Md., 1994, pp. 592-605.

[39] Limitations of HEP and WET, as applied to wetlands, are outlined in B.F. Birkitt and S. Gray, "Wetland Impact Evaluation and Mitigation: Comparing Apples and Oranges," in D.W. Fisk (ed.), *Proceedings of the Symposium on Wetlands: Concerns and Successes*, American Water Resources Association, Bethesda, Md., 1989, pp. 259-267.

[40] I.J. Steinblums, H.A. Froehlich, and J.K. Lyons, "Designing Stable Buffer Strips for Stream Protection," *Journal of Forestry*, Vol. 81, 1984, pp. 49-52; R. Lowrance, R. Leonard, and J. Sheridan, "Managing Riparian Ecosystems to Control Nonpoint Pollution," *Journal of Soil and Water Conservation*, Vol. 40, 1985, pp. 87-91; J.R. Cooper, J.W. Gilliam, and T.C. Jacobs, "Riparian Areas as a Control of Nonpoint Pollutants," in D.L. Correll (ed.), *Watershed Research Perspectives*, Smithsonian Environmental Research Center, Edgewater, Md., 1986, pp. 166-190; R.L. Beschta and R.L. Taylor, "Stream Temperature Increases and Land Use in a Forested Oregon Watershed," *Water Resources Bulletin*, Vol. 24, 1988, pp. 19-25; Dames & Moore, *Buffer Zone Study for Suwannee River Water Management District*, Live Oak, Fla., 1988; M.T. Brown et al., *Econlockhatchee River Basin Natural Resources Development and Protection Plan*, Center for Wetlands, University of Florida, Gainesville, 1989; M.T. Brown, J.

Schaefer, and K. Brant, *Buffer Zones for Water, Wetlands, and Wildlife in East Central Florida*, Center for Wetlands, University of Florida, Gainesville, 1990; D.J. Welsch, *Riparian Forest Buffers—Function and Design for Protection and Enhancement of Water Resources*, United States Department of Agriculture, Radnor, Pa., 1991; and J.M. Schaefer and M.T. Brown, "Designing and Protecting River Corridors for Wildlife," *Rivers*, Vol. 3, 1992, pp. 14-26.

[41] Dames & Moore, op. cit., pp. 7-10; M.F. Small and W.N. Johnson, "Wildlife Management in Riparian Habitats," in J.A. Bissonette (ed.), *Is Good Forestry Good Wildlife Management?* Maine Agricultural Experiment Station, University of Maine, Orono, 1986, pp. 69-79; G.H. Belt, J. O'Laughlin, and T. Merrill, *Design of Forest Riparian Buffer Strips for the Protection of Water Quality: Analysis of Scientific Literature*, Idaho Forest, Wildlife, and Range Policy Group, University of Idaho, Moscow, 1992, pp. 7-11; and D. Salvesen, *Wetlands: Mitigating and Regulating Development Impacts*, Urban Land Institute, Washington, D.C., 1994, p. 93.

[42] Belt et al., op. cit., pp. 16-17; Brinson et al., op. cit., pp. 71, 76-78; C.T. Roman and R.E. Good, *Buffer Delineation Model for New Jersey Pinelands Wetlands*, Center for Coastal and Environmental Studies, Rutgers University, New Brunswick, N.J., 1985, pp. 10-46; J.K. Sullivan, "Using Buffer Zones to Battle Pollution," *EPA Journal*, Vol. 12, May 1986, pp. 8-10; W.W. Budd et al., "Stream Corridor Management in the Pacific Northwest: Determination of Stream-Corridor Widths," *Environmental Management*, Vol. 11, 1987, pp. 587-597; C.A. Elliot, "Riparian Zones and Wetlands," in C.A. Elliot (ed.), *A Forester's Guide to Managing Wildlife Habitats in Maine*, Cooperative Extension Service, University of Maine, Orono, 1988, pp. 12-14; D.J. Nilson and R.S. Diamond, "Wetland Buffer Delineation Method for Coastal New Jersey," *Proceedings of an International Symposium—Wetlands and River Corridor Management*, Association of Wetland Managers, Berne, N.Y., 1989, pp. 381-386; M.H. McDade et al., "Source Distances for Coarse Woody Debris Entering Small Streams in Western Oregon and Washington," *Canadian Journal of Forest Research*, Vol. 20, 1990, pp. 326-330; and M.W. Binford and M.J. Buchenau, "Riparian Greenways and Water Resources," in D.S. Smith and P.C. Hellmund (eds.), *Ecology of Greenways*, University of Minnesota Press,

Minneapolis, 1993, pp. 69-104.

43 M.T. Brown and Henigar & Ray, Inc., *Vegetative Buffer Zones*, Southwest Florida Water Management District, Brooksville, 1991, pp. III-12 through III-23.

44 At observed rates of loss, longleaf pine forests will disappear entirely from unprotected lands within a few years, and sand pine scrub forests will disappear by the middle of the next century. R.S. Kautz, "Trends in Florida Wildlife Habitat 1936-1987," *Florida Scientist*, Vol. 56, 1993, pp. 7-24.

45 Florida Natural Areas Inventory, *Element Rank Explanations*, Tallahassee, Fla., 1992. Also see Cox et al., op. cit.

46 Bluewater Bay developed most of its 265 acres of sandhill community, once home to two endangered or threatened species. Hunter's Creek plans to develop nearly all of its mesic hardwoods and mixed upland forests, over protests from the East Central Florida Regional Planning Council and Florida Game and Freshwater Fish Commission.

47 R.F. Noss and A.Y. Cooperrider, "Selecting Reserves," *Saving Nature's Legacy—Protecting and Restoring Biodiversity*, Island Press, Washington, D.C., 1994, pp. 99-128.

48 R.F. Noss and L.D. Harris, "Nodes, Networks, and MUMs: Preserving Diversity at All Scales," *Environmental Management*, Vol. 10, 1986, pp. 299-309.

49 Wetlands, streams, and other water bodies in urbanizing basins can never be restored to a pristine state, only "rehabilitated" to a functional state. The term "restoration" is used loosely in this document, as it is throughout the literature.

50 Kusler and Kentula, op. cit.; J. Zedler, M. Josselyn, and C. Onuf, "Restoration Techniques, Research, and Monitoring: Vegetation," in M. Josselyn (ed.), *Wetland Restoration and Enhancement in California*, California Sea Grant College Program, University of California, La Jolla, 1982, pp. 63-72; J.S. Larson, "Wetland Creation and Restoration: An Outline of the Scientific Perspective," in J. Zelazny and J.S. Feierabend (eds.), *Increasing Our Wetland*

Resources, National Wildlife Federation, Washington, D.C., 1988, pp. 73-79; Committee on Restoration of Aquatic Ecosystems, "Wetlands," in *Restoration of Aquatic Ecosystems—Science, Technology, and Public Policy*, National Academy Press, Washington, D.C., 1992, pp. 262-340; L.H. Fredrickson and M.K. Laubhan, "Managing Wetlands for Wildlife," in T.A. Bookhout (ed.), *Research and Management Techniques for Wildlife and Habitats*, The Wildlife Society, Bethesda, Md., 1994, pp. 623-647; and M.W. Weller, "Management and Restoration," *Freshwater Marshes—Ecology and Wildlife Management*, University of Minnesota Press, Minneapolis, 1994, pp. 69-86.

51 Binford and Buchenau, op. cit.; N.R. Nunnally, "Improving Channel Efficiency Without Sacrificing Fish and Wildlife Habitat: The Case for Stream Restoration," in *Strategies for Protection and Management of Floodplain Wetlands and Other Riparian Ecosystems*, Forest Service, U.S. Department of Agriculture, Washington, D.C., 1978, pp. 394-399; O. Fagen and J.L. Robinson, *Stream Corridor Management—A Proposed Response to Streambank Erosion*, Soil Conservation Service, U.S. Department of Agriculture, Columbia, Mo., 1985, pp. 5-10; E.E. Herricks and L.L. Osborne, "Water Quality Restoration and Protection in Streams and Rivers," in J.A. Gore (ed.), *The Restoration of Rivers and Streams—Theories and Experience*, Butterworth Publishers, Boston, 1985, pp. 1-20; A. Brookes, "Restoring the Sinuosity of Artificially Straightened Stream Channels," *Environmental Geology and Water Sciences*, Vol. 10, 1987, pp. 33-41; J.A. Gore and F.L. Bryant, "River and Stream Restoration," in J. Cairns (ed.), *Rehabilitating Damaged Ecosystems*, CRC Press, Boca Raton, Fla., 1988, pp. 23-38; K. Baird, "High Quality Restoration of Riparian Ecosystems," *Restoration and Management Notes*, Vol. 7, 1989, pp. 60-64; G.M. Kondolf, "Hydrologic and Channel Stability Considerations in Stream Habitat Restoration," in J.J. Berger (ed.), *Environmental Restoration—Science and Strategies for Restoring the Earth*, Island Press, Washington, D.C., 1990, pp. 214-227; and Committee on Restoration of Aquatic Ecosystems, "Rivers and Streams," in *Restoration of Aquatic Ecosystems—Science, Technology, and Public Policy*, National Academy Press, Washington, D.C., 1992, pp. 165-261.

52 Articles by Uttormark, Peterson, Theis, Fast, Funk and Gibbons, Hickok, and Burton et al. in *Lake Restoration—*

Proceedings of a National Conference, U.S. Environmental Protection Agency (EPA), Washington, D.C., 1979; articles by Kothandaraman and Evans, Kroll, and Summerfelt, Holt, and McAlexander in *Proceedings of the Symposium on Surface Water Impoundments, Volumes I and II*, American Society of Civil Engineers (ASCE), New York, 1981; articles by Harper et al., Cooke, and Conyers and Cooke in *Lake Restoration, Protection, and Management—Proceedings of the Second Annual Conference*, U.S. Environmental Protection Agency (EPA), Washington, D.C., 1983; G.D. Cooke et al., *Lake and Reservoir Restoration*, Butterworth Publishers, Boston, 1986; and Committee on Restoration of Aquatic Ecosystems, "Lakes," in *Restoration of Aquatic Ecosystems—Science, Technology, and Public Policy*, National Academy Press, Washington, D.C., 1992, pp. 71-164.

53 T. King, R. Stout, and T. Gilbert, *Habitat Reclamation Guidelines*, Florida Game and Fresh Water Fish Commission, Bartow, 1985, pp. 42-54; K. Baird, "High Quality Restoration of Riparian Ecosystems," *Restoration & Management Notes*, Vol. 7, Winter 1989, pp. 60-64; and articles by Horowitz, Perry and Amaranthus, and Mahler and Walther in J.J. Berger (ed.), *Environmental Restoration—Science and Strategies for Restoring the Earth*, Island Press, Washington, D.C., 1990.

54 Hunter, op. cit., pp. 157-199; Payne and Bryant, op. cit., Chapters 7, 9, 13, and 15; Salvesen, op. cit., p. 114-119; B.W. Anderson, R.D. Ohmart, and J. Disano, "Revegetating the Riparian Floodplain for Wildlife," in *Strategies for Protection and Management of Floodplain Wetlands and Other Riparian Ecosystems*, Forest Service, U.S. Department of Agriculture, Washington, D.C., 1978, pp. 318-331; M.W. Weller, "Management of Freshwater Marshes for Wildlife," in R.E. Good, D.F. Whigham, and R.L. Simpson (eds.), *Freshwater Wetlands—Ecological Processes and Management Potential*, Academic Press, New York, 1978, pp. 267-284; A.R. Geier and L.B. Best, "Habitat Selection by Small Mammals of Riparian Communities: Evaluating Effects of Habitat Alterations," *Journal of Wildlife Management*, Vol. 44, 1980, pp. 16-24; D.F. Stauffer and L.B. Best, "Habitat Selection by Birds of Riparian Communities: Evaluating Effects of Habitat Alterations," *Journal of Wildlife Management*, Vol. 44, 1980, pp. 1-15; J. Yoakum et al., "Habitat Improvement Techniques," in S.D. Schemnitz (ed.), *Wildlife Management Techniques Manual*,

The Wildlife Society, Washington, D.C., 1980, pp. 329-403; T.A. Wesche, "Stream Channel Modifications and Reclamation Structures to Enhance Fish Habitat," in J.A. Gore (ed.), *The Restoration of Rivers and Streams—Theories and Experience*, Butterworth Publishers, Boston, 1985, pp. 103-163; N.F. Payne and F. Copes, *Wildlife and Fisheries Habitat Improvement Handbook*, Forest Service, U.S. Department of Agriculture, Washington, D.C., 1986; M.W. Weller, "Waterfowl Management Techniques for Wetland Enhancement, Restoration and Creation Useful in Mitigation Procedures," in J.A. Kusler and M.E. Kentula (eds.), *Wetland Creation and Restoration—The Status of the Science*, Island Press, Washington, D.C., 1990, pp. 517-528; D.A. Hammer, *Creating Freshwater Wetlands*, Lewis Publishers, Boca Raton, Fla., 1992, pp. 195-256; R.L. Knight, "Ancillary Benefits and Potential Problems with the Use of Wetlands for Nonpoint Source Pollution Control," in R.K. Olson (ed.), *Created and Natural Wetlands for Controlling Nonpoint Source Pollution*, CRC Press, Inc., Boca Raton, Fla., 1993, pp. 131-150; R.W. Newbury and M.N. Gaboury, *Stream Analysis and Fish Habitat Design—A Field Manual*, Newbury Hydraulics Ltd., Gibsons, B.C., 1993, pp. 91-182; N.F. Payne and F.C. Bryant, *Techniques for Wildlife Management of Uplands*, McGraw-Hill, New York, 1993, Chapters 7, 9, 13, and 15; and R.W. Mannan et al., "Managing Forestlands for Wildlife," in T.A. Bookhout (ed.), *Research and Management Techniques for Wildlife and Habitats*, The Wildlife Society, Bethesda, Md., 1994, pp. 689-721.

55   Complexity has been described as "fine-grained patchiness." Old-growth forests are patchy in this sense. The other kind of patchiness, the kind with the negative ramifications, differs from this kind in three respects: It is coarse-grained, has abrupt edges, and has highly contrasting habitats next to one another. See P.V. August, "The Role of Habitat Complexity and Heterogeneity in Structuring Tropical Mammal Communities," *Ecology*, Vol. 64, 1983, pp. 1495-1507; and R.F. Noss, "Effects of Edge and Internal Patchiness on Avian Habitat Use in an Old-Growth Florida Hammock," *Natural Areas Journal*, Vol. 11, 1991, pp. 34-47.

56   Askins et al., op. cit., 1987; Blake and Karr, op. cit., 1987; Boecklen, op. cit.; Forman and Baudry, op. cit.; Freemark and Merriam, op. cit.; Geier and Best, op. cit.;

Kitchener, op. cit.; Lynch and Whigham, op. cit.; Martin, op. cit., 1980; Martin, op. cit., 1988; Merriam and Lanoue, op. cit.; Noss, op. cit., 1991; Robbins et al., op. cit.; Stauffer and Best, op. cit.; Stevens et al., op. cit.; Tilghman, op. cit.; Williams, op. cit.; J.R. Karr and R.R. Roth, "Vegetation Structure and Avian Diversity in Several New World Areas," *The American Naturalist*, Vol. 105, 1971, pp. 423-435; B. Ortego, R.B. Hamilton, and R.E. Noble, "Bird Usage by Habitat Types in a Large Freshwater Lake," in *Proceedings of the Thirtieth Annual Conference of the Southeastern Association of Fish and Wildlife Agencies*, Montgomery, Ala., 1976, pp. 627-633; J.T. Rotenberry and J.A. Wiens, "Habitat Structure, Patchiness, and Avian Communities in North America Steppe Vegetation: A Multivariate Analysis," *Ecology*, Vol. 61, 1980, pp. 1228-1250; J. Rice, R.D. Ohmart, and B.W. Anderson, "Habitat Selection Attributes of an Avian Community: A Discriminant Analysis Investigation," *Ecological Monographs*, Vol. 53, 1983, pp. 263-290; A. Shmida and M.V. Wilson, "Biological Determinants of Species Diversity," *Journal of Biogeography*, Vol. 12, 1985, pp. 1-20; R.D. Dueser and J.H. Porter, "Habitat Use by Insular Small Mammals: Relative Effects of Competition and Habitat Structure," *Ecology*, Vol. 67, 1986, pp. 195-201; and E.L. Goldstein, M. Gross, and R.M. DeGraaf, "Breeding Birds and Vegetation: A Quantitative Assessment," *Urban Ecology*, Vol. 9, 1986, pp. 377-385. A few studies have reached the contrary conclusion that after controlling for patch size, habitat variables have little independent effect on species richness or abundance. This is a minority opinion, however, and a small minority at that.

57   S. Schauman, S. Penland, and M. Freeman, "Public Knowledge of and Preferences for Wildlife Habitats in Urban Open Spaces," in L.W. Adams and D.L. Leedy (eds.), *Integrating Man and Nature in the Metropolitan Environment*, National Institute for Urban Wildlife, Columbia, Md., 1987, pp. 113-118. Also see P.J. Pudelkewicz, "Visual Response to Urban Wildlife Habitat," in *Transactions of the 46th North American Wildlife and Natural Resources Conference*, Wildlife Management Institute, Washington, D.C., 1981, pp. 381-389.

58   J.M. Harbor, "A Practical Method for Estimating the Impact of Land-Use Change on Surface Runoff, Groundwater Recharge and Wetland Hydrology," *Journal*

of the American Planning Association, Vol. 60, 1994, pp. 95-108.

59   B.K. Ferguson, "Stormwater Management: Hydraulic Design or Environmental Process?" *Ars Natura*, Vol. 3, No. 2, 1990, pp. 6-8; and B.K. Ferguson, M.M. Ellington, and P.R. Gonnsen, "Evaluation and Control of the Long-Term Water Balance on an Urban Development Site," in K.J. Hatcher (ed.), *Proceedings of the 1991 Georgia Water Resources Conference*, Institute of Natural Resources, University of Georgia, Athens, 1991, pp. 217-220.

60   New York State Department of Environmental Conservation, "Best Management Practices," in *Stream Corridor Management: A Basic Reference Manual*, Albany, N.Y., 1986, pp. 65-93; Northern Virginia Regional Planning Commission, *BMP Handbook for the Occoquan Watershed*, Annandale, Va., 1987; T.R. Schueler, *Controlling Urban Runoff: A Practical Manual for Planning and Designing Urban BMPs*, Metropolitan Washington Council of Governments, Washington, D.C., 1987; E. Livingston et al., *The Florida Development Manual: A Guide to Sound Land and Water Management*, Florida Department of Environmental Protection, Tallahassee, 1988, Chapter 6; B.K. Ferguson and T.N. Debo, *On-Site Stormwater Management—Applications for Landscape and Engineering*, Van Nostrand Reinhold, New York, 1990; Maine Department of Environmental Protection, *Best Management Practices for Stormwater Management*, Sanford, Me., 1990; D.W. Dreher and T.H. Price, *Best Management Practice Guidebook for Urban Development*, Northeastern Illinois Planning Commission, Chicago, 1992; E.H. Livingston and E. McCarron, *Stormwater Management—A Guide for Floridians*, Florida Department of Environmental Protection, Tallahassee, 1992; and T.R. Schueler, P.A. Kumble, and M.A. Heraty, *A Current Assessment of Urban Best Management Practices—Techniques for Reducing Non-Point Source Pollution in the Coastal Zone*, Metropolitan Washington Council of Governments, Washington, D.C., 1992.

61   A third category of BMPs is sometimes defined: BMPs for *filtration* of stormwater. Filtration devices include filter strips, grassed swales, and sand filters. Following the more common convention, we have classified these as infiltration and/or detention devices, depending on the ultimate

disposition of the stormwater (whether on-site or off-site).

62 A concise summary of the literature on BMP applicability, cost, and effectiveness is provided in U.S. Environmental Protection Agency (EPA), *Guidance Specifying Management Measures for Sources of Nonpoint Pollution in Coastal Waters*, Washington, D.C., 1993, pp. 4-12 through 4-35.

63 B.K. Ferguson, "Urban Stormwater Infiltration—Purposes, Implementation, Results," *Journal of Soil and Water Conservation*, Vol. 45, 1990, pp. 605-609; and B.K. Ferguson, "Infiltration Performance," *Stormwater Infiltration*, Lewis Publishers, Boca Raton, Fla., in press, pp. 153-184.

64 M.M. Ellington and B.K. Ferguson, "Comparison of Infiltration and Detention in the Georgia Piedmont Using Recent Hydrologic Models," in K. Hatcher (ed.), *Proceedings of the 1991 Georgia Water Resources Conference*, Institute of Natural Resources, University of Georgia, Athens, 1991, pp. 213-216.

65 I.L. McHarg and J. Sutton, "Ecological Plumbing for the Texas Coastal Plain," *Landscape Architecture*, Vol. 65, 1975, pp. 78-89; N. Juneja and J. Veltman, "Natural Drainage in The Woodlands," *Environmental Comment*, November 1979, pp. 7-14; and W.G. Lynard et al., "Management of a Natural Drainage System—The Woodlands, Texas," in *Urban Stormwater Management and Technology: Case Histories*, U.S. Environmental Protection Agency, Washington, D.C., 1980, pp. 119-135.

66 Ferguson, op. cit., in press, pp. 35-88; R.J. Weaver, *Recharge Basins for Disposal of Highway Storm Drainage—Theory, Design Procedure, and Recommended Practices*, New York State Department of Transportation, Albany, 1971; J.B. Hannon, *Underground Disposal of Stormwater Runoff—Design Guidelines Manual*, Federal Highway Administration, Washington, D.C., 1980; H.E. Shaver, "Infiltration as a Stormwater Management Component," in B. Urbonas and L.A. Roesner (eds.), *Urban Runoff Quality—Impact and Quality Enhancement Technology*, American Society of Civil Engineers, New York, 1986, pp. 270-280; B.W. Harrington, "Design and Construction of Infiltration Trenches," in L.A. Roesner, B. Urbonas, and M.B. Sonnen (eds.), *Design of*

Urban Runoff Quality Controls, American Society of Civil Engineers, New York, 1989, pp. 290-304; P. Stahre and B. Urbonas, "Local Disposal by Infiltration and Percolation," in *Stormwater Detention for Drainage, Water Quality, and CSO Management*, Prentice-Hall, Englewood Cliffs, N.J., 1990, pp. 7-23; and F.G. Galli, *Preliminary Analysis of the Performance and Longevity of Urban BMPs Installed in Prince George's County*, Department of Environmental Resources, Prince George's County, Md., 1992.

67 Occoquan Watershed Monitoring Laboratory (OWML), *An Evaluation of the Performance of Porous Pavement for Stormwater Quality Control*, Manassas, Va., 1986; J. Cox, L.A. Roberts, and J.E. Paine, *Portland Cement Pervious Pavement—Surface Water Management Design Example*, Tarmac Florida, Deerfield Beach, 1991, p. ii; and J.E. Paine, "Portland Cement Pervious Pavement Construction," *Concrete Construction*, Vol. 37, September 1992, pp. 655-659.

68 Schueler, op. cit., Chapter 7; E. Thelen et al., *Investigation of Porous Pavements for Urban Runoff Control*, U.S. Environmental Protection Agency, Washington, D.C., 1972, pp. 19-33; E. Thelen and L.F. Howe, *Porous Pavement—Principles of Development and a Porous Pavement Design Manual*, Franklin Institute Press, Philadelphia, 1978, pp. 3-4 and 13-16; R. Field, H. Masters, and M. Singer, "Porous Pavement: Research; Development; and Demonstration," *Transportation Engineering Journal*, Vol. 108, 1982, pp. 244-258; Maryland Department of Natural Resources, *Maryland Standards and Specifications for Infiltration Practices*, Annapolis, Md., 1984, pp. 3-24 through 3-37; and D.B. Nichols, "Paving," in S.S. Weinberg and G.A. Coyle (eds.), *Handbook of Landscape Architectural Construction, Volume 4—Materials*, Landscape Architecture Foundation, Washington, D.C., 1992, pp. 69-138.

69 J.S. Baldwin, "Use of Open-Graded, Free-Draining Layers in Pavement Systems: A National Synthesis Report," *Transportation Research Record 1121*, 1987, pp. 86-89; articles in the collection "Porous Asphalt Pavements: An International Perspective," *Transportation Research Record 1265*, 1990; R.A. Forsyth, *Asphalt Treated Permeable Material—Its Evolution and Application*, National Asphalt Pavement Association, Lanham, Md., 1991, pp. 6-9; F.A. Kozeliski, "Permeable Bases Help Solve Pavement Drainage

Problems," *Concrete Construction*, Vol. 37, September 1992, pp. 660-667; W.J. Tappeiner, *Open-Graded Asphalt Friction Course*, National Asphalt Pavement Association, Lanham, Md., 1993, pp. 1-4; and E. Schlect, "Open-Graded Asphalt Surfaces Offer Safety and Environmental Advantages," *Stone Review*, April 1994, pp. 10-11.

70 Performance charateristics of open-celled pavers are described in G.E. Day, "Investigation of Concrete Grid Pavements," in W.L. Downing (ed.), *Proceedings of the National Conference on Urban Erosion and Sediment Control: Institutions & Technology*, Great Lakes National Program Office, U.S. Environmental Protection Agency (EPA), Chicago, 1980, pp. 127-136; G.E. Day, D.R. Smith, and J. Bowers, *Runoff and Pollution Abatement Characteristics of Concrete Grid Pavements*, Bulletin 135, Virginia Water Resources Research Center, Virginia Polytechnic Institute, Blacksburg, 1981, pp. 24-35; R.J. Southerland, "Construction—Concrete Grid Pavers," *Landscape Architecture*, Vol. 74, 1984, pp. 97-99; and D. Nichols, "Porous Paving: Stormwater Management Alternative," *Landscape Design*, Vol. 6, January 1993, pp. 22-24.

71 K. Sorvig, "Porous Paving," *Landscape Architecture*, Vol. 83, February 1993, pp. 66-69. Also see Thelen et al., op. cit., pp. 75-122; and Florida Concrete and Products Association, *Portland Cement Pervious Pavement Manual*, Orlando, Fla., undated, pp. 16-17.

72 Sorvig, op. cit.

73 T. Cahill, "A Second Look at Porous Pavement/Underground Recharge," *Watershed Protection Techniques*, Vol. 1, 1994, pp. 76-78. For detailed design and installation guidelines, see Maryland Department of Natural Resources, op. cit.; and Cahill Associates, *Stormwater Management Systems: Porous Pavement System with Underground Recharge Beds—Engineering Design Report*, West Chester, Pa., 1993, pp. 14-30.

74 Cahill, op. cit.; Cahill Associates, op. cit., pp. 31-34; and Schueler, op. cit., p. 7.21. For maintenance requirements of porous concrete, see R. Wingerter and J.E. Paine, *Field Performance Investigation—Portland Cement Pervious Pavement*, Florida Concrete and Products Association, Orlando, 1989.

[75] J. Horanic, "Re-Using Scarce Waters for Suburban Offices," *Landscape Architecture*, Vol. 70, 1980, pp. 389-391; G.W. Frasier and W.L.E. Myers, *Handbook of Water Harvesting*, Agricultural Research Service, U.S. Department of Agriculture, Washington, D.C., 1983; B.K. Ferguson, "Urban Stormwater Harvesting: Applications and Hydraulic Design," *Journal of Environmental Management*, Vol. 25, 1987, pp. 71-79; and C.L. Ellefson, T.L. Stephens, and D. Welsh, "Efficient Irrigation: Making Every Drop Count," in *Xeriscape Gardening: Water Conservation for the American Landscape*, Macmillan Publishing Company, New York, 1992, pp. 103-116.

[76] Infiltrating the first flush can accomplish so much for two reasons. First, small storms are so much more common than big ones; 90 percent of all storm events in Florida produce less than one inch of rainfall. Second, even when the occasional big storm comes along, the first flush picks up most of the pollutants deposited since the last rainfall, 90 percent according to some estimates. B.H. McArthur, "The Use of Isolated Wetlands in Florida for Stormwater Treatment," in D.W. Fisk (ed.), *Proceedings of the Symposium on Wetlands: Concerns and Successes*, American Water Resources Association, Bethesda, Md., 1989, pp. 185-193.

[77] Florida studies of stormwater treatment efficiencies are reviewed by P.J. Whalen and M.G. Cullum, *An Assessment of Urban Land Use/Stormwater Runoff Quality Relationships and Treatment Efficiencies of Selected Stormwater Management Systems*, South Florida Water Management District, West Palm Beach, 1988, pp. 36-44. National studies are summarized in Schueler et al., op. cit., pp. 105-113; and E.W. Strecker et al., *The Use of Wetlands for Controlling Stormwater Pollution*, The Terrene Institute, Washington, D.C., 1992, pp. 7-32. Also see R.P. Akeley, "Retention Basins for Control of Urban Stormwater Quality," in W.L. Downing (ed.), *Proceedings of the National Conference on Urban Erosion and Sediment Control: Institutions & Technology*, Great Lakes National Program Office, U.S. Environmental Protection Agency, Chicago, 1980, pp. 69-78; R.H. McCuen, "Water Quality Trap Efficiency of Storm Water Management Basins," *Water Resources Bulletin*, Vol. 16, 1980, pp. 15-21; E.A. Hickok, "Wetlands for the Control of Urban Stormwater," in W.L. Downing (ed.), *Proceedings of the National Conference on Urban Erosion and Sediment Control: Institutions & Technology*, Great Lakes National Program Office, U.S. Environmental Protection Agency, Chicago, 1980, pp. 79-88; E. Chan et al., *The Use of Wetlands for Water Pollution Control*, Municipal Environmental Research Laboratory, U.S. Environmental Protection Agency, Cincinnati, 1981, pp. 165-175; S.M. Luzkow, D.A. Scherger, and J.A. Davis, "Effectiveness of Two In-Line Urban Stormwater Best Management Practices," in *Proceedings of the 1981 International Symposium on Urban Hydrology, Hydraulics, and Sediment Control*, University of Kentucky, Lexington, 1981, pp. 193-206; G.L. Oberts, "Impact of Wetlands on Watershed Water Quality," in B. Richardson (ed.), *Selected Proceedings of the Midwest Conference on Wetland Values and Management*, Freshwater Society, Navarre, Minn., 1981, pp. 213-226; L.J. Oliver and S.G. Grigoropoulos, "Control of Storm-Generated Pollution Using a Small Urban Lake," *Journal of the Water Pollution Control Federation*, Vol. 53, 1981, pp. 594-603; T. Wang, *Transport, Deposition and Control of Heavy Metals in Highway Runoff*, Master's Thesis, Department of Civil Engineering, University of Washington, Seattle, 1981, pp. 59-83; D.L. Hey, "Lake Ellyn and Urban Stormwater Treatment," in W. DeGroot (ed.), *Proceedings of the Conference on Stormwater Detention Facilities*, American Society of Civil Engineers, New York, 1982, pp. 220-235; G.L. Oberts, "Impact of Wetlands on Nonpoint Source Pollution," in *Proceedings of the 1982 International Symposium on Urban Hydrology, Hydraulics, and Sediment Control*, University of Kentucky, Lexington, 1982, pp. 225-232; C.W. Randall, "Stormwater Detention Ponds for Water Quality Control," in W. DeGroot (ed.), *Proceedings of the Conference on Stormwater Detention Facilities*, American Society of Civil Engineers, New York, 1982, pp. 200-204; D.A. Scherger and J.A. Davis, "Control of Stormwater Runoff Pollutant Loads by a Wetland and Retention Basin," in *Proceedings of the 1982 International Symposium on Urban Hydrology, Hydraulics, and Sediment Control*, University of Kentucky, Lexington, 1982, pp. 109-123; J. Barten, "Nutrient Removal from Urban Stormwater by Wetland Filtration: The Clear Lake Restoration Project," in *Lake Restoration, Protection, and Management—Proceedings of the Second Annual Conference*, U.S. Environmental Protection Agency, Washington, D.C., 1983, pp. 23-30; R.A. Ferrara and P. Witkowski, "Stormwater Quality Characteristics in Detention Basins," *Journal of Environmental Engineering*, Vol. 109, 1983, pp. 428-447; W.C. Kercher, J.C. Landon, and R. Massarelli, "Grassy Swales Prove Cost-Effective for Water Pollution Control," *Public Works*, Vol. 114, April 1983, pp. 53-54; P.H. Oakland, "An Evaluation of Urban Storm Water Pollutant Removal Through Grassed Swale Treatment," *Proceedings of the 1983 International Symposium on Urban Hydrology, Hydraulics and Sediment Control*, University of Kentucky, Lexington, 1983, pp. 183-185; U.S. Environmental Protection Agency (EPA), *Results of the Nationwide Urban Runoff Program, Volume 1—Final Report*, Washington, D.C., 1983, pp. 8-1 through 8-25; R.L. Knight, "Wetlands—A Natural Land Treatment Alternative," in D. Gillespie and O.K. Buros (eds.), *Reuse and the Protection of Florida's Waters: The Dilemma—The Challenge*, CH2M Hill, Deerfield Beach, Fla., 1984, pp. 117-129; R.G. Brown, "Effects of an Urban Wetland on Sediment and Nutrient Loads in Runoff," *Wetlands*, Vol. 4, 1985, pp. 147-158; W.D. Weidenbacher and P.R. Willenbring, "Limiting Nutrient Flux into an Urban Lake by Natural Treatment and Diversion," *Lake and Reservoir Management*, Vol. 3, 1984, pp. 525-526; T.E. Jordon et al., "Nutrient Flux in a Landscape: The Rhode River Watershed and Receiving Waters," in D.L. Correll (ed.), *Watershed Research Perspectives*, Smithsonian Institution Press, Washington, D.C., 1986, pp. 57-76; D.F. Whigham et al., "Modification of Runoff from Upland Watersheds: The Influences of a Diverse Riparian Ecosystem," in D.L. Correll (ed.), *Watershed Research Perspectives*, Smithsonian Institution Press, Washington, D.C., 1986, pp. 305-332; P.J. Wigington, C.W. Randall, and T.J. Grizzard, "Accumulation of Selected Trace Metals in Soils of Urban Runoff Swale Drains," *Water Resources Bulletin*, Vol. 22, 1986, pp. 73-79; R.G. Striegl, "Suspended Sediment and Metals Removal from Urban Runoff by a Small Lake," *Water Resources Bulletin*, Vol. 23, 1987, pp. 985-996; E.H. Martin, "Effectiveness of an Urban Runoff Detention Pond-Wetlands System, *Journal of Environmental Engineering*, Vol. 114, 1988, pp. 810-827; E.J. Kuenzler, "Value of Forested Wetlands as Filters for Sediments and Nutrients," in D.D. Hook and R. Lea (eds.), *The Forested Wetlands of the Southern United States*, Southeastern Forest Experimental Station, Forest Service, U.S. Department of Agriculture, Asheville, N.C., 1989, pp. 85-96; A.E. Maristany and R.L. Bartel, "Wetlands and Stormwater Management: A Case Study of Lake Munson—Part I: Long-Term Treatment Efficiencies," in D.W. Fisk (ed.), *Proceedings of the Symposium on Wetlands: Concerns and Successes*, American Water Resources Association, Bethesda, Md., 1989, pp. 215-229; G.L. Oberts, P.J. Wotzka,

and J.A. Hartsoe, *The Water Quality Performance of Select Urban Runoff Treatment Systems*, Metropolitan Council of the Twin Cities Area, St. Paul, Minn., 1989, pp. 45-57; T.R. Schueler and M. Helfrich, "Design of Extended Detention Wet Pond Systems," in L.A. Roesner, B. Urbonas, and M.B. Sonnen (eds.), *Design of Urban Runoff Quality Controls*, American Society of Civil Engineers, New York, 1989, pp. 180-200; J.S. Wu, B. Holman, and J. Dorney, "Water Quality Study on Urban Wet Detention Ponds," in L.A. Roesner, B. Urbonas, and M.B. Sonnen (eds.), *Design of Urban Runoff Quality Controls*, American Society of Civil Engineers, New York, 1989, pp. 280-289; and W.J. Mitsch, "Landscape Design and the Role of Created, Restored, and Natural Riparian Wetlands in Controlling Nonpoint Source Pollution," in R.K. Olson (ed.), *Created and Natural Wetlands for Controlling Nonpoint Source Pollution*, CRC Press, Inc., Boca Raton, Fla., 1993, pp. 43-70.

[78] NAHB National Research Center, *Affordable Residential Land Development: A Guide for Local Government and Developers*, Upper Marlboro, Md., 1987, pp. 72-89.

[79] Adams et al., op. cit.; R.S. Hankin and D.A. Daily, "Pleasant Grove: A Case Study in Innovative Stormwater Management," in H.G. Stefan (ed.), *Proceedings of the Symposium on Surface Water Impoundments*, American Society of Civil Engineers, New York, 1981, pp. 985-994; and E.H. Baxter, G. Mulamoottil, and D. Gregor, "A Study of Residential Stormwater Impoundments: Perceptions and Policy Implications," *Water Resources Bulletin*, Vol. 21, 1985, pp. 83-88.

[80] Weller, op. cit., 1978; W.C. Hobaugh and J.G. Teer, "Waterfowl Use Characteristics of Flood Prevention Lakes in North Central Texas," *Journal of Wildlife Management*, Vol. 45, 1981, pp. 16-26; L.W. Adams and L.E. Dove, *Urban Wetlands for Stormwater Control and Wildlife Enhancement*, National Institute for Urban Wildlife, Columbia, Md., 1984, pp. 7-9; J.M. Duffield, "Waterbird Use of a Stormwater Wetland System in Central California, USA," *Colonial Waterbirds*, Vol. 9, 1986, pp. 227-235; J.P. Ball and T.D. Nudds, "Mallard Habitat Selection: An Experiment and Implications for Management," in R.R. Sharitz and J.W. Gibbons (eds.), *Freshwater Wetlands and Wildlife*, U.S. Department of Energy, Oak Ridge, Tenn., 1989, pp. 659-671; M.T. Brown, "Forested Wetlands in Urbanizing

Landscapes," in D.D. Hook and R. Lea (eds.), *The Forested Wetlands of the Southern United States*, Southeastern Forest Experimental Station, Forest Service, U.S. Department of Agriculture, Asheville, N.C., 1989, pp. 19-26; J.P. Hartigan, "Basis for Design of Wet Detention Basin BMPs," in L.A. Roesner, B. Urbonas, and M.B. Sonnen (eds.), *Design of Urban Runoff Quality Controls*, American Society of Civil Engineers, New York, 1989, pp. 122-143; M. Brittingham, *Providing Wetlands for Wildlife While Controlling Stormwater*, College of Agriculture, Pennsylvania State University, University Park, 1990; and T.R. Schueler, *Design of Stormwater Wetland Systems: Guidelines for Creating Diverse and Effective Stormwater Wetlands in the Mid-Atlantic Region*, Metropolitan Washington Council of Governments, Washington, D.C., 1992, pp. 27-28.

[81] Chan et al., op. cit.; D.S. Nichols, "Capacity of Natural Wetlands to Remove Nutrients from Wastewater," *Journal of the Water Pollution Control Federation*, Vol. 55, 1983, pp. 495-505; H.H. Harper et al., *Stormwater Treatment by Natural Systems*, Florida Department of Environmental Regulation, Tallahassee, 1986, pp. 6-11 through 6-13; E.C. Stockdale, *The Use of Wetlands for Stormwater Management and Nonpoint Pollution Control: A Review of Literature*, Washington State Department of Ecology, Seattle, 1986, pp. 16-18; and E.J. Kuenzler, "Wetlands as Sediment and Nutrient Traps for Lakes," in *Proceedings of a National Conference on Enhancing the State's Land and Wetland Management Programs*, 1990, pp. 105-112.

[82] Knight, op. cit.; Mitsch and Gosselink, op. cit., p. 589-590; Schueler, op. cit., 1992, pp. 19-21; and O.L. Loucks, "Restoration of the Pulse Control Function of Wetlands and Its Relationship to Water Quality Objectives," in J.A. Kusler and M.E. Kentula (eds.), *Wetland Creation and Restoration: The Status of the Science*, Island Press, Washington, D.C., 1990, pp. 467-478.

[83] R.P. Brooks, "Optimal Designs for Restored Wetlands," in J.E. Burris (ed.), *Treatment of Mine Drainage by Wetlands*, Department of Biology, Pennsylvania State University, University Park, 1984, pp. 19-29.

[84] Adams and Dove, op. cit., 1984, pp. 8 and 13; Hobaugh and Teer, op. cit.; L.W. Adams, L.E. Dove, and T.M. Franklin, "Use of Urban Stormwater Control

Impoundments by Wetland Birds," *Wilson Bulletin*, Vol. 97, 1985, pp. 120-122; L.W. Adams et al., "Design Considerations for Wildlife in Urban Stormwater Management," *Transactions of the 51st North American Wildlife and Natural Resources Conference*, Wildlife Management Institute, Washington, D.C., 1986, pp. 249-259; and L.H. Fredrickson and F.A. Reid, "Wetland and Riparian Habitats: A Nongame Management Overview," in J.B. Hale, L.B. Best, and R.L. Clawson (eds.), *Management of Nongame Wildlife in the Midwest: A Developing Art*, BookCrafters, Chelsea, Mich., 1986, pp. 59-96.

[85] Duffield, op. cit.; Weller, op. cit., 1978; Williams, op. cit.; M.W. Weller and L.H. Fredrickson, "Avian Ecology of a Managed Glacial Marsh," in D.A. Lancaster (ed.), *The Living Bird*, Laboratory of Ornithology, Cornell University, Ithaca, N.Y., 1973, pp. 269-291; and R.M. Kaminski and H.H. Prince, "Dabbling Duck and Aquatic Macroinvertebrate Responses to Manipulated Wetland Habitat," *Journal of Wildlife Management*, Vol. 45, 1981, pp. 1-15.

[86] Ferguson and Debo, op. cit., p. 126; and Schueler, op. cit., 1987, p. 4.9.

[87] Brittingham, op. cit., 1990, p. 5; and Schueler, op. cit., 1987, pp. 4.9-4.10.

[88] Livingston et al., op. cit., p. 2-25.

[89] The apparent contradiction between this guideline, which calls for more edge on lakes and ponds, and *Environmental Practice 3*, which calls for less edge on forest patches, is explained by the different species of concern in the two cases and their very different habitat requirements.

[90] Adams and Dove, op. cit., 1984, pp. 8-9, 13; Adams et al., op. cit., 1986; Anderson and Gutzwiller, op. cit.; Brittingham, op. cit., p. 5; Duffield, op. cit.; and Knight, op. cit.

[91] Wilcove, op. cit.; D. Gill, "The Feral House Cat as a Predator of Varying Hares," *Canadian Field Naturalist*, Vol. 89, 1975, pp. 78-79; A.S. Leopold and M.F. Dedon, "Resident Mourning Doves in Berkeley, California," *Journal*

of *Wildlife Management*, Vol. 47, 1983, pp. 780-789; B.M. Fitzgerald and C.R. Veitch, "The Cats of Herekopare Island, New Zealand; Their History, Ecology and Effects on Birdlife," *New Zealand Journal of Zoology*, Vol. 12, 1985, pp. 319-330; and P.B. Churcher and J.H. Lawton, "Beware of Well-Fed Felines," *Natural History 7*, Vol. 89, pp. 40-47.

[92] Adams, op. cit., pp. 113-114; Adams et al., op. cit., 1986; Brittingham, op. cit., p. 5; Schueler, op. cit., 1987, p. 4.18; and C.N. Palmer and J.D. Hunt, "Greenwood Urban Wetland—A Manmade Stormwater Treatment Facility," in D.W. Fisk (ed.), *Wetlands Concerns and Successes*, American Water Resources Association, Tampa, Fla., 1989, pp. 1-10.

[93] A. Duany and E. Plater-Zyberk, "The Second Coming of the American Small Town," *The Wilson Quarterly*, Vol. 16, Winter 1992, pp. 19-48.

[94] Florida Department of Environmental Regulation (DER), *Land Application of Domestic Wastewater Effluent in Florida*, Tallahassee, 1982, pp. 1-2; J. Crook, "Health and Regulatory Considerations," in G.S. Pettygrove and T. Asano (eds.), *Irrigation with Municipal Wastewater—A Guidance Manual*, Lewis Publishers, Boca Raton, Fla., 1985, pp. 10-1 through 10-49; Florida Department of Environmental Regulation (DER), "Reuse of Reclaimed Water and Land Application—Part III: Reuse; Slow-Rate Land Application Systems; Public Access Areas, Residential Irrigation, and Edible Crops," Chapter 17-610, Florida Administrative Code, Tallahassee, 1990; J. Crook, D.K. Ammerman, and D. Okun, *Manual: Guidelines for Water Reuse*, U.S. Environmental Protection Agency/U.S. Agency for International Development, Washington, D.C., 1992, pp. 133-138; and C.F. Mancino and I.L. Pepper, "Irrigation of Turfgrass with Wastewater," in *Wastewater Reuse for Golf Course Irrigation*, Sponsored by the United States Golf Association, Lewis Publishers, Boca Raton, Fla., 1994, pp. 174-191. A balanced assessment of irrigation with wastewater, both pluses and minuses, is presented by C.H. Peacock, "Wastewater Irrigation for Golf Courses: Advantages versus Disadvantages," in *Wastewater Reuse for Golf Course Irrigation*, Sponsored by the United States Golf Association, Lewis Publishers, Boca Raton, Fla., 1994, pp. 204-220.

[95] L.B. Baldwin and D.A. Comer, *Utilizing Treated Sewage for Irrigation of Urban Landscapes*, Institute of Food and Agricultural Sciences, University of Florida, Gainesville, 1986, pp. 5-10. Also see American Water Works Association (AWWA), *Dual Water Systems*, Denver, 1994, pp. 76-78; R.A. Mills and T. Asano, "The Economic Benefits of Using Reclaimed Water," *Journal of Freshwater*, Vol. 10, 1986/87, pp. 14-15; and D.W. Prasifka, "Water Reuse Can Turn a Liability into an Asset," *Land Development*, Vol. 3, Spring 1990, pp. 27-30.

[96] Dade County at one point shut down its smaller plants in favor of super-regional ones, but has since found it difficult to supply high-quality effluent when the waste stream includes a mix of industrial and residential sewage. Reportedly, Dade County is now considering recommissioning small plants.

[97] Reuse projects in St. Petersburg, Tampa, Orlando/Orange County, and other areas are described in W. Johnson, "St. Petersburg—Experiences with a Dual Water System," in D. Gillespie and O.K. Buros (eds.), *Reuse and the Protection of Florida's Waters: The Dilemma—The Challenge*, CH2M Hill, Deerfield Beach, Fla., 1984, pp. 153-160; M. Morrisette, "Water Reuse in St. Petersburg: A 10-Year Success Story," *Journal of Freshwater*, Vol. 10, 1986/87, pp. 25-26; J.V. Towry and D. Shulmister, "Water Conservation Pioneers," *Quality Cities*, Vol. 63, May 1990, pp. 44-47; and A.B. Marcous, "Project APRICOT Blooms in Altamonte Springs," *Quality Cities*, Vol. 63, May 1990, pp. 46-50.

[98] D. Brandes, *Wastewater Treatment and Reuse Inventory in the St. Johns River Water Management District*, St. Johns River Water Management District, Palatka, Fla., 1991.

[99] For IPM principles and practices, see D.A. Potter, "Urban Landscape Pest Management," in G.W. Bennett and J.M. Owens (eds.), *Advances in Urban Pest Management*, Van Nostrand Reinhold, New York, 1986, pp. 219-251; A.R. Leslie and R.L. Metcalf (eds.), *Integrated Pest Management for Turfgrass and Ornamentals*, Golf Course Superintendents Association of America, Washington, D.C., 1989; W. Olkowski, S.S. Daar, and H. Olkowski, *Common-Sense Pest Control*, The Taunton Press, Newtown, Conn., 1991, Chapters 2-4 and 29-30; J.C. Balogh et al., "Development

of Integrated Management Systems for Turfgrass," in J.C. Balogh and W.J. Walker (eds.), *Golf Course Management and Construction—Environmental Issues*, Sponsored by the United States Golf Association, Lewis Publishers, Boca Raton, Fla., 1992, pp. 355-439; A.H. Bruneau, J.E. Watkins, and R.L. Brandenburg, "Integrated Pest Management," in D.V. Waddington, R.N. Carrow, and R.C. Shearman (eds.), *Turfgrass*, American Society of Agronomy, Madison, Wis., 1992, pp. 501-533; L.B. McCarty et al., *Integrated Pest Management Strategies for Golf Courses*, Institute of Food and Agricultural Sciences, University of Florida, Gainesville, 1992; and A.R. Leslie (ed.), *Handbook of Integrated Pest Management for Turf and Ornamentals*, Lewis Publishers, Boca Raton, Fla., 1994. For a critical appraisal of IPM, see D.A. Potter and S.K. Braman, "Ecology and Management of Turfgrass Insects," *Annual Review of Entomology*, Vol. 36, 1991, pp. 383-406.

[100] D.E. Short, J.A. Reinert, and R.A. Atilano, "Integrated Pest Management for Urban Turfgrass Culture—Florida," in H.D. Niemczyk and B.G. Joyner (eds.), *Advances in Turfgrass Entomology*, ChemLawn Corporation, Columbus, Ohio, 1982, pp. 25-30. Other studies showing large reductions in pesticide use with IPM include Olkowski et al., 1976; J.J. Holmes and J.A. Davidson, "Integrated Pest Management for Arborists: Implementation of a Pilot Program," *Journal of Arboriculture*, Vol. 10, 1984, pp. 65-70; M.J. Raupp and R.M. Noland, "Implementing Landscape Plant Management Programs in Residential and Institutional Settings, *Journal of Arboriculture*, Vol. 10, 1984, pp. 161-169; J.L. Sherald and C.L.J. DiSalvo, "Integrated Pest Management in the National Capital Region of the National Park Service," *Journal of Arboriculture*, Vol. 13, 1987, pp. 229-235; and Z. Grant, "Integrated Pest Management in the Golf Course Industry: A Case Study and Some General Considerations," in A.R. Leslie and R.L. Metcalf (eds.), *Integrated Pest Management for Turfgrass and Ornamentals*, Golf Course Superintendents Association of America, Washington, D.C., 1989, pp. 85-91.

[101] D.C. Smith and M.J. Raupp, "Economic and Environmental Assessment of an Integrated Pest Management Program for Community-Owned Landscape Plants," *Journal of Economic Entomology*, Vol. 79, 1986, pp. 162-165.

102 T.M. Buttler et al., *Turf - Golf Courses—Managing Pesticides for Crop Production and Water Quality Protection*, Institute of Food and Agricultural Sciences, University of Florida, Gainesville, 1991; P.W.M. Augustijn-Beckers et al., *Turf - Lawn Care Industry—Managing Pesticides for Crop Production and Water Quality Protection*, Institute of Food and Agricultural Sciences, University of Florida, Gainesville, 1991; and A.G. Hornsby, T.M. Buttler, and R.B. Brown, "Managing Pesticides for Crop Production and Water Quality Protection: Practical Grower Guide," *Agriculture, Ecosystems and Environment*, Vol. 46, 1993, pp. 187-196.

103 See the literature review in D.A. Potter, S.D. Cockfield, and T.A. Morris, "Ecological Side Effects of Pesticide and Fertilizer Use on Turfgrass," in A.R. Leslie and R.L. Metcalf (eds.), *Integrated Pest Management for Turfgrass and Ornamentals*, Golf Course Superintendents Association of America, Washington, D.C., 1989, pp. 33-44.

104 See literature reviews in J.A. Reinert, "Insecticide Resistance in Epigeal Insect Pests of Turfgrass: 1. A Review," in H.D. Niemczyk and B.G. Joyner (eds.), *Advances in Turfgrass Entomology*, Hammer Graphics, Piqua, Ohio, 1982, pp. 71-76; and R.L. Metcalf, "Insect Resistance to Insecticides," in A.R. Leslie and R.L. Metcalf (eds.), *Integrated Pest Management for Turfgrass and Ornamentals*, Golf Course Superintendents Association of America, Washington, D.C., 1989, pp. 3-31.

105 Incidents of pest resurgences or secondary pest outbreaks are recounted in M.J. Raupp, C.S. Koehler, and J.A. Davidson, "Advances in Implementing Integrated Pest Management for Woody Landscape Plants," *Annual Review of Entomology*, Vol. 37, 1992, pp. 561-585.

106 The following long list of articles is presented for two reasons: first, to illustrate the many facets of IPM and, second, as a guide to some of the most useful literature on IPM. Z. Grant, "Integrated Pest Management Update: The Sherman Hollow Story," *Golf Course Management*, Vol. 55, November 1987, pp. 6-16, 81-82; D. Borland, "Using Alternative Plant Materials," *Golf Course Management*, Vol. 56, March 1988, pp. 68-76; R.N. Carrow, "Managing Turf for Maximum Root Growth," *Golf Course Management*, Vol.

57, July 1989, pp. 18-26; G. Witteveen, "Disposal of Grass Clippings," *Golf Course Management*, Vol. 57, July 1989, pp. 64-70; D. Gadd, "Deep Aerification: A Power Play with Promise?" *Golf Course Management*, Vol. 57, August 1989, pp. 6-16; D. Bishop, "Building Successful Programs: The Dimensions of IPM Today," *Golf Course Management*, Vol. 58, March 1990, pp. 56-64; K. Delahaut and C.F. Koval, "Nature's Aerator," *Golf Course Management*, Vol. 58, March 1990, pp. 136-140; D. Gadd, "Current Trends in Cultural Programs," *Golf Course Management*, Vol. 58, March 1990, pp. 66, 70, 72 and 76; R.L. Duble, "Managing Turfgrass Insects," *Golf Course Management*, Vol. 58, April 1990, pp. 96-114; M.M. Boaz, "Soil Modification and Its Role in Integrated Pest Management," *Golf Course Management*, Vol. 59, February 1991, pp. 133-136; D. Eskelson, "Implementing IPM Strategies," *Golf Course Management*, Vol. 60, February 1992, pp. 68-75; M.L. Agnew, "Slow-Release Fertilizers: Natural Organic Nitrogen Sources," *Golf Course Management*, Vol. 60, March 1992, pp. 70-75; E.B. Nelson, "The Biological Control of Turfgrass Diseases," *Golf Course Management*, Vol. 60, April 1992, pp. 78-90; D.J. Shetlar, "The Biological Control of Insects," *Golf Course Management*, Vol. 60, April 1992, pp. 92-98; W.K. Hock, "Unraveling the Mysteries: Horticultural Spray Adjuvants," *Golf Course Management*, Vol. 60, September 1992, pp. 56, 58, and 60; "Aerification Options Continue to Expand," *Golf Course Management*, Vol. 61, March 1993, pp. 108-124; J. Nus, "Coming to Terms with Surface Insects," *Golf Course Management*, Vol. 61, May 1993, pp. 6-20; M.J. Carroll, "Determining Pesticide Mobility and Persistence in Soil," *Golf Course Management*, Vol. 61, June 1993, pp. 103-107; and M.L. Agnew, "Thatch Control," *Golf Course Management*, Vol. 61, August 1993, pp. 60, 62, and 64.

107 M.M. Smart et al., "Working with Nature for Better Golf Developments," *Urban Land*, Vol. 52, March 1993, pp. 17-22.

108 For Xeriscape principles and practices, see Ellefson et al., op. cit.; G.O. Robinette, *Water Conservation in Landscape Design & Maintenance*, Van Nostrand Reinhold Company, New York, 1984; K. Ball, *Xeriscape^TM—Programs for Water Utilities*, American Water Works Association, Denver, 1990; E.F. Gilman and S.P. Brown, *Florida Guide to Environmental Landscapes*, Institute of Food and

Agricultural Sciences, University of Florida, Gainesville, 1991; J. Kelly et al., *Xeriscape—Landscape Water Conservation in the Southeast*, Cooperative Extension Service, Clemson University, Clemson, SC, 1991; G.L. Wade et al., *Xeriscape—A Guide to Developing a Water-Wise Landscape*, Cooperative Extension Service, University of Georgia, Athens, 1992; R.E. Bennett and M.S. Hazinski, *Water-Efficient Landscape Guidelines*, American Water Works Association, Denver, 1993; and U.S. Environmental Protection Agency (EPA), *Xeriscape Landscaping—Preventing Pollution and Using Resources Efficiently*, Washington, D.C., 1993.

109 A. Davidson, "Xeriscaping—The Art of Water-Conserving Landscaping," *Land Development*, Vol. 4, Fall 1991, pp. 11-14. Other studies showing marked water savings with Xeriscape landscaping include J.O. Nelson, "Water Conserving Landscapes Show Impressive Savings," *Journal of the American Water Works Association*, Vol. 79, March 1987, pp. 35-42; J.C. Kruta, "Landscape Comparison: A Follow-Up Study," Unpublished paper available from the author, Mathematics Department, California Polytechnic State University, San Luis Obispo, 1993; and T. Gregg, *Xeriscaping: Promises and Pitfalls—A Multivariate Research Study of Xeriscape Practices, Water Consumption, and Water Quality*, Environmental and Conservation Services Department, City of Austin, Tex., 1994, pp. 19-25.

110 G. Caputo, L. Kavouras, and Y. Wang, *A Water-Efficient Landscaping Guide for Local Governments*, St. Johns River Water Management District/Southwest Florida Water Management District/South Florida Water Management District, Palatka/Brooksville/West Palm Beach, 1994, pp. 75-88.

111 D.G. Morrison, "Use of Native Vegetation in Urban and Suburban Landscaping," in W.L. Downing (ed.), *Proceedings of the National Conference on Urban Erosion and Sediment Control: Institutions & Technology*, Great Lakes National Program Office, U.S. Environmental Protection Agency, Chicago, 1980, p. 119.

112 M. Hough, *Out of Place—Restoring Identity to the Regional Landscape*, Yale University Press, New Haven, Conn., 1990, p. 92.

[113] J.I. Nassauer, "Ecological Function and the Perception of Suburban Residential Landscapes," in P.H. Gobster (ed.), *Managing Urban and High-Rise Settings*, North Central Forest Experimental Station, Forest Service, U.S. Department of Agriculture, Chicago, 1992, pp. 55-60.

[114] Three of Florida's water management districts publish Xeriscape plant guides. South Florida Water Management District (SFWMD), *Xeriscape Plant Guide II*, Palm Beach, Fla., undated; Southwest Florida Water Management District (SWFWMD), *Plant Guide*, Brooksville, Fla., undated; and St. Johns River Water Management District (SJRWMD), *Xeriscape Plant Guide*, Palatka, Fla., undated. The Florida Cooperative Extension Service, Institute of Food and Agricultural Sciences, University of Florida, has sets of reports for different climate zones. A.W. Meerow and R.J. Black, *Enviroscaping to Conserve Energy: Ground Covers for South Florida*, Institute of Food and Agricultural Sciences, University of Florida, 1993; A.W. Meerow and R.J. Black, *Enviroscaping to Conserve Energy: Trees for South Florida*, Institute of Food and Agricultural Sciences, University of Florida, 1993; A.W. Meerow and R.J. Black, *Enviroscaping to Conserve Energy: Ground Covers for Central Florida*, Institute of Food and Agricultural Sciences, University of Florida, 1993; R.J. Black and A.W. Meerow, *Enviroscaping to Conserve Energy: Trees for Central Florida*, Institute of Food and Agricultural Sciences, University of Florida, 1993; A.W. Meerow and R.J. Black, *Enviroscaping to Conserve Energy: Ground Covers for North Florida*, Institute of Food and Agricultural Sciences, University of Florida, 1993; and R.J. Black and A.W. Meerow, *Enviroscaping to Conserve Energy: Trees for North Florida*, Institute of Food and Agricultural Sciences, University of Florida, 1993. Finally, the Association of Florida Native Nurseries publishes listings of native plant associations as they occur in different climate zones of Florida. Plants are grouped by landscape forms and use (trees, shrubs, groundcovers, etc.). M. Jameson and R. Moyroud (eds.), *Xeric Landscaping with Florida Native Plants*, Association of Florida Native Nurseries, San Antonio, Fla., 1991.

[115] J.B. Beard, "An Assessment of Water Use by Turfgrasses," in V.A. Gibeault and S.T. Cockerham (eds.), *Turfgrass Water Conservation*, Division of Agriculture and Natural Resources, University of California, Oakland, 1985, pp. 45-60; R.N. Carrow et al., "Turfgrass," in B.A. Stewart and Nielsen (eds.), *Irrigation of Agricultural Crops*, American Society of Agronomy, Madison, Wis., 1990, pp. 889-919; L.B. McCarty and J.L. Cisar, "Selecting a Turfgrass for Florida Lawns," in L.B. McCarty, R.J. Black, and K.C. Ruppert (eds.), *Florida Lawn Handbook—Selection, Establishment and Maintenance of Florida Lawngrasses*, Institute of Food and Agriculture Sciences, University of Florida, Gainesville, 1990, pp. 3-5; and M.P. Kenna and G.L. Horst, "Turfgrass Water Conservation and Quality," *International Turfgrass Society Research Journal*, Vol. 7, 1993, pp. 99-113.

[116] Bennett and Hazinski, op. cit., pp. 58-67; Kelly et al., op. cit., pp. 4, 20; R.L. Thayer and T. Richman, "Water-Conserving Landscape Design," in E.G. McPherson (ed.), *Energy-Conserving Site Design*, American Society of Landscape Architects, Washington, D.C., 1984, pp. 185-213; and Florida Irrigation Society, *Standards and Specifications for Turf and Landscape Irrigation Systems*, Winter Park, Fla., 1988, p. 9.

[117] Caputo et al., op. cit., p. 24.

[118] Caputo et al., op. cit.

VI. BEST HOUSING PRACTICES

Practice 1: Offer "life cycle" housing.

Practice 2: Achieve an average net residential density of six to seven units per acre (without the appearance of crowding).

Practice 3: Use cost-effective site development and construction practices.

Practice 4: Design in energy-saving features.

Practice 5: Supply affordable single-family homes for moderate-income households.

Practice 6: Supply affordable multifamily and accessory housing for low-income households.

Practice 7: Tap government housing programs to broaden and deepen the housing/income mix.

Practice 8: Mix housing to the extent the market will bear.

These *Best Housing Practices* are designed to increase the *affordability* and *diversity* of the housing stock. Affordability is promoted for all Floridians, but particularly those with moderate, low, and very low incomes; for them, documented housing shortages exist.[1]

Promoting affordable housing serves transportation as well as social purposes. Low-skilled workers are concentrated in cities, while low-skilled jobs are, increasingly, concentrated in the suburbs.[2] At best, the mismatch means a lot of long-distance commuting for those who can least afford it. At worst, it means perennial joblessness. Low-income households will move closer to their jobs if affordable housing is available.[3]

Diversity of the housing stock is sought so people can "age in place" rather than moving at each stage in the life cycle...also, because diversity breeds vitality in all systems, natural and man-made.[4] We were originally attracted to Bluewater Bay as a study site, even before we knew much about it, by a published quote from the developer: "Other developments were ghost cities with no neighbors. We wanted to create a real community. We want to avoid the feeling of an artificial place. If it is just rich people, it is too limited..."[5]

While controversial, the goal of diversity was endorsed recently by the state's Affordable Housing Study Commission. The commission made a point of adding, to its previously adopted guidelines, one new one: "State housing programs should maximize opportunities for people to live in mixed income developments or socioeconomically diverse neighborhoods, and further, the State should oppose the negative impacts of the NIMBY syndrome."[6]

Practice 1: Offer "life cycle" housing.

Contemporary suburban developments segregate people at different stages in life by segregating housing by type, size, and price range. Large complexes of studio and one-bedroom apartments, large subdivisions of three- and four-bedroom homes, and large condominium projects guarantee that young singles, young families, and empty nesters will have minimal contact.

Contemporary suburban developments offer little opportunity to put down roots; neither the homes nor the neighborhoods are equipped to see families through the life cycle. When families move up (or down), they move out.

This is in contrast to traditional towns, where a fine mix of housing leads to a fine mix of people. The generations are mixed to the point of "granny flats" or "teenager cottages" behind family homes. It is also in contrast to new communities started in the 1960s, an idealistic time when the idea of *three generational* or *life cycle* housing caught on. In such communities, senior, multifamily, and single-family housing were sited within the same villages and sometimes even within the same neighborhoods. The result, according to a sociological study of Columbia, Maryland, is a "stable and working pluralism that respects and builds on the variations in its population."[7]

Life cycle housing serves a useful social purpose. "Some families wish to move within the same housing development or neighborhood when their space needs change. (With life cycle

Multigenerational Housing in Downtown Dade City

Mixed Housing Within Villages and Neighborhoods of Columbia, MD

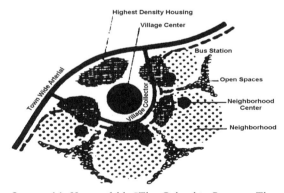

Source: M. Hoppenfeld, "The Columbia Process: The Potential for New Towns" *The Architects Yearbook*, Garden City Press Limited, Letchworth, England, 1972.

housing) social networks can remain intact; children need not be uprooted from familiar schools; and elderly persons can remain near friends and families."[8]

In addition, life cycle housing makes good business sense. For large developers, the key to profitability is rapid land absorption, and the key to rapid land absorption is to tap many market segments.[12] "Life cycle" housing creates its own demand. Renters feed the starter home market. Families in starter homes buy move-up homes. When the kids move out, the parents become candidates for townhouses or condominiums. And eventually they may move into a retirement home or congregate care facility.

New communities nationally report that 14 to 50 percent of all new homebuyers come from within the communities themselves.[13] More than a quarter of the homebuyers at Hunter's Creek's newest subdivision are already residents of the community. In reporting the phenomenon, the community newsletter proclaimed: "...for Hunter's Creek residents, moving *up* doesn't have to mean moving *out*."

If a community developer cannot find anyone else to build life cycle housing, he always has the option of building it himself (using a general contractor or an in-house builder). This is exactly what Haile Plantation, Miami Lakes, and Oakbridge have done, and they have ended up with enviable housing mixes. Seven years after opening, Oakbridge has 106 conventional single-family homes; 45 zero lot line homes; 110 du-

VARIED HOUSING (MOSTLY DEVELOPER BUILT) AT OAKBRIDGE

Zero Lot Line

Single-Family Duplex

Stacked Flats

Congregate Care Facility

plexes/triplexes/quadplexes; 300 apartments; and a 240-unit congregate care facility. In contrast, after eight years, Hunter's Creek is only now seeing its first apartments built; relying on other developers and builders, Hunter's Creek has had five apartment deals fall through and seen its goal of 50 percent multifamily housing slip away.

Practice 2: Achieve an average net residential density of six to seven units per acre (without the appearance of crowding).

The harsh reality of housing is that density is necessary for affordability.[14] Higher densities mean less land per unit, less site preparation, less infrastructure, and typically less floor and wall area, all of which hold down the hard costs of housing. It is a "harsh" reality because the mere mention of density sends shivers down the spines of suburban residents and their elected officials.

Falling Site Development Costs with Rising Density

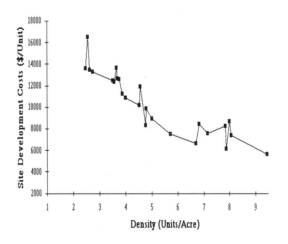

Source: National Association of Home Builders, *Cost Effective Site Planning—Single Family Development*, Washington, D.C., 1986, p. 56-97. Reprinted with permission from Home Builders Press, National Association of Home Builders, 1201 15th St., NW, Washington, DC 20005; 800-223-2665.

In this regard, density has gotten a bum rap. People confuse density with crowding, high density with high rise, and *perceived* density with *measured* density.[15] "The preference for low density seems to arise out of needs for privacy, quiet, and outdoor space, needs which are met in varying degrees by different site arrangements."[16] If such needs can be met at somewhat higher densities than the suburban norm, it is all the better for affordability.

We know, for example, that densities are perceived to be lower where there is open space nearby. Even a small commons provides a feeling of spaciousness. Other urban design elements that create the perception of spaciousness include small housing clusters, short blocks, low buildings, and natural landscaping.[18]

Individual floor plans and lot layouts also affect perceived densities and acceptance in the marketplace. The Urban Land Institute and the National Association of Home Builders have published entire volumes filled with examples of dense housing that afford privacy, quiet, outdoor space, and interior light and airiness.[19] These qualities are achieved through ample landscaping; judicious use of fences and walls; vaulted or cathedral ceilings; and decks, patios, porches, and yards that extend indoor living space.

Monotony can be avoided at higher densities through what the Urban Land Institute has called "density by design." Zero lot line homes can be staggered or zigzagged, and setbacks and garage locations can be varied. Duplexes and triplexes can have entrances separated from one another and oriented, alternately, toward the street and side yards; this, plus landscape elements to break up building masses, make attached homes fit nicely into detached home neighborhoods. Quadplexes and townhouses can have varying ceiling heights, roof lines, setbacks, and colors; units can be placed side-by-side, back-to-back, or over-under for, once again, variety. Examples of "density by design" can be found in nearly all our exemplary developments.

How dense is dense enough? How dense is too dense? From surveys, residents are as satisfied with housing at six or seven units per acre as they are at three or four units per acre.[20] Site development costs per unit are nearly halved at the higher densities.[21] As a bonus, travel patterns begin to shift from almost total auto-dependence to some use of alternative modes.[22]

Average net residential densities within this range—six to seven units per acre—make a nice target for suburban developers.[23] Two of our exemplary developments meet the target and three others come close. Note the strong relationship between net residential density and housing mix in the following tables. Bluewater Bay, with 78 percent detached housing, does not come close to meeting our target density, while The Hammocks, with 27 percent detached housing, almost doubles it.

Spaciousness Through Site Design at Haile Plantation

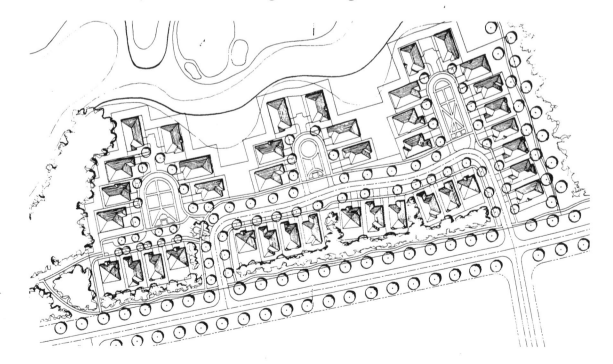

Average Net Residential Densities of Exemplary Developments
(planned at build-out)[*]

Bluewater Bay	2.5
Haile Plantation[**]	4.0
Hammocks	11.5
Hunter's Creek	5.7
Miami Lakes	8.6
Oakbridge	5.7
Palmer Ranch[***]	5.3

[*] Net residential acreage, from which net residential density is computed, excludes commercial areas, rights-of-way of major roads, parks, golf courses, lakes, and natural areas.

[**] The density figure for Haile Plantation applies to the original site. Plans for the new addition are not yet finalized.

[***] The density figure for Palmer Ranch relates to the west side only. Plans for the east side are not yet finalized.

Planned Housing Mix in Exemplary Developments
(# and % of units at build-out)

	Detached Single-Family	Attached Single-Family	Multifamily	Total
Bluewater Bay	2,566 (78%)	332 (10%)	379 (12%)	3,277
Haile Plantation	1,595 (59%)	——1,091—— (41%)		2,686
Hammocks	1,732 (27%)	1,488 (23%)	3,232 (50%)	6,452
Hunter's Creek	3,954 (45%)	197 (2%)	4,764 (53%)	8,915
Miami Lakes	1,935 (27%)	1,511 (21%)	3,802 (52%)	7,248
Oakbridge	1,333 (48%)	270 (10%)	1,158[*] (42%)	2,761
Palmer Ranch[**]	1,810 (51%)	128 (4%)	1,607 (45%)	3,545

[*] Includes congregate care units.

[**] Applies only to the west side of Palmer Ranch; the exact product mix for the east side will be determined by merchant builders, responding to market conditions, as they seek final approvals under planned unit development (PUD) zoning.

DENSITY BY DESIGN

*Angled Z-Lot Homes
at Palmer Ranch*

Duplex at Palmer Ranch

Townhouses at Bluewater Bay

*Patio Homes with Rear Parking at
Bluewater Bay*

Townhouses at Haile Plantation

Apartments at The Hammocks

Hiding the Garage at Higher Densities

Subdivisions have gone almost full circle, from narrow lots with shallow building setbacks at the beginning of this century, to wide lots with deep setbacks after World War II, and back to narrower lots with shallower setbacks recently as the economics of development have forced residential densities upward. This would seem a positive trend for streetscapes but for the fact that garages, which used to be out of sight in back, are now the most prominent visual features in many small-lot subdivisions.[24] It leaves the impression that "cars live here," not people.

To enhance streetscapes in small-lot neighborhoods, neo-traditional planners favor a return to the alleys of yesteryear.[25] Some traffic engineers agree.[26] With alleys, residential streetscapes need not be interrupted by driveways nor cluttered with garages. Houses can be moved up to the street to form a "street wall," enclosing street space and making it more intimate. More frontage is available for parked cars, which form a metal wall buffering sidewalks and front yards from traffic.

Given the aesthetic advantages, one must wonder why alleys fell out of favor. One possibility is that even with reduced street widths, too much land is lost to public rights-of-way when alleys are tacked onto streets.[27] It is also possible that property is perceived as less secure when public access is from two directions, front and back.[28] Whatever the reason, alleys have a negative "urban" image that must be overcome in the suburbs.[29]

Bluewater Bay is reintroducing alleys in its newest development, Magnolia Village. It will be interesting to see how the market responds. Bluewater Bay has already proven the market appeal of another traditional alternative to garage-dominated streetscapes, the side driveway with a recessed garage. This layout is used, with visually striking results, in Bluewater Bay's traditional Village of Bolton.

Garage-Dominated Zero Lot Line Homes at Palmer Ranch

Side Driveway and Recessed Garage at Bluewater Bay

Practice 3: Use cost-effective site development and construction practices.

Housing can be made more affordable with cost-effective site development and construction practices. We have already called for narrow residential streets (*Transportation Practice 6*) and for cluster development (*Land Use Practice 4*). The latter can knock a third off site development costs by reducing the length of streets and utilities, allowing natural drainage, and keeping the area to be cleared and graded to a minimum.[30]

Lot frontage is probably the single most important determinant of site development costs since street lengths and utility runs vary with front footage. Front setbacks are next most important since driveways and utility service lines vary with setbacks. Thus, for affordable housing, lots should be as narrow as possible and front setbacks as shallow as possible.

Small frontages and setbacks have other advantages. They make streets more walkable by "enclosing" street space, visual enclosure being one of the foremost principles of urban design: "...enclosure of street space as an outdoor room or corridor would appear to emerge as a precondition for street activity."[31] And according to at least one criminologist, small setbacks (less than 25 feet) add to street security by giving residents a more protective attitude toward the street.[32]

Minimum Lot Frontages and Front Setbacks

Conventional single-family zoning establishes minimum front setbacks and lot frontages which are, in one way or another, an accommodation of the automobile. With deep setbacks, residents can park in their driveways and the home environment is less affected by passing traffic. With wide lots, visitors can park between driveways and streetscapes are less visually dominated by garages and driveways.

While the automobile must somehow be accommodated, it should not be at expense of other considerations. Most jurisdictions offer planned unit development (PUD) options that relax frontage and setback requirements. Thus, it is possible for developers and builders in most jurisdictions to balance the storage needs of automobiles against the housing needs of their owners.

The following average values, from nationally recognized affordable single-family housing projects, represent such a balance. Front setbacks may be even shallower when garages are recessed. Both setbacks and frontages may be smaller when garages are accessed from alleys.

	Smallest	Largest	Average
Lot Frontage	24'	60'	47'
Front Setback	0'	30'	17'

Source: W. Sanders et al., *Affordable Single-Family Housing—A Review of Development Standards*, American Planning Association, Chicago, 1984, pp. 6-7.

Small Setbacks at Haile Plantation

Other cost-saving ideas include (depending on densities) use of rolled curbs or no curbs at all, T-shaped turnarounds rather than circular cul-de-sacs, shared driveways, thin street pavements, common trenching, common laterals, etc.[33]

Discussions of affordable housing always seem to focus on land and site development costs. Yet, even for detached housing, construction costs typically exceed land and site development costs combined by a factor of 2:1.

Through the "Joint Venture for Affordable Housing," dozens of construction techniques have been shown to save money without sacrificing structural integrity.[34] In different applications, $1,200 was saved with optimum value engineered (OVE) wall construction; $400 with clustered plumbing; even more with pre-assembled roof trusses.

All told, cost savings of 12 percent are achievable with cost-effective construction techniques (see accompanying figure for a breakdown of savings).[35] Some cost-effective techniques run counter to often-antiquated local building codes and will require special exceptions or modernizing amendments. Many can be implemented as is.

Breakdown of "Hard Costs" of Detached Housing Projects

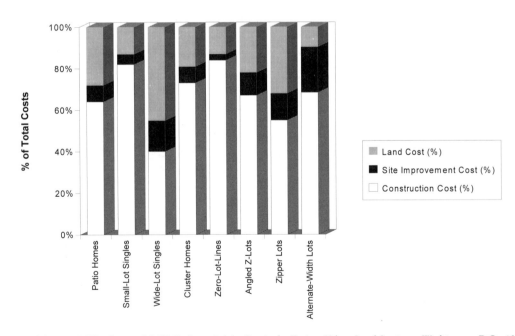

Source: Derived from J.W. Wentling and L.W. Bookout (eds.), *Density by Design*, Urban Land Institute, Washington, D.C., 1988, pp. 22-75.

Breakdown of Cost Savings with Cost-Effective Construction

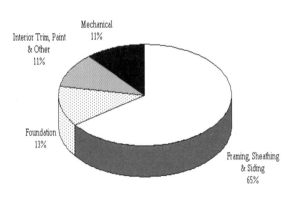

Source: NAHB Research Center, *Cost-Effective Home Building—A Design and Construction Handbook*, National Association of Home Builders, Washington, D.C., 1994, p. 3. Reprinted with permission of Home Builders Press, National Association of Home Builders, 1201 15th St., NW, Washington, DC 20005; 800-223-2665.

Practice 4: Design in energy-saving features.

This best practice goes hand-in-hand with *Transportation Practice 7*, which recommends that roads be aligned for optimum building orientation vis-a-vis the sun and prevailing winds. Any energy savings make housing that much more affordable for owners and renters.

Already, all new construction in Florida must conform to the Florida Energy Efficiency Code for Building Construction.[36] Additional energy savings are possible by following guidelines in the Florida Solar Energy Center's *Energy-Efficient Florida Home Building* and the National Association of Home Builders' *Energy-Smart Building for Increased Quality, Comfort, and Sales*.[37]

Shade trees should be preserved and/or planted near the house, particularly on east and west exposures to block the sun in the morning and late afternoon, when it is low in the sky. One large tree produces the cooling effect of 10 room-sized air conditioners running 20 hours a day.[38] Trees are also helpful for humidity control and as a windbreak in extreme weather. On top of all that, they are one of the best investments for home appreciation, adding thousands of dollars to the value of homes.[39] Where trees leave off, shrubs can shade the lower portions of east-west walls and windows, stop hot breezes from infiltrating windows, moderate heat conduction from adjacent air, and block indirect radiation from adjacent grounds. These same trees and shrubs can be pruned in the spring and fall to maximize natural ventilation. The careful siting of trees and shrubs for energy conservation has been called, quite appropriately, "precision landscaping"; precision landscaping can reduce home cooling bills by 40 percent.[40]

Florida homes should be designed for natural ventilation, as they were before air conditioning. Wide porches, windows on opposite walls, and screens on doors and windows allow homes to be opened up and catch prevailing breezes. No one is suggesting that natural ventilation can replace air conditioning entirely, but it can extend the months when air conditioning is not required. This period can be further extended with whole house fans that draw in cool night air (natural breezes dying down at night, as they do).[41]

Home interiors should be laid out with time-of-day occupancy in mind.[42] Living and high-activity rooms go on the south side where they are heated by the low winter sun and shaded from the high summer sun. Morning rooms go on the west side, afternoon rooms go on the east side. Garages, utility rooms, and closets provide nice insulating barriers on the east and west sides of buildings.

Cooling Effect of a Shade Tree and Shrub

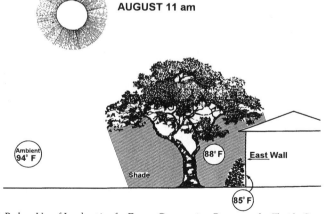

Source: J. H. Parker, *Use of Landscaping for Energy Conservation*, Report to the Florida Governor's Energy Office, Tallahassee, Fla., 1981, p. 3-16.

Time-of-Day Room Layouts

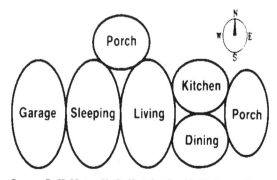

Source: R. K. Vieira, K. G. Sheinkopf and J. K. Sonne, *Energy-Efficient Florida Home Building*, Florida Solar Energy Center, Cape Canaveral, 1992, p. 4-11.

Heat flow from sun-baked roofs must be blocked, and attics must be well-ventilated to remove heat that would otherwise flow through ceilings to living areas below. An attic radiant barrier costs about $325. For this small investment, home builders can reduce heat flow through ceilings by more than 40 percent.[43] A similar rate of return can be achieved with high-grade roof insulation (R-30 rather than R-19, the Florida statewide minimum). Super-heated air can be removed from attics most efficiently with a combination of continuous ridge and soffit vents.[44]

The list of energy-saving features is too long to be reviewed here.[45] We would only note that several additional features both save energy and cut the cost of home construction. Use of slab-on-grade foundations (in southern climates only), modular framing, insulated prehung doors, and simple building shapes are promoted by both the National Association of Home Builders (for their cost savings) and the Florida Solar Energy Center (for their energy savings).

The developer of Haile Plantation has discovered that energy-efficiency matters to homebuyers, and is building and marketing houses accordingly. Tree clearing is usually limited to the front of lots; even in front, mature trees are preserved. Homes built by the developer himself boast R-30 ceiling insulation and ceiling fans. Many homes have

porches for shading and wide-shallow designs for cross-ventilation. A few are even placed at an angle to the street for optimal solar orientation (per *Transportation Practice 7*).

While not blessed with a heavily wooded site like Haile Plantation's, Palmer Ranch requires planting of native shade trees on all residential lots and requires structural shading (e.g., trellises, awnings, or roof overhangs) in the absence of natural shading.

Tree Planting Program on a Treeless Site at Palmer Ranch

Tree Preservation Around a Cul-de-Sac at Haile Plantation

Porch Home Angled for Optimal Solar Orientation at Haile Plantation

Pioneering Energy-Efficient Homes at Bluewater Bay

Exemplary developers innovate. One of the best examples among our seven developments is the use of aerated concrete in new homes at Bluewater Bay (the U.S. debut of a 50-year-old technology used around the world). Aerated concrete blocks have millions of tiny air pockets that make them light, easy to cut, well-insulating, and unaffected by sudden changes in temperature. They reduce by about half the time air conditioning is required in Bluewater Bay's warm and humid climate.

The German manufacturer of aerated concrete, with the involvement of the developer of Bluewater Bay, a German himself, has built its first U.S. plant. The plant was completed in late 1995 and began supplying the U.S. market in early 1996.

In addition, one of only 10 Energy Smart demonstration homes in the entire Southeast will be built at Bluewater Bay. The Energy Smart program is demonstrating the energy savings possible using off-the-shelf technology and materials. Bluewater Bay was selected as a demonstration site due to its high volume of visitors (including many foreigners) and its innovation with aerated concrete.

Aerated Concrete in Its U.S. Debut at Bluewater Bay

Practice 5: Supply affordable single-family housing for moderate-income households.

Not to dismiss niche markets, but the American public has shown a preference for single-family housing, preferably detached; it is a preference that cuts across income classes.[46] We would like to make single-family housing available to as many market segments as possible. Detached housing should be within reach of moderate-income households, provided densities are high enough.

Consider Haile Plantation; its housing is more affordable than most. The median household income in Alachua County, the location

Affordable Patio Homes at Haile Plantation

of Haile Plantation, is $34,500. At 80 percent to 120 percent of median income, moderate-income households can afford housing payments of $690 to $1,035 per month.[47] Such payments will cover principal and interest, taxes and insurance, on new homes priced from $89,000 to $134,000.[48]

Plotting new home prices at Haile Plantation vs. net residential densities, prices generally follow a downward curve with rising density. The moderate-income price range corresponds to net densities of about two to five units per acre. Much of Haile

Plantation's detached housing is simply not dense enough to be affordable for moderate-income households. Its attached housing is plenty dense, and affordable even for some low-income households, but current offerings are limited to one project.

Zero lot line homes can be built at densities of 10 to 15 units per acre (the upper end if homes are small and parking is supplied via parking courts).[49] Densities of seven to 10 units per acre are attainable with standard living space and built-in garages.[50]

Creative Lot Configurations for Detached Homes

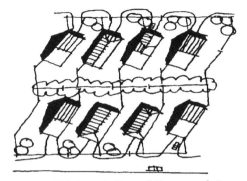

■ The Z-lot variation of the zero-lot-line concept is intended to reduce the negative visual effect of garage doors, thus enhancing the street appeal.

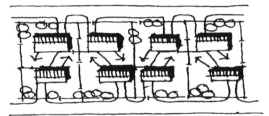

■ Zipper-lot houses are placed on wider lots. Typically, only garages are located on lot lines.

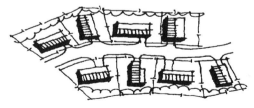

■ The alternate-width lot allows variety in the streetscape and in unit plans.

Source: J. W. Wentling and L. W. Bookout (eds.), *Density By Design*, Urban Land Institute, Washington, D.C., 1988, p. 53.

New Home Prices vs. Net Density at Haile Plantation

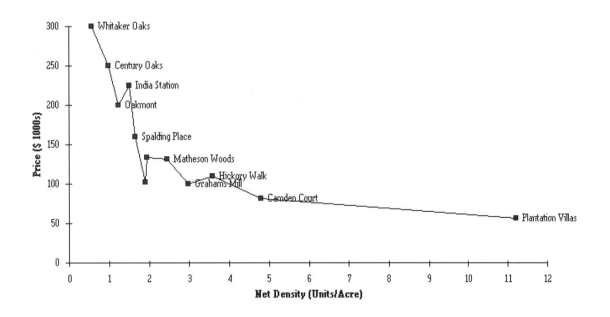

Vast Market for Moderate-Income Housing

Lack of affordable detached housing limits a developer's market share. Being located on a reclaimed phosphate mine, Oakbridge has site development costs 20-30% higher than its competitors. Construction costs are also higher due to the need for radon gas-proofing. Hence, while Oakbridge is able to capture an impressive share of any market segment for which it aggressively competes, it has as yet offered only attached products in the under-$120,000 price range (where 84% of Lakeland's new home sales fall). The following table illustrates the problem:

	# of New Units Sold in Lakeland Market (1993)	Oakbridge's Unit Sales (1993)	Oakbridge's Market Share
Less than $80,000	1,092	0	0%
$80,000-120,000	672	12	2%
$120,000-200,000	244	33	14%
More than $200,000	92	27	29%
Total	2,100	72	3%

Practice 6: Supply affordable multifamily and accessory housing for low-income households.

As we shift from single-family to multifamily housing, there is a quantum increase in density and hence affordability. Densities at Oakbridge range up to 6.8 units per acre for detached housing and 8.2 units per acre for attached singles, but rise as high as 16.8 units per acre for apartments. The least expensive detached homes at Oakbridge sell for $125,000; this translates into housing costs of $965 per month. The least expensive attached homes sell for $92,000, still well beyond the reach of low-income households. But Oakbridge has two-bedroom apartments renting for $550 a month, an affordable rent for many low-income households in Polk County.

Developers who include apartment sites in their plans will be ready when the multifamily market heats up and single-family market cools off, as happens periodically. An expectedly strong multifamily market allowed The Hammocks to rebound financially from recessions of the early 1980s. As vacancy rates in Orlando have fallen to 6-7 percent, Hunter's Creek has seen a surge of interest in its multifamily parcels; as of late 1994, it finally closed on its first apartment deal. Some of the nation's hottest apartment markets are in Florida.[51] Thus, large Florida developers have every reason to include multifamily housing in their product mix.

"Low-Income" Housing at Oakbridge

Another affordable housing option for low-income households is accessory apartments.[52] These backyard cottages, garage apartments, and second-story apartments effectively double the residential densities of neighborhoods. They do so, in theory, without changing the basic character of single-family neighborhoods. Herein lies the rub. The character of neighborhoods is not altered by "granny flats" occupied by grannies. However, the character will suffer if such flats become "transient" housing.

In surveying traditional towns, we asked about experiences with accessory apartments. Results were mixed. Arcadia and DeLand report problems with transient populations now occupying the bulk of their accessory housing; Arcadia allows no new units anywhere, and DeLand allows no new units in residential zones. On the other hand, Dade City now encourages accessory apartments downtown; it wants the street activity and customers for downtown businesses. Key West sees no alternative to accessory apartments, given the high cost of land; accessory apartments are permitted with a density variance.

The very problems experienced by Arcadia and DeLand are testimony to the value (from an affordability standpoint) of the housing involved. Our informal survey of rentals in DeLand showed that accessory apartments typically rent for $100 to $350 per month; by comparison, apartments in apartment buildings or complexes start at about $350 per month.

Thus, accessory housing should not be banned but rather regulated (through ordinances or deed restrictions) and limited to appropriate areas. Problems arise in Arcadia when homes cease to be owner-occupied, leaving no one in charge of accessory units. Why not require owner-occupancy of the main units? DeLand has found accessory apartments well-suited to areas of mixed use. Why not so limit them? Additional requirements and restrictions, aimed at safeguarding neighborhoods while permitting accessory units, are suggested in reports issued by the American Planning Association.[53]

ACCESSORY APARTMENTS IN TRADITIONAL TOWNS

Arcadia

Key West

Accessory Housing at Rivendell

Rivendell, the semi-traditional project at Palmer Ranch, will have a broad mix of housing within its 380 acres. Outlying areas are planned for conventional detached homes on 85' x 120' lots. Moving inward, townhouses will be sited in small clusters on 40' x 100' lots. The village center will have detached "village homes" on 50' x 100' lots, plus townhouses and accessory housing above shops and offices. A third of the village homes will have additional accessory units—backyard cottages or garage apartments—to supplement the supply of affordable housing.

Practice 7: Tap government housing programs to broaden and deepen the housing/income mix.

Anyone can produce cheap housing on fringe land with few amenities and government supplied infrastructure. But exemplary developers have relatively high cost bases, supplying all needed infrastructure themselves, offering nice amenity packages, and preserving open space. And they have the ability to charge a premium for their housing, the market paying more for quality. Supply and demand being what they are, housing in exemplary developments tends to run 5 percent to 15 percent higher than identical housing in neighboring subdivisions.

Fortunately, an array of government housing programs is now available to help broaden and deepen the housing mix in exemplary developments. After divesting itself of programs in the early 1980s, the federal government reentered the housing arena by enacting the low-income housing tax credit in 1986 and the HOME Program in 1990. The State of Florida has become a national leader in housing assistance, starting in 1982 with various revenue bond programs and culminating in 1992 with the Sadowski Affordable Housing Act. Used in combination with one another, as they often are, the various government programs provide subsidies deep enough to bring high-quality housing within reach of moderate-, low-, and even very low-income households.[55]

Several new communities around the state, including The Hammocks, have tapped the state's revenue bond programs for multifamily housing. One Florida Quality Development, Southlake outside Orlando, is financing much of its housing and infrastructure with state revenue bonds and a loan from the State Apartment Incentive Loan (SAIL) program.

Subsidized and Market Rate Rental Housing Side-By-Side at The Hammocks

Selected Affordable Housing Programs in Florida

Program	Type of Assistance	Target Groups
State Apartment Incentive Loan (SAIL) Program	low-interest mortgage loans for apartment developers	at least 20% very low-income households
HOME Investment Partnerships Program	zero- or low-interest loans for housing developers who pass them on to homebuyers and renters	very low- and low-income households[*]
Single-Family Mortgage Revenue Bond Program	below-market interest mortgage loans for first-time homebuyers	very low- and low-income households (though those with slightly higher incomes qualify)
Homeownership Assistance Program	zero- or low-interest second mortgage loans for homebuyers; below-market construction loans for home builders	very low- and low-income households
Rental Housing Bond Program	below-market interest mortgage loans for developers of rental housing	at least 20% very low-income households[**]
Low-Income Housing Tax Credit Program	federal tax credits for developers of rental housing	at least 20% very low-income households[**]
State Housing Initiatives Partnership (SHIP) Program	downpayment, closing cost, and other assistance for homebuyers	at least 30% for very low-income households, another 30% for very low- or low-income households, and the balance for very low-, low-, or moderate-income households

[*] In the rental program, 20% of units must be set aside for households at 50% or less of the area median income; 70% for households at 60% or less of the area median income; and 10% for households at 80% or less of the area median income. In the homeownership program, it is simply necessary that all households be at 80% or less of the area median income, without regard to proportions.

[**] As an alternative, 40% of the units may be set aside for households at 60% or less (rather than 50%) of the area median income.

State Housing Initiatives Partnership (SHIP) Program

Under Florida's SHIP Program, all 101 eligible counties and cities around the state have established Local Housing Assistance programs to help finance new home purchases (among other things). Local governments may assist in the purchase of new homes priced at up to 90 percent of the area's median home price. In 1994, the price ceilings were $107,000 for the Sarasota area and $119,000 for the Miami area. Palmer Ranch's Rivendell and many projects at The Hammocks could qualify under these ceilings.

Practice 8: Mix housing to the extent the market will bear.

There are differing opinions about the extent to which housing for different socioeconomic groups can and should be mixed within developments. There are some who argue for maximum economic integration in the interest of social justice. "...[E]conomic segregation has far-reaching effects. A whole generation of Americans has now reached adulthood cut off from direct contact with people from other social classes."[56]

At the other end of the spectrum are those who advocate neighborhood homogeneity in the interest of social compatibility or crime prevention.[57] "...[H]omogeneity will improve the tenor of neighbor relations, and will thus make it easier—although not easy—to realize heterogeneity at the community level."[58]

We come down in the middle. *Land Use Practices 3 and 4* call for fine-grained development. Applied to residential areas, this suggests small clusters of housing, similar in type and price, next to other small clusters, themselves similar but different from other clusters in the same area. If one wishes to promote interaction, it is only necessary to have common areas and common facilities.

Mixed-income projects can be good for large developers because several market segments are tapped at once, yet only a small area need be under development at any time, minimizing infrastructure costs. All seven exemplary developments have housing clusters of different types and price ranges near one another. The Hammocks and Palmer Ranch even mix housing within the same subdivisions, with a high degree of market acceptance.

Mixed Housing at Palmer Ranch

Mixed Housing Around Common Recreational Facilities at The Hammocks

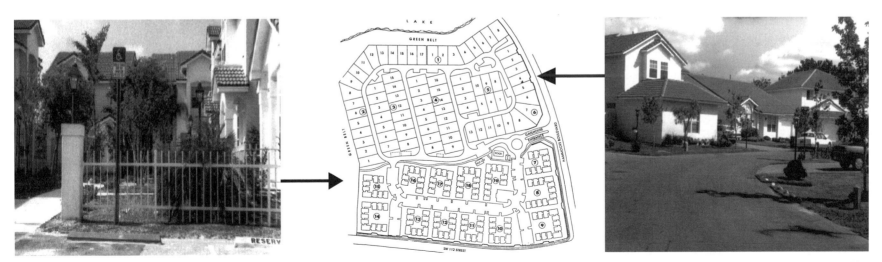

Nowhere is the need for mixing greater than with low-income housing. The failure to mix incomes may stigmatize certain areas, making them into ghettos. Or worse, it may generate so much public opposition that low-income housing never gets built. As a condition of development approval, The Hammocks was required to set aside several parcels for low-income housing. When it came time to develop the parcels, public opposition was so strident the developer ended up donating the parcels to the county for subsequent sale, with the proceeds used to build affordable housing elsewhere.

There is a growing sense that mixed-income housing is healthier for low-income households and no problem for their higher-income neighbors, this suggested by low vacancy rates among market-rate units in mixed-income projects.[59] In one study, resident satisfaction levels were found to be higher in mixed-income housing than in purely subsidized housing, not because of the mix *per se* (which was a neutral factor) but because developers had to offer superior design, management, and maintenance in order to attract market-rate renters.[60] Since affordable rental housing programs—the State Apartment Incentive Loan Program, Rental Housing Bond Program, and Low-Income Housing Tax Credit Program—promote the mixing of below-market and market-rate units, exemplary developers will want to follow this best practice.

ENDNOTES

1 In Florida, over 1.2 million low- and moderate-income households are paying over 30 percent of their gross monthly income for housing. There is an immediate need for another 250,000 units affordable to very low-income households, which will grow to over 320,000 units by the year 2000. Department of Community Affairs, *State of Florida CHAS— Comprehensive Housing Affordability Strategy*, Tallahassee, Fla., 1994, pp. 32-37.

2 The literature on jobs-housing mismatch is reviewed by H.J. Holzer, "The Spatial Mismatch Hypothesis: What Has the Evidence Shown?" *Urban Studies*, Vol. 28, 1991, pp. 105-122; J.F. Kain, "The Spatial Mismatch Hypothesis: Three Decades Later," *Housing Policy Debate*, Vol. 3, 1992, pp. 371-460; and R.W. Burchell and E. Schmeidler, "The Demographic and Social Difference Between Central Cities and Suburbs as They Relate to the Job Fulfillment of Urban Residents," in B. Chinitz (ed.), *Metropolitan America in Transition: Implications for Land Use and Transportation Planning*, Lincoln Institute of Land Policy, Cambridge, Mass., 1994. An example of jobs-housing mismatch in Florida is discussed by J.E. Lindsey, "Sector Planning as a Method of Managing and Paying for Growth," Specialty Conference on Successful Land Development, American Society of Civil Engineers, New York, 1991.

3 J.M. Quigley, "Consumer Choice of Dwelling, Neighborhood and Public Services," *Regional Science and Urban Economics*, Vol. 15, 1985, pp. 41-63; and J.C. Levine, "Decentralization of Jobs and the Emerging Suburban Commute," *Transportation Research Record 1364*, 1992, pp. 71-80.

4 See literature reviews in I. Allen, "The Ideology of Dense Neighborhood Redevelopment—Cultural Diversity and Transcendent Community Experience," *Urban Affairs Quarterly*, Vol. 15, 1980, pp. 409-428; and D.R. Hill, "Jane Jacobs' Ideas on Big, Diverse Cities: A Review and Commentary," *Journal of the American Planning Association*, Vol. 54, 1988, pp. 302-314.

5 D.J. Godwin, "Land Planning—A Blueprint By Design," *Business Climate*, Vol. 4, 2nd Quarter 1993, pp. 20-22 and 50-51.

6 Governor's Affordable Housing Study Commission, *Final Report*, Tallahassee, Fla., 1992, p. 4.

7 L.C. Burkhart, *Old Values in a New Town—The Politics of Race and Class in Columbia, Maryland*, Praeger, New York, 1981, p. 152.

8 C.C. Marcus and W. Sarkissian, *Housing As If People Mattered*, University of California Press, Berkeley, 1986, p. 44.

9 Called the "Adequate Housing Uniform Standard Rule," it can be found in Chapter 9J-2.048, Florida Administrative Code. The rule was adopted in March 1994, as part of DCA's efforts to standardize requirements for developments of regional impact (DRIs).

10 G. Bauman, A.R. Kahn, and S. Williams, "Inclusionary Housing Programs in Practice," *Urban Land*, Vol. 42, November 1983, pp. 14-19; S.I. Schwartz and R.A. Johnston, "Inclusionary Housing Programs," *Journal of the American Planning Association*, Vol. 49, 1983, pp. 3-21; A. Mallach, *Inclusionary Housing Programs—Policies and Practices*, Center for Urban Policy Research, Rutgers University, New Brunswick, N.J., 1984, pp. 196-264; M.A. Stegman and J.D. Holden, "Inclusionary Housing Programs," in *Nonfederal Housing Programs—How States and Localities Are Responding to Federal Cutbacks in Low-Income Housing*, Urban Land Institute, Washington, D.C., 1987, pp. 49-74; F. Schnidman et al., *The Housing Linkage Study*, FAU/FIU Joint Center for Environmental and Urban Problems, Ft. Lauderdale, Fla., 1990, pp. 102-103; and S.M. White, *Affordable Housing —Proactive & Reactive Planning Strategies*, Planning Advisory Service Report Number 441, American Planning Association, Chicago, 1992, pp. 17-26 and 62-65.

11 Stegman and Holden, op. cit.; and R. Collin and M. Lytton, "Linkage: An Evaluation and Exploration," *The Urban Lawyer*, Vol. 21, 1989, pp. 413-446.

12 R. Ewing, *Developing Successful New Communities*, Urban Land Institute, Washington, D.C., 1993, pp. 67-70 and 119-121.

13 Ewing, op. cit., p. 67.

14 C.B. Schaake, "Affordable Housing: Fantasy or Possibility?" *Land Development*, Vol. 1, December 1988, pp. 14-18; and NAHB National Research Center, *Affordable Housing—Development Guidelines for State and Local Government*, U.S. Department of Housing and Urban Development, Washington, D.C., 1991, pp. 17-18.

15 T. Banerjee and P.G. Flachsbart, "Factors Influencing Perceptions of Residential Density," in V. Kouskoulas and R. Lyle (eds.), *Urban Housing and Transportation*, Wayne State University, Detroit, 1975; A. Rapoport, "Toward a Redefinition of Density," *Environment and Behavior*, Vol. 7, 1975, pp. 133-158; A. Rapoport, *Human Aspects of Urban Form: Toward a Man -Environment Approach to Urban Form and Design*, Pergamon Press, Oxford, England, 1977, pp. 201-207; S.L. Kirmeyer, "Urban Density and Pathology," *Environment and Behavior*, Vol. 10, 1978, pp. 247-269; D.E. Schmidt, R.D. Goldman, and N.R. Feimer, "Perceptions of Crowding—Predicting at the Residence, Neighborhood, and City Levels," *Environment and Behavior*, Vol. 11, 1979, pp. 105-130; P.G. Flachsbart, "Residential Site Planning and Perceived Densities," *Journal of Urban Planning and Development*, Vol. 105, 1979, pp. 103-117; P. Newman and T. Hogan, "A Review of Urban Density Models: Toward a Resolution of the Conflict Between Populace and Planner," *Human Ecology*, Vol. 9, 1981, pp. 269-303; E.R. Alexander and K.D. Reed, *Density Measures and Their Relation to Urban Form*, Center for Architecture and Urban Planning Research, University of Wisconsin-Milwaukee, 1988, pp. 3-8; E.E. Lonzano, *Community Design and the Culture of Cities—The Crossroad and the Wall*, Cambridge University Press, New York, 1990, pp. 166-172; and E.R. Alexander, "Density Measures: A Review and Analysis," *Journal of Architectural and Planning Research*, Vol. 10, 1993, pp. 181-202.

16 J.B. Lansing, R.W. Marans, and R.B. Zehner, *Planned Residential Environments*, Survey Research Center, University

of Michigan, Ann Arbor, 1970, p. 122. A similar conclusion was reached in a survey of British new town residents. P. Willmott, "Housing Density and Town Design in a New Town—A Pilot Study at Stevenage," *Town Planning Review*, Vol. 33, 1962, pp. 115-127.

[17] C.A. Hales, "Higher Density + Certainty = Affordable Housing for Portland, Oregon," *Urban Land*, Vol. 50, September 1991, pp. 12-15; and P. Ketcham and S. Siegel, *Managing Growth to Promote Affordable Housing: Revisiting Oregon's Goal 10*, 1000 Friends of Oregon, Portland, Ore., 1991.

[18] Banerjee and Flachsbart, op. cit.; Flachsbart, op. cit.; and Rapoport, op. cit.

[19] D.R. Jensen, *Zero Lot Line Housing*, Urban Land Institute, Washington, D.C., 1981; National Association of Home Builders, *Higher Density Housing—Planning-Design-Marketing*, Washington, D.C., 1986a; and J.W. Wentling and L.W. Bookout, *Density By Design*, Urban Land Institute, Washington, D.C., 1988.

[20] Flachsbart, op. cit.; and R.W. Marans and W. Rodgers, "Toward an Understanding of Community Satisfaction," in A.H. Hawley and V.P. Rock (eds.), *Metropolitan America in Contemporary Perspective*, John Wiley and Sons, New York, 1975, pp. 299-352. Also see A.C. Nelessen, *Visions for a New American Dream—Process, Principles, and an Ordinance to Plan and Design Small Communities*, American Planning Association, Chicago, 1994, pp. 99-102.

[21] National Association of Home Builders, *Cost Effective Site Planning—Single Family Development*, Washington, D.C., 1986b, p. 25.

[22] Wilbur Smith and Associates, *Patterns of Car Ownership, Trip Generation and Trip Sharing in Urbanized Areas*, U.S. Department of Transportation, Washington, D.C., 1968, pp. 108-110; B.S. Pushkarev and J.M. Zupan, *Public Transportation and Land Use Policy*, Indiana University Press, Bloomington, 1977, pp. 30-31; P. Newman and J. Kenworthy, *Cities and Automobile Dependence: An International Sourcebook*, Gower Technical, Brookfield, Vt., 1991, pp. 47-50; R.T. Dunphy and K.M. Fisher, "Transportation, Congestion, and Density: New Insights," Paper presented at the 73rd Annual Meeting, Transportation Research Board, Washington, D.C., 1994; and L.D. Frank and G. Pivo, "Impacts of Mixed Use and Density on the Utilization of Three Modes of Travel: The Single-Occupant Vehicle, Transit, and Walking," *Transportation Research Record 1466*, 1994, pp. 44-52.

[23] The case for densities in this range is made by M.N. Corbett, *A Better Place to Live—New Designs for Tomorrow's Communities*, Rodale Press, Emmaus, PA, 1981, pp. 33-37. Here, as elsewhere, "net residential density" is defined as the number of dwelling units divided by the net residential acreage. The latter includes internal subdivision streets but excludes perimeter roads, public parks and playgrounds, neighborhood commercial areas, schools, vacant unbuildable land, and community facilities. See Alexander and Reed, op. cit., pp. 10-12.

[24] M. Southworth and P.M. Owens, "The Evolving Metropolis—Studies of Community, Neighborhood, and Street Form at the Urban Edge," *Journal of the American Planning Association*, Vol. 59, 1993, pp. 271-287.

[25] P. Calthorpe, *The Next American Metropolis—Ecology, Community, and the American Dream*, Princeton Architectural Press, New York, 1993, p. 100; A. Duany and E. Plater-Zyberk, "The Second Coming of the American Small Town," *The Wilson Quarterly*, Vol. 16, Winter 1992, pp. 19-48; and A. Duany, E. Plater-Zyberk, and R. Shearer, "Zoning for Traditional Neighborhoods," *Land Development*, Vol. 5, Fall 1992, pp. 20-26.

[26] ITE Technical Council Committee 5P-8, *Traffic Engineering for Neo-Traditional Neighborhood Design*, Institute of Transportation Engineers, Washington, D.C., 1994, p. 8. Two generally accepted residential street design manuals provide for alleys, but on very different terms. One manual recommends that alleys be considered whenever lots are less than 50 feet wide; paved widths of 12 feet are judged adequate. This manual concludes that with "the increased use of narrow lots and a renewed concern for the streetscape, alleys may enjoy a renaissance in the next few years." Another manual cites a variety of problems with alleys, calls for 20-foot minimum pavement widths, and declares that "even well-constructed and maintained alleys may play a limited role in future residential construction." Residential Streets Task Force, *Residential Streets*, American Society of Civil Engineers/ National Association of Home Builders/Urban Land Institute, Washington, D.C., 1990, pp. 41-42; and ITE Technical Council Committee 5A-25A, *Guidelines for Residential Subdivision Street Design*, Institute of Transportation Engineers, Washington, D.C., 1990, pp. 25-26.

[27] This seems to be the main reason developers shy away from alleys. W. Sanders et al., *Affordable Single-Family Housing—A Review of Development Standards*, American Planning Association, Chicago, 1984, p. 17. Belmont, Virginia, was redesigned as a neo-traditional development complete with alleys (having originally been planned as a standard-issue subdivision). The denser street network and addition of alleys increased right-of-way requirements from 12 percent to 20 percent of total site area. M.J. Wells, "Neo-Traditional Neighborhood Developments: You Can Go Home Again," Unpublished paper available from the author, Wells & Associates, Inc., Arlington, Va., 1993. A similar comparison for Magnolia Village at Bluewater Bay shows that alleys increase right-of-way requirements by 4-5 percent of total site area (in the sections where alleys are planned).

[28] The literature on crime prevention through environmental design (CPTED) calls for restricted access to the rear of properties, where natural surveillance is limited. See Newman, op. cit., 1976, pp. 78-80; H. Rubenstein et al., *The Link Between Crime and the Built Environment—The Current State of Knowledge, Volume I*, U.S. Department of Justice, Washington, D.C., 1980, p. 36; B. Poyner, *Design Against Crime—Beyond Defensible Space*, Butterworths, New York, 1983, pp. 13-14; and P. Stollard, *Crime Prevention Through Housing Design*, E&F N Spon, London, 1991, pp. 68-70.

[29] In a visual preference survey, alleys were reported to rank at the very bottom of urban design elements, down there with factories. T.R. Herzog, S. Kaplan, and R. Kaplan, "The Prediction of Preference for Unfamiliar Urban Places," *Population and Environment*, Vol. 5, 1982, pp. 43-59.

[30] See the comparison of conventional and cluster site development costs in National Association of Home Builders, op. cit., 1986b, p. 119.

[31] T. Schumacher, "Buildings and Streets: Notes on

Configuration and Use," in S. Anderson (ed.), *On Streets*, MIT Press, Cambridge, Mass., 1986, pp. 133-150. Also see C. Alexander, S. Ishikawa, and M. Silverstein, "Positive Outdoor Space," *A Pattern Language*, Oxford University Press, New York, 1977, pp. 517-523; R. Hedman and A. Jaszewski, *Fundamentals of Urban Design*, American Planning Association, Chicago, 1984, pp. 53-60; K. Lynch and G. Hack, *Site Planning*, MIT Press, Cambridge, Mass., 1984, pp. 156-158; R. Trancik, *Finding Lost Space—Theories of Urban Design*, Van Nostrand Reinhold, New York, 1986, pp. 60-78; A. Rapoport, *History and Precedent in Environmental Design*, Plenum Press, New York, 1990, pp. 282-287; and A.B. Jacobs, *Great Streets*, MIT Press, Cambridge, Mass., 1993, pp. 277-281.

[32] O. Newman, *Design Guidelines for Creating Defensible Space*, U.S. Department of Justice, Washington, D.C., 1976, p. 77; and O. Newman, *Community of Interest*, Anchor Press, Garden City, N.J., 1980, p. 171.

[33] A plethora of manuals on cost-effective site development have been prepared by the National Association of Home Builders. National Association of Home Builders, op. cit., 1986b; NAHB National Research Center, op. cit., 1991, pp. 39-106; NAHB Research Foundation, *Building Affordable Homes—A Cost Savings Guide for Builder/Developers*, U.S. Department of Housing and Urban Development, Washington, D.C., 1982, pp. 5-15; NAHB National Research Center, *Affordable Residential Land Development: A Guide for Local Government and Developers*, U.S. Department of Housing and Urban Development, Washington, D.C., 1987a.

[34] NAHB Research Foundation, op. cit., pp. 17-53; NAHB National Research Center, op. cit., 1991, pp. 115-156; and NAHB National Research Center, *Affordable Residential Construction: A Guide for Home Builders*, U.S. Department of Housing and Urban Development, Washington, D.C., 1987b.

[35] NAHB Research Center, *Cost-Effective Home Building—A Design and Construction Handbook*, National Association of Home Builders, Washington, D.C., 1994, p. 3.

[36] Department of Community Affairs, *State of Florida—Energy Efficiency Code for Building Construction*, Tallahassee, Fla., 1993.

[37] R.K. Vieira, R. Sheinkopf, and J.K. Sonne, *Energy-Efficient Florida Home Building*, Florida Solar Energy Center, Cape Canaveral, Fla., 1988; and P. Russell, *Energy-Smart Building for Increased Quality, Comfort, and Sales*, National Association of Home Builders, Washington, D.C., 1993.

[38] L. Lord, *Guide to Florida Environmental Issues and Information*, Florida Conservation Foundation, Winter Park, 1993, p. 47.

[39] Division of Forestry, *Tree Protection Manual for Builders and Developers*, Florida Department of Agriculture and Consumer Services, Tallahassee, 1980, pp. 2-3. Also see B.R. Payne and S. Strom, "The Contribution of Trees to the Appraised Value of Unimproved Residential Land," *Valuation*, Vol. 22, 1975, pp. 36-45; D.J. Morales, B.N. Boyce, and R.J. Favretti, "The Contribution of Trees to Residential Property Value: Manchester, Connecticut," *Valuation*, Vol. 23, October-November 1976, pp. 26-43; D.J. Morales, F.R. Micha, and R.L. Weber, "Two Methods of Valuating Trees on Residential Sites," *Journal of Arboriculture*, Vol. 9, 1983, pp. 21-24; and L.M. Anderson and H.K. Cordell, "Residential Property Values Improved by Landscaping with Trees," *Southern Journal of Applied Forestry*, Vol. 9, 1985, pp. 162-166. The many contributions of trees to the urban environment are reviewed in R.C. Smardon, "Perception and Aesthetics of the Urban Environment: Review of the Role of Vegetation," *Landscape and Urban Planning*, Vol. 15, 1988, pp. 85-106.

[40] J.H. Parker, *Use of Landscaping for Energy Conservation*, Governor's Energy Office, Tallahassee, Fla., 1981, pp. 1-1 through 1-12, 3-1 through 3-17.

[41] D.M. Burch and S.J. Treado, "Ventilating Residences and Their Attics for Energy Conservation—An Experimental Study," in M.H. Reppert (ed.), *Summer Attic and Whole-House Ventilation*, National Bureau of Standards, U.S. Department of Commerce, Washington, D.C., 1979, pp. 73-100; T. Kusuda and J.W. Bean, *Savings in Electric Cooling Energy by the Use of a Whole-House Fan*, National Bureau of Standards, Washington, D.C., 1981; H.A. Ingley, R.W. Dixon, and D.E. Buffington, *Residential Conservation Demonstration Program*, University of Florida, Gainesville,

1983; M. Olszewski and H.A. McLain, *Using a Whole-House Fan to Decrease Air Conditioning Energy Use*, Oak Ridge National Laboratory, Oak Ridge, Tenn., 1983; and D. Parker, *Florida Cooling—The Natural Way*, Florida Solar Energy Center, Cape Canaveral, 1990.

[42] Vieira et al., op. cit., p. 4-11; G.Z. Brown, *Sun, Wind, and Light—Architectural Design Strategies*, John Wiley & Sons, New York, 1985, pp. 110-111 and 116-117; and Passive Solar Industries Council, *Passive Solar Design Strategies: Guidelines for Home Building*, Washington, D.C., 1994, p. 18.

[43] A radiant barrier consists of an aluminum-foil liner facing a vented attic air space. The foil blocks radiation from the hot roof to the ceiling or attic insulation above the ceiling, the primary source of ceiling heat flow. See P. Fairey, "Building Design Considerations," in *Principles of Low Energy Building Design in Warm, Humid Climates*, Florida Solar Energy Center, Cape Canaveral, 1984, pp. 7-13.

[44] Russell, op. cit., p. 55.

[45] For checklists of energy-saving features, and estimates of potential energy savings (from the last two references), see Russell, op. cit., pp. 33, 41, 45, 52, 55, 62-63, and 78-79; Vieira et al., op. cit., pp. 3-1, 4-1, 5-1, 6-1, and 7-1; and J.B. Cummings, *The Economics of Energy-Saving Features in Home Construction*, Florida Solar Energy Center, Cape Canaveral, 1990, Appendix A.

[46] See, for example, G.S. Rent and C.S. Rent, "Low-Income Housing—Factors Related to Residential Satisfaction," *Environment and Behavior*, Vol. 10, 1978, pp. 459-488; A.B. Shlay, "Taking Apart the American Dream: The Influence of Income and Family Composition on Residential Evaluations," *Urban Studies*, Vol. 23, 1986, pp. 253-270; J.J. Dillman and D.A. Dillman, "Private Outside Space as a Factor in Housing Acceptability," *Housing and Society*, Vol. 14, 1987, pp. 20-29; "Housing Preferences—Results of a Poll," *Urban Land*, Vol. 47, May 1988, pp. 32-33; and I. Audirac, A.H. Shoemyen, and M.T. Smith, "Consumer Preference and the Compact Development Debate," Paper presented at the National Planning Conference, April 29-May 3, 1989 (available from the authors at the Real Estate Research Center, University of Florida, Gainesville).

[47] Consistent with federal and state laws and regulations, and private underwriting criteria, we consider housing affordable if housing expenses do not exceed 30 percent of gross household income. In owner-occupied housing, the 30 percent standard applies to monthly principal and interest payments, taxes, and insurance; sometimes utilities are included as well, though not here. In rental housing, the 30 percent standard applies to monthly rent and utilities.

[48] These figures assume 10 percent down, a 30-year fixed-rate mortgage at 8 percent interest, and property taxes and insurance at rates of $10 and $5 per $1,000 in value, respectively.

[49] S. Bradford, "Pushing the Density Envelope," *Builder*, Vol. 16, February 1993, pp. 148-152.

[50] National Association of Home Builders, op. cit., 1986a, pp. 41-42; W.J. Richardson, "Designing High-Density Single-Family Housing - Variations on the Zero-Lot-Line Theme," *Urban Land*, Vol. 47, February 1988, pp. 15-20; and L.W. Bookout and J.W. Wentling, "Density By Design," *Urban Land*, Vol. 47, June 1988, pp. 10-15.

[51] L. Howland, "Apartment Niches," *Urban Land*, Vol. 53, January 1994, pp. 25-30.

[52] P.H. Hare, *Accessory Apartments—Using Space in Single-Family Houses*, Planning Advisory Service Report Number 365, American Planning Association, Chicago, 1981; M. Gellen, *Accessory Apartments in Single-Family Housing*, Center for Urban Policy Research, Rutgers University, New Brunswick, N.J., 1985; J. Lawrence and L. Watson, "Two by Two," *Planning*, Vol. 54, November 1988, pp. 22-23; P.H. Hare, *Accessory Units: The State of the Art, Report I—Summary of Experience with Accessory Units in the U.S. and Canada*, Patrick H. Hare Planning and Design, Washington, D.C., 1989; and P.H. Hare, "Homes within Homes: Making Accessory Units Work in the Marketplace," *Land Development*, Vol. 5, Spring-Summer 1992, pp. 31-33.

[53] Hare, op. cit., 1981, pp. 9-20; and P.H. Hare, *Accessory Units: The State of the Art, Report III—Model Zoning*, American Planning Association, Chicago, 1991, pp. 1-28.

[54] Ewing, op. cit., pp. 106-107.

[55] In particular, federal low-income tax credits may not have sufficient value to bridge the gap between the cost of housing and the amount of conventional financing that can be supported with low- and moderate-income rents. To make tax credit deals work often requires low-interest loans or grants on top of tax credits. See K. McClure, "Low and Moderate Income Housing Tax Credits—Calculating Their Value," *Journal of the American Planning Association*, Vol. 56, 1990, pp. 363-369. For examples of affordable housing projects in Florida, many tapping multiple funding sources, see J. Ross, *Planning and Financing Affordable Housing in Florida*, 1000 Friends of Florida, Tallahassee, 1995, pp. 29-74.

[56] Duany and Plater-Zyberk, op. cit.

[57] Lonzano, op. cit., pp. 144-148; Marcus and Sarkissian, op. cit., p. 42; Newman, op. cit., 1980, pp. 16-22; Poyner, op. cit., pp. 36-39; Stollard, op. cit., p. 24; H.J. Gans, "Planning and Social Life—Friendship and Neighbor Relations in Suburban Communities," *Journal of the American Institute of Planners*, Vol. 27, 1961, pp. 134-140; H.J. Gans, "The Balanced Community: Homogeneity or Heterogeneity in Residential Areas," *Journal of the American Institute of Planners*, Vol. 27, 1961, pp. 176-184; G. Herbert, "The Neighborhood Unit Principle and Organic Theory," *The Sociological Review*, Vol. 11, 1961, pp. 165-213; S. Keller, *The Urban Neighborhood: A Sociological Perspective*, Random House, New York, 1968, pp. 79-85; R.B. Taylor, S.D. Gottfredson, and S. Brower, "The Defensibility of Defensible Space: A Critical Review and Synthetic Framework for Future Research," in T. Hirschi and M. Gottredson (eds.), *Understanding Crime—Current Theory and Research*, Sage Publications, Beverly Hills, Calif., 1980, pp. 53-71; G.C. Galster and G.W. Hesser, "Residential Satisfaction—Compositional and Contextual Correlates," *Environment and Behavior*, Vol. 13, 1981, pp. 735-758; and T. Banerjee and W.C. Baer, *Beyond The Neighborhood Unit - Residential Environments and Public Policy*, Plenum Press, New York, 1984, pp. 187-190.

[58] H.J. Gans, *The Levittowners—Ways of Life and Politics in the New Suburban Community*, Pantheon Books, New York, 1967, p. 172.

[59] T. Doerr and J. Siegel, "Mixing Incomes at Timberlawn Crescent," *Urban Land*, Vol. 49, April 1990, pp. 8-11; E.A. Mulroy, "Mixed-Income Housing in Action," *Urban Land*, Vol. 50, May 1991, pp. 2-7; and D. Sachs and J. Siegel, "Assisted Living with a Twist—Mixed-Income Residents," *Urban Land*, Vol. 53, February 1994, pp. 21-23.

[60] In a related finding, residents at different income levels displayed surprisingly similar values, social attitudes, and life styles. It was this similarity that explained the apparent lack of relationship between income mix and resident satisfaction level. See the dated but seminal evaluation by W. Ryan et al., *All In Together: An Evaluation of Mixed-Income Multi-Family Housing*, Massachusetts Housing Finance Agency, Boston, 1974.

APPENDIX A
ANNOTATED BIBLIOGRAPHY OF DEVELOPMENT GUIDELINES

(1) David Jensen Associates, *Community Design Guidelines—Responding to a Changing Market*, National Association of Home Builders, Washington, D.C., 1985. Contains dozens of general guidelines aimed at market image and affordability.

(2) Model Code Task Force, *Australian Model Code for Residential Development*, Department of Health, Housing and Community Services, Commonwealth of Australia, Canberra, 1990; and Regulatory Reform Working Group, *AMCORD URBAN—Guidelines for Urban Housing*, Department of Health, Housing and Community Services, Commonwealth of Australia, Canberra, 1992. Offers the most comprehensive set of development guidelines and standards available anywhere. Several Australian states have prepared codes based on the central government's model. The Victorian Model Code is noteworthy for its incorporation of neo-traditional concepts.

(3) E.L. Fisher, *Affordable Housing Development Guidelines for State and Local Government*, U.S. Department of Housing and Urban Development, Washington, D.C., 1991. Suggests specific ordinance language relating to land use, streets, sidewalks and walkways, storm drainage systems, sanitary sewers, water supplies, and building design and construction.

(4) C.S. Doble and G.M. McCulloch, *Community Design Guidelines Manual*, The Tug Hill Commission, Watertown, N.Y., 1991. Offers 71 guidelines related mostly to site planning and development.

(5) S. Weissman and J. Corbett, *Land Use Strategies for More Livable Places*, The Local Government Commission, Sacramento, Calif., 1992. Outlines the so-called Ahwahnee Principles formulated by leading neo-traditional planners; 15 relate to community design, site planning, and development.

(6) P. Calthorpe, *The Next American Metropolis—Ecology, Community, and the American Dream*, Princeton Architectural Press, New York, 1993. Presents 72 guidelines and standards for new development around transit stops, culminating work begun in Sacramento County, California, and refined in San Diego, California, and Portland, Oregon.

(7) NAHB Research Center, *Proposed Model Land Development Standards and Accompanying Model State Enabling Legislation*, U.S. Department of Housing and Urban Development, Washington, D.C., 1993. Contains dozens of numerical standards for streets, drainage, and utilities, all aimed at reducing the costs of land development.

(8) Marshall Macklin Monaghan Limited, *Making Choices—Alternative Development Standards*, Ministry of Housing/Ministry of Municipal Affairs, Toronto, Ont., 1994. Provides general guidelines, mostly related to streets and streetscapes.

APPENDIX B
SURVEY OF STATE GROWTH MANAGEMENT PROGRAMS

The mutually supportive relationship between growth management programs and development of new communities was appreciated as far back as 1966, when the Council of State Governments published *State Community Development Policy: The Case of New Communities.* Quoting: "New communities—large-scale, planned communities—provide the opportunity for states to use their constitutional powers and intergovernmental positions to encourage sound patterns of community development, and to optimize the sometimes conflicting goals of environmental protection and economic development."

Accordingly, as the present effort to formulate quality development guidelines began, we had reason to hope that our work had been done for us by other growth management states. This, it turned out, was not the case. Even Oregon, with years of experience in growth management, has yet to offer any guidance to large-scale developers, perhaps because the state's slow growth rate has made it unnecessary. Administrators in several state planning offices indicated that rules for large-scale developments would be useful and may be necessary in the future.

The statutes of eight states with comprehensive growth management programs were reviewed, and officials who administer these statutes were then interviewed. The purpose was, first, to identify state goals, policies, and plans that might encourage or discourage planned communities; and second, to check for any supporting standards or guidelines governing the location, phasing, and/or design of planned communities.

The states examined were, in alphabetical order, Georgia, Maine, Maryland, New Jersey, Oregon, Rhode Island, Vermont, and Washington. Our findings:

1. *Seven states have goals and policies for curbing urban sprawl, which have implications for planned communities.*

The state growth management statutes and/or plans of Maine, Maryland, New Jersey, Oregon, Rhode Island, Vermont, and Washington all encourage or require compact development and strive to protect rural and natural areas. When and if these goals and policies filter down to local plans and regulations, they may influence the location, phasing, and design of planned communities. To this point, they have had no discernable effect.

2. *Vermont's and Georgia's statutes provide for special review and approval of large-scale developments but offer no review criteria.*

Vermont's Act 250, enacted in 1970, established district environmental commissions to review and approve large-scale developments. Despite a lengthy history, their reviews have remained strictly ad hoc. Georgia's statutes governing developments of regional impact, enacted in 1989, have yet to be implemented in most regions. In the regions where they have been implemented, notably Atlanta, review is limited to the issue of infrastructure needs and available capacities.

3. *Washington and New Jersey have criteria for assessing new community proposals, but they are not at a level of detail and specificity required for guideline or standard setting.*

The 1991 amendments to Washington's statute restrict development to urban growth areas, but make an exception for designated "new fully contained communities." New communities must have adequate infrastructure and open space buffers around them. They must incorporate transit-oriented planning, travel demand management, mixed uses, affordable housing, and mitigation of environmental and natural resource impacts. These are nominal requirements, though; no operational guidance has been provided.

New Jersey's plan provides for designation of growth areas. To date, 66 new communities have been proposed as growth areas. Procedures for delineating community boundaries and for preparing a community impact analysis must be submitted along with a designation request. The analysis must include population and employment projections, resource inventories and capacity analyses, design guidelines, and proposed growth management mechanisms. Details are left up to applicants.

APPENDIX C
QUESTIONNAIRE FOR EXEMPLARY DEVELOPMENTS

Name of Project

Location
Contact Person
Date Construction Began
Date First Residents Moved In
Projected Date of Residential Buildout
Projected Date of Commercial Buildout

I. GENERAL DESCRIPTION

a. Population: current   at buildout

b. Dwelling units: current   at buildout

c. Jobs: current   at buildout

d. Net Res Density: current   at buildout

e. Acreage   current   at buildout
   Residential
   Retail
   Office
   Industrial
   Public/Institutional
   Recreation/Conservation
   Right-of-way
   Total

f. How many dwelling units were sold in 1991? 1992?
g. How many acres of land were sold to other developers or builders in 1991? 1992?
h. How do vacancy rates, property values, property appreciation, and sales prices compare to neighboring developments?
i. How is the project doing financially? Has it defaulted on any loan obligations? Has ownership of the project changed hands?
j. What are the most important special conditions imposed on the project by local government? Who recommended them (DCA, FDOT, RPC, etc.)? When must they be met?
k. What were the most important changes in the project's development program imposed or negotiated during the development approval process?
l. What are the most important contributions of the project to the region (affordable housing, regional open space, shopping or job opportunities for nearby areas, etc.)?
m. What is the expected internal/external split for trips generated by the project? Please indicate what was assumed in the development approval process and what you actually expect.

II. LOCATION

a. Does the controlling jurisdiction have an urban service boundary, and if so, where was/is the boundary relative to the project?
b. Is the project within an urbanized area (population of 50,000 or more) and if not, how close is the nearest urbanized area?
c. Was sprawl an issue during the development approval process, and if so, how did you distinguish the project from sprawl?
d. How far is the closest central business district? Which CBD?
e. How far is the closest major employment center? Which employment center?
f. How far is the closest commercial airport? Which airport?
g. How far is the closest Interstate highway or other freeway? Which freeway?
h. What land uses surround the project? What kinds of buffers have been established to separate incompatible uses and discourage sprawl? Are farmlands among the incompatible uses? What pedestrian and open space connections exist to surrounding land uses?

III. DEVELOPMENT PHASING

a. Is there an approved master plan for the overall project, and if so, when was it approved?
b. How many times has the master plan been amended, and what were the amendments?
c. Was the entire site rezoned at once or are rezonings requested with each phase? How large are the phases, and how many phases will there be?
d. To what extent and in what way is commercial development phased to coincide with residential development? Affordable housing development phased to coincide with job development?

IV. DEVELOPMENT PATTERN

a. Under what type of zoning ordinance is development occurring (conventional/Euclidean, cluster subdivision, PUD, traditional neighborhood development, satellite community)?
b. Was the developer involved in drafting of the ordinance? If so, what specific provisions were written into the ordinance that were not available under the pre-existing land development code?
c. Is the project organized into "self-contained" units (such as villages/neighborhoods with a mix of housing and internal facilities)? What facilities are incorporated into these villages/neighborhoods?
d. What characteristics distinguish neighborhoods/villages from one another?

e. What separates and buffers neighborhoods/villages from one another and from nonresidential uses?
f. What connects neighborhoods/villages to one another and to nonresidential uses?
g. If development is not organized into villages/neighborhoods, how would you describe the development pattern?
h. Is there an overall commercial, civic, or recreational focal point to the development (a town center, village square, main street, etc.). If so, what is it? What uses does it or will it contain? What connections (pedestrian, open space, etc.) exist between this focal point and the rest of the development?

V. ACCESSIBILITY

a. Currently, what are typical distances (in miles) from residential areas to the closest:
Elementary school?
Middle school?
High school?
Day care center?
Convenience store?
Supermarket?
Regional shopping mall?
Discount center?
Fast food restaurant?
Sit down restaurant?
Golf course?
Tennis courts?
Public swimming pool?
Neighborhood park?
Community park?

b. At buildout, what will typical distances be from residential areas to the closest:
Elementary school?
Middle school?
High school?
Day care center?
Convenience store?
Supermarket?
Regional shopping center?
Discount center?
Fast food restaurant?
Sit down restaurant?
Golf course?
Tennis courts?
Public swimming pool?
Neighborhood park?
Community park?

c. Do you or your governing jurisdiction have accessibility standards for parks, schools, or other facilities? If so, what are they?

VI. EXACTIONS

a. Has the developer donated sites for schools? Churches? Parks? Other?
b. Who is building on-site infrastructure and providing on-site services, and who is paying for them?

	building them	*paying for them*
water		
sewer		
stormwater		
roads		
parks		

schools
public safety facilities
affordable housing

c. What contributions have been or will be made to off-site infrastructure? Note type and amount of impact fees.
d. What special assessment or taxing districts, or community or neighborhood associations, have been or will be established to help pay for infrastructure and services?
e. Has an overall fiscal impact study been done or is one to be done? What does it show? May we get a copy?

VII. HOUSING

a. Are you (the master developer) building or planning to build any housing?
b. What is being done to hold down the cost of housing? Will prices/rents be above or below the regional norm? If so, how much?
c. What is being done to provide low- or moderate-income housing? Achieve a balance of jobs and housing? Are government incentives available (for example, density bonuses or tax subsidies)?
d. Does/will the project have any subsidized housing? If so, which federal, state, and/or local programs are being tapped?
e. What will ensure that any "affordable housing" stays affordable?

f. Residential development program
Numbers   *current* *buildout*
Single-family Detached
Single-family Attached
Multifamily
Density Ranges
Single-family Detached
Single-family Attached
Multifamily
Prices (owner-occupied)
less than $80,000
$80,000 - $100,000
$100,000 - $150,000
$150,000 - $200,000
$200,000 plus
Rents (renter-occupied)
less than $250/month
$250 - $450
$450 - $650
$650 plus

VIII. JOBS (if the project has an economic development component)

a. What are the competitive advantages of the project in attracting jobs? Has a marketing study been done? If so, may we get a copy?
b. What programs are in place or contemplated to attract businesses to the project?
c. What retail or other uses or amenities are incorporated into business parks/districts?
d. Are buildings clustered and connected within business parks/districts?
e. Is anything being done to reduce the amount of solo commuting into and out of the project (commuter bus service/pedestrian connections/parking limitations/ridesharing programs)?
f. Is anything being done to promote telecommuting or home-based businesses?
g. How many people are expected to both live and work within the project at buildout?

IX. TRANSPORTATION

a. If known, what is the current mode split for all trips generated by the project? What is the projected mode split at buildout?
b. How many lane miles of road are there/will there be within the project? Local? Collector? Arterial?
c. How many connections are there between the project and the external road network? How many are signalized?
d. How many signalized intersections are there/will there be within the project? What is being done to ensure minimum delay at signalized intersections?
e. What are the levels of service on internal and external roads today and at buildout? May we get a copy of your traffic impact study (if not in the Application for Development Approval)?
f. Do subdivisions have multiple connections to major internal roads and direct connections to one another?
g. What are the standard road cross-sections? May we get diagrams?
h. What access controls are applied to collectors and arterials within the project?

i. What traffic calming measures are applied to residential and local commercial streets?

j. Were any variances sought from city/county/state road design standards? If yes, what variances? If no, were you happy in all respects with the standards or simply resigned to them?

k. Is on-street parking allowed in residential areas? In commercial areas?

l. Does/will the development have any internal transit service?

m. Does/will the development have transit service within one-quarter mile of its boundaries?

n. What special provisions have been made by the developer for transit availability and access? Do/will transit stops have shelters and other amenities?

o. How many miles of sidewalk and off-street walkway will be provided? Which types of roads have/will have sidewalks? How wide?

p. How many miles of bikeways will be internal to the development? Which types of roads have/will have bike lanes, extra-wide curb lanes, or paved shoulders for bikes? How wide?

q. Are direct pedestrian/bike connections provided from residential areas to schools? Shopping areas? Parks and recreational facilities?

X. ENERGY CONSERVATION

a. Which of the following energy conservation measures are featured in the project? Optimal building orientation?

Preservation/use of shade trees and other vegetation?
Extra insulation?
Minimum paved surfaces?
Energy-efficient building materials?
Other?

XI. RECREATION

What park and recreational facilities are already in place or will be at buildout?

	today # acres	buildout # acres
mini/pocket parks		
neighborhood parks		
community parks		
regional parks		
public squares/plazas		
golf courses		

	today (#)	buildout (#)
tennis courts		
public swimming pools		
recreational lakes		
other		

XII. RESOURCE CONSERVATION

a. What are the major environmental problems of the project? What are the major environmental strengths of the project?

b. What special (endangered) upland habitat existed on-site and what portion has been preserved?

c. What was the total acreage of wetlands on-site and what portion has been preserved?

d. What, if anything, is built/will be built in 100-year floodplains of rivers and streams?

e. Were any listed species observed on-site? If yes, which ones and how were their habitats protected?

f. Have conservation areas been established? What legal mechanisms are being used to ensure that conservation areas are preserved in perpetuity?

g. Have upland buffers been established around wetlands? If yes, which ones and how wide?

h. Are conservation areas connected to larger ecosystems, and if so, which ecosystems?

i. Have any natural areas or water bodies been restored or enhanced? If yes, describe.

j. What prime farmlands existed on-site and what portion has been preserved?

k. Is use of fertilizers or pesticides limited in any way?

l. Is removal of topsoil or trees limited in any way?

m. Does/will the community have an on-site recycling center?

n. Does/will the community have the capacity for on-site shredding or mulching green waste?

o. Is reclaimed water available as a non-potable water source, and if so, where is it used?

p. Are special water saving measures being taken, and if so, what and where?

q. Is the use of native plants encouraged in any way?

r. Is the amount of turf restricted in any way?

s. Are septic systems or package wastewater treatment plants used? How is groundwater protected?

t. To what extent are natural drainage channels being maintained?

XIII. SENSE OF COMMUNITY/ AESTHETICS

a. Does the development preserve and/or relate to the history and culture of the area? If so, how?

b. Have special design/architectural guidelines been established for the project? May we get a copy?

c. Does the project have special landscaping requirements and sign controls for commercial properties? May we get a copy?

d. Does the project have well-defined entries and edges?

e. Does the project have landmarks?

f. Are all utilities placed underground?

g. What public access is provided to water bodies?

h. Does the project have self-governing mechanisms?

i. Does the project provide special indoor or outdoor places/spaces for meetings/gatherings?

APPENDIX D
QUESTIONNAIRE FOR TRADITIONAL TOWNS

1. Has your town received any official recognition for its quality of life, downtown revitalization efforts, historic preservation program, or anything else related to its historic status? For example, Arcadia was cited in a recent publication as one of the "100 Best Small Towns in America."

2. Traditional towns have main streets, town squares, or traffic circles with bordering buildings forming a continuous "street wall" uninterrupted by driveways and parking lots. How many blocks of such streets does your downtown have? What retail uses are present along them? Are these stores used primarily by locals or tourists? How are downtown stores doing financially? How are vacancy rates? How well have downtown stores withstood competition from strip centers and other auto-oriented commercial developments? If downtown stores are not doing well, how much of the problem is due to physical layout of buildings and parking rather than, say, location? How much is due to the absence of auto-oriented uses such as supermarkets and discount stores? How is parking accommodated downtown? What has been done to make the downtown more competitive?

3. Traditional towns have narrow streets by today's standards. What are typical residential and commercial street widths in older parts of town? What are minimum widths in the current code? What are typical corner curb radii in older parts of town? What are minimums in the current code? What are typical street tree clearances in older parts of town? What are minimums in the current code? Have the narrower street widths, smaller curb radii and smaller tree clearances caused any traffic problems (accidents, complaints, lawsuits, etc.)? Do emergency or service vehicles have a problem with them? In your opinion, do the narrower streets, smaller curb radii, and smaller tree clearances slow down traffic, encourage walking, or have any other effects?

4. Traditional towns have grids of straight, parallel streets running at right angles. What proportion of the town is gridded? Do you have more or less traffic congestion in the older gridded parts of town compared to the newer parts with their cul-de-sacs, loops, and other discontinuous streets? Have you had problems with through-traffic, excessive speeds, or accidents on residential streets that are part of the grid? Have you done anything to discourage the use of residential streets by through-traffic or to slow down traffic? Do houses on the grid sell as well as houses in newer areas sitting on streets without through-traffic?

5. Traditional towns allow or even encourage on-street parking in commercial and residential areas. Is on-street parking banned on any streets in the older parts of town? Has on-street parking been removed in older areas to create additional lanes for traffic? Do residents and businesses like or dislike on-street parking? Have you had any "dart out" type accidents as a result of parallel parked cars? Have you had many "pull out" or "back out" type accidents as a result of on-street parking?

6. Traditional towns have small blocks by today's standards. What are typical block dimensions in the older parts of town? In the newer parts of town? Does the land development code specify block dimensions for new subdivisions? If so, what are they? What are the advantages or disadvantages to the shorter blocks? Have any small blocks been consolidated to form superblocks?

7. Traditional towns have relatively small building setbacks. What are typical setbacks of homes and businesses in older parts of town? What are minimum setbacks in the current land development code? What are the advantages and disadvantages of the smaller setbacks? Are traffic noise, fumes, etc. a problem with small setbacks? Do small setbacks create a better or worse pedestrian environment?

8. Traditional towns mix rather than separate residential and commercial land uses. To what extent are residential and commercial land uses mixed in the older parts of town (placed next to or across from each other on the same street)? To what extent are they mixed in the newer parts of town? Does the current land development code allow different uses to be mixed in the same building or same zone? If not, why not? Is the greater mixing in older parts of town a plus or minus from the standpoint of the local real estate market?

9. Traditional towns mix rather than separate housing by type and house/lot size. To what extent are different housing types and house/lot sizes mixed in the older parts of town (small and large, attached and detached, single family and multifamily next to or across from each other)? How about in the newer parts of town? Does the land development code allow different housing types and house/lot sizes to be mixed in the same zone? If not, why not? Is the greater mixing in older parts of town a plus or minus from the standpoint of the local real estate market?

10. Traditional towns have accessory apartments behind single-family homes or above stores. Does your town have many accessory apartments (upstairs apartments/garage apartments/backyard cottages/granny flats) with its older homes? Above its older stores? Are these apartments a significant source of affordable housing? Are they a problem in any way for neighbors or local government? Does your town allow accessory apartments on new homes or businesses? If not, why not?

11. Traditional towns have single-family homes fronting on arterial and collector roads that, in suburbia, would have only commercial uses, apartments, or single-family homes backing up to them and separated by berms or walls. Is traffic a problem for residences on arterials and collectors? Are residences being converted to other uses or turning over rapidly? What has been done to slow traffic on these roads or otherwise reduce the impacts on abutting residences? Is it the town's policy that these properties should remain residential?

12. Traditional towns are organized around prominant public open spaces (town squares, village greens, town parks, etc.)? What public open spaces are present in or near your downtown? What facilities are provided in your downtown parks? Are your downtown parks heavily utilized? If so, who uses them and for what purposes? If not, is the reason poor location, lack of recreational facilities found in suburban parks, or some other factor? Do these public open spaces create any problems for neighbors or local government?

13. In your opinion, are people in the older parts of town more likely to walk or bike than those in the newer parts of town? For recreation? For shopping? To school? Is the amount of walking/biking significant as a proportion of total travel by residents of older neighborhoods?

How do land use patterns affect household travel behavior? One would assume that a question this basic had been asked and answered long ago, and that any first-year planning student could recite the answer. Yet, in fact, few planning issues have generated such diverse opinions and so little definitive research.

TWO SCHOOLS OF THOUGHT

There are those who believe that accessibility affects every aspect of household travel behavior, from trip rates to mode choices (as in the accompanying figure). They advocate *compact development, urban villages, neo-traditional neighborhoods, pedestrian pockets, transit-oriented developments, mixed-use activity centers,* and *jobs-housing balance.* Their ideological leaders are the new urbanists, notably architects Andres Duany and Peter Calthorpe.[2] Followers include many (perhaps most) urban planners, bicycle and pedestrian activists, and environmentalists with urban concerns. The advocates' viewpoint has acquired academic respectability thanks to a plethora of recent studies:

- Studies relating urban densities to mode choices, gasoline consumption, or vehicle miles of travel.[3]

Advocates' View of Land Use-Travel Relationships

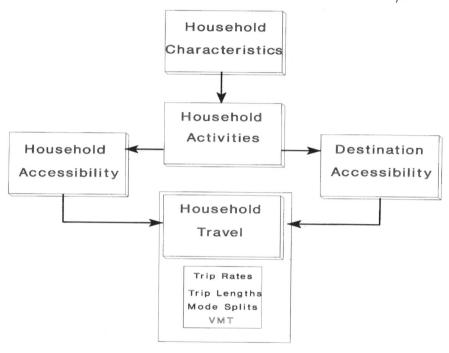

- Studies relating neighborhood design (pedestrian-oriented vs. auto-oriented) to mode choices or trip lengths.[4]
- Studies relating the land-use mix of suburban employment centers to mode choices of employees.[5]
- Studies relating jobs-housing balance to the length of work trips.[6]

On the other side of the issue is a small but influential group of skeptics. Most hail from the field of economics and seem to delight in challenging the conventional wisdom of planners. They have argued that land planning isn't worth the effort.[7] They have argued *against* compact development.[8] They have gone so far as to question whether accessibility—the common thread connecting pedestrian pockets, jobs-housing balance, and other land planning initiatives—is important in this age of automobiles, superhighways, and low-cost travel.[9] Corollaries include:

- Americans will not live at high densities (without massive government interference in land markets).
- Americans will not use alternative modes (without a dramatic increase in the cost of automobile use).
- Americans will not live close to their places of work (given the many other factors more important to them such as the cost of housing and quality of schools).

According to the skeptics, the studies upon which the advocates rely fail to prove their point. Sure, households in dense cities make less use of automobiles and more use of alternative modes. But these households are also smaller and poorer than suburban households and therefore would make less use of automobiles wherever they lived. Until studies control for household income, size, and other sociodemographic variables, the independent effect of land use patterns will be unknown and unknowable.[10]

Faced with such divergent views, one might suppose that the truth lies in-between—that land use patterns have less effect on household travel than claimed by one group and more effect than admitted by the other. But the truth may be more complex than this, just as household travel behavior is more complex. Land use patterns may be important, but not in the way envisioned by the advocates. Government's ability to affect density, mode choice, and the single-purpose commute may be limited, as the skeptics argue, yet greater accessibility may still be achievable and effective in reducing vehicular travel.

ACCESSIBILITY AND TRAVEL-ACTIVITY PATTERNS

Accessibility is defined in terms of ease of access to desired activities. The more activities available within a given travel time, the better the "accessibility" of a location. Good accessibility offers the potential for "maximum contact with minimum effort."[11]

Two types of accessibility may affect household travel behavior. *Residential accessibility* refers to ease of access to activities from one's place of residence, *destination accessibility* to ease of access to activities from other activities, whether work, school, shopping, or recreational sites. Destination acces-

Skeptics' View of Land Use-Travel Relationships

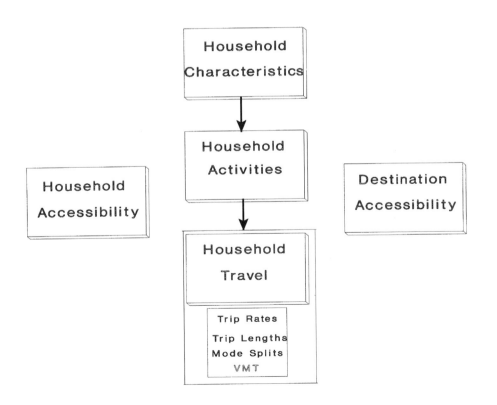

sibility is potentially significant in that it affects travelers' ability to efficiently link trips for different purposes into tours, or better still, complete more than one activity at a single stop.

TRIP CLASSIFICATION

This study deviates from standard practice in its classification of trips. Standard practice, which has its origin in conventional travel modeling, classifies trips as either home-based or nonhome-based. Home-based and nonhome-based trips are treated as independent of each other, when in fact they are necessarily linked.

Here, trips are classified as part of tours. In Palm Beach County, almost two-thirds of all trips are part of multistop, usually multipurpose, tours. High to begin with, the proportion of linked trips appears to be increasing.[12] As development becomes more dispersed, household members can economize on travel by cooperating in the scheduling of trips and by linking obligatory and discretionary trips into multipurpose tours. Obligatory activities act as "pegs" around which the household's discretionary activities are "arranged and shuffled."[13]

A tour may have only one stop away from home or may have many stops. If at least one stop is for purposes of work (the most important "peg"), the tour is classified in this study as *work-related*. Otherwise, it is classified as *nonwork-related*. This is not a perfect classification scheme, but it comes closer to capturing households' complex travel behavior than does the standard scheme.

COMMUNITY TRAVEL COMPARISON

Against this backdrop, a 16,000-record travel survey for Palm Beach County, Florida, has been analyzed for the effects of location and land use on household travel. Six communities were culled from the larger data base, low-income households were dropped from the resulting samples, and household travel data were then tested for significant differences in *trip frequencies*, *travel times*, *mode shares*, *trip linkage*, and *overall vehicle hours of travel*. We wanted to know if, after controlling for household income, location and land use influence household travel patterns, and if so, in what ways.[14]

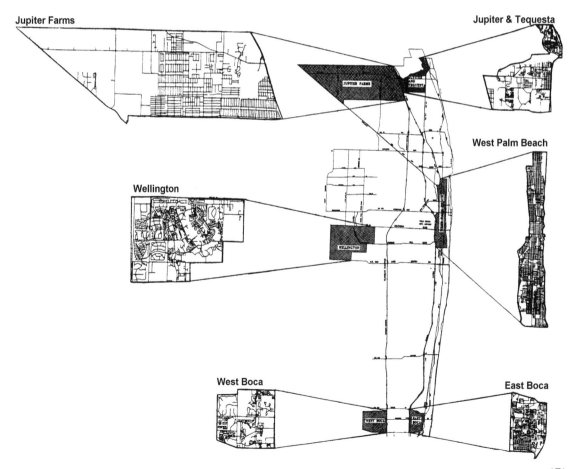

Communities of Palm Beach County

Study Area

The study area, Palm Beach County, was chosen in part for convenience. A recent diary-based travel survey was available for the county, at that time the only general travel survey in Florida to ask about walk and bike trips. Earlier surveys had focused exclusively on vehicular travel (being undertaken for the purpose of highway and transit planning).

Palm Beach County has another advantage as a study area. It is a large county that offers some diversity of development within an urban form often characterized as "sprawl." Within the larger county, six communities have been singled out. It is for these communities that travel patterns are compared.

West Palm Beach

West Palm Beach is as "traditional" (not neo-traditional, but the real thing) as any place in the county. Its housing stock varies from detached single-family homes to high-rise apartments, all within view of each other. Streets form a very dense grid and are narrow by today's standards. The community has corner stores, small building setbacks, rear parking, alleys, accessory apartments, and other hallmarks of traditional development. It is the only community with much mass transit service and the only one with a real central business district. In terms of density and accessibility, it is the most urban of the six communities.

Wellington

Wellington is a classic 1970s PUD (planned unit development). It has curvilinear streets, loop roads, and cul-de-sacs galore. It has "pods" of residential development,

walled off, inward-oriented, with only one way in and out. It has beautifully landscaped collector roads with meandering sidewalks. In short, it has everything that the new urbanists love to hate. At the same time, Wellington has a good mix of attached and multifamily housing, and comes complete with its own shopping centers, schools, recreational facilities, and medical offices, making it "self-contained" with respect to all daily activities except basic employment. For employment, residents must make the long trek into the urbanized area.

East Boca

East Boca is one of Florida's early master-planned communities, dating back to Addison Mizner and Florida's land boom of the 1920s. It has a small, almost-walkable downtown, historic neighborhoods on a rectilinear grid, and newer neighborhoods on a modified grid. It is well-endowed with public recreational facilities, schools, and small shopping centers. Its streets are tree-lined, often with sidewalks, making walking a option for some utilitarian trips (even though distances are longer than ideal for walking). Employment is located nearby at Florida Atlantic University, in a large industrial area just west of I-95, and to the south in Broward County. In terms of density and accessibility, it is the second most urban of the six communities.

West Boca

West Boca is a suburb of residential PUDs—each well-designed and well-landscaped but inward-oriented and independent of the others. The community has a fair number of schools and parks, four golf courses within a remarkably small area, and several large community shopping centers within or nearby. Subdivision and PUD streets are discontinuous to exclude through-traffic, but arterials form a grid with good connections to the rest of the region. While further from employment than East Boca, West Boca is accessible to the same employment centers.

Jupiter and Tequesta

Jupiter and Tequesta are twin strip cities; small strip centers line their major thoroughfares, Indiantown Road and Federal Highway. Streets are strictly for automobiles; landscaping, medians, sidewalks, and pedestrian amenities are in short supply. Basic employment opportunities are limited, as are recreational facilities. But the community is well-supplied with schools and local service employment, is reasonably dense, and mixes land uses in a fashion (with residential areas running up to the edges of the commercial strips).

Jupiter Farms

Jupiter Farms is the epitome of urban sprawl. It has large-lot, single-family homes; only one school, one park, and one convenience shopping center; and very limited employment nearby. Almost regardless of their trip purposes, residents must travel to Indiantown Road and then head for the Florida Turnpike or I-95. Jupiter Farms is closer to the ocean and the county's urbanized area boundary than is Wellington but is even less accessible for most purposes since it sits across from the relatively minor urban centers of Jupiter and Tequesta.

Results

For the six communities, household travel characteristics are summarized in the following figures. All statistics relate to the two-day period covered by the travel diaries. Mode splits vary only slightly across communities, less than one might expect given the differences in land use patterns. Average travel times show more variation, particularly for work trips. Total vehicle hours of travel (VHT) per person also vary considerably, due mostly to differences in average travel times.[15] VHT per person is inversely related to accessibility, measured with a gravity model.[16]

Our samples are small, and travel characteristics vary considerably from household to household within each community. Thus, apparent differences among communities could be solely due to chance (sampling variability).

To test for significant differences, analysis of variance was performed on our samples. At the 0.05 level, mean values of only three travel characteristics differ significantly across communities:

- travel time for work trips;
- travel time for nonwork trips; and
- total hours of travel per person.

A fourth characteristic, VHT per person, approaches significance at the 0.05 level.

One other important difference is evident across communities. The time savings realized through trip chaining appear to be much greater for the less accessible communities. For the county as a whole, average travel times decline only slightly as extra stops are added to tours. However, for Jupiter Farms, the declines are dramatic for both work-related and nonwork-related tours. And for Wellington, the decline is sizable for work-related tours, work places being relatively inaccessible.

174

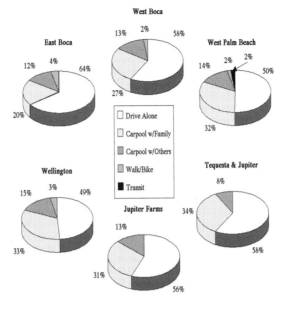

Mode Splits
in Different Communities

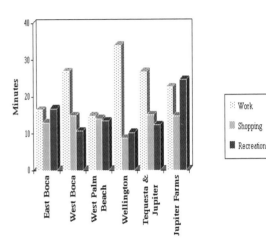

Average Travel Times
in Different Communities

Analysis of Variance Across Communities

Variable Tested	F-Statistic	Significance Level
Trips/Person (Work-Related)	0.76	0.58
Trips/Person (Nonwork-Related)	1.02	0.41
Trips/Tour (Work-Related)	0.65	0.66
Trips/Tour (Nonwork-Related)	0.53	0.75
% Drive Alone	1.26	0.29
% Carpool w/ Others	0.34	0.89
% Walk or Bike	1.51	0.19
Travel Time (Work)	2.79	0.02
Travel Time (Nonwork)	3.12	0.01
Total Hours of Travel/Person	2.72	0.02
Total Vehicle Hours of Travel/Person	2.16	0.06

Interpretation

Stepping back from the statistical tests and eyeballing the community averages, we can refine our understanding of travel patterns even as we become slightly less confident in our conclusions. There is an inverse relationship between accessibility and VHT per person. Density, mixed use, and a central location all appear to depress vehicular travel. Even so, VHT does not reflect accessibility to the extent one might expect. While Jupiter Farms has one-tenth the accessibility of West Palm Beach, it generates only two-thirds more VHT per person. Urbanites drive a lot whether they need to or not, and sprawl dwellers can reduce the amount of driving they do through coordinated trip scheduling.

West Palm Beach's relative accessibility fails to induce large numbers of auto users to switch to walking, biking, or transit; apparently, even the best accessibility in Palm Beach County is not good enough for travel by these modes. Yet, due to their short auto trips, West Palm Beach residents still save on vehicular travel.

The community with the worst accessibility, Jupiter Farms, produces the highest average vehicle hours per person. What saves Jupiter Farms from even more vehicular travel is its longer-than-average trip chains and, more importantly, the time savings realized with each additional stop in these chains.

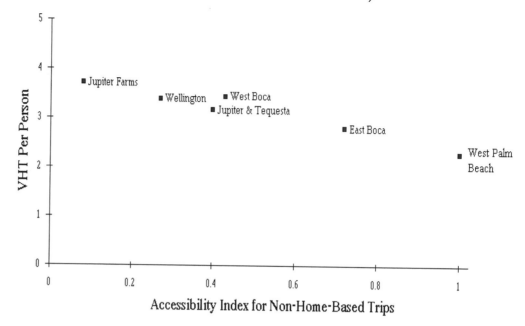

VHT Per Person vs. Accessibility

Wellington is an interesting case study. It has the longest work trips by far, yet still manages to generate less vehicular travel than West Boca or Jupiter Farms. The availability of on-site shopping and recreational facilities produces the shortest shopping and recreational trips of any community, more than offsetting the longer work trips.

Jupiter and Tequesta generate some very long nonwork trips, a result no doubt of their strip development patterns. Even so, Jupiter and Tequesta produce less vehicular travel than the best of the outlying communities. This makes the case for infill development generally, though one might prefer it take the form of East Boca or West Palm Beach.

Implications for land planning are more complex than simply "pedestrianizing" or "transitizing" the suburbs. Communities should *internalize as many facilities and services* as possible. This is true even where the automobile reigns supreme, as in Wellington. Land uses should be arranged to *facilitate efficient auto trips and tours*. The more sprawling the area, like Jupiter Farms, the more important this becomes. And infill development should be encouraged, for it promises much less vehicular travel than does outlying development (given comparable community designs).

HOUSEHOLD TRAVEL STUDY

The preceding comparison of community travel patterns has illustrative value that a more rigorous analysis cannot match. Use of community prototypes provides a graphic means of portraying land use characteristics (via photos, land use maps, and street maps). Use of community averages affords a simple means of summarizing diverse travel behavior.

Yet, because real communities are not perfect prototypes, and because community averages mask the complexities of household travel behavior, a follow-up study has been undertaken. In this study, travel data for individual households countywide are analyzed. Multiple regression analysis allows us to quantify the independent effects of land use characteristics on household travel behavior, controlling for socio-demographic characteristics of households. Complete data sets are available for 422 Palm Beach County households. They are our sample.

Here, only regression results for *vehicle hours of travel* are reported.[17] Regression results for *trip frequencies*, *travel times*, and *mode shares* are reported elsewhere.[18]

Four household characteristics are treated as explanatory variables. They are household income and autos/person, and also the number of household members in total and number who are employed. While related, these particular pairs are not so highly correlated as to preclude treating them as independent variables.[19]

Eight land use characteristics are treated as explanatory variables. They fall into four distinct classes, as shown in the accompanying table. Each variable relates either to

Variables Used in the Regressions

Travel Variable Modeled (for all household members combined over the two-day period of the travel survey)
- Total vehicle hours of travel (VHT)

Household Variables Tested
- Number of persons in household (PERSONS)
- Number of workers in household (WORKERS)
- Household income - the midpoint of the household's income range in thousands (INCOME)
- Number of vehicles per household member (AUTOS/PERSON)

Land Use Variables Tested for Place of Residence (traffic analysis zones in which households reside)
- Gross overall density ($OVERDEN_{home}$) = (population + jobs)/acres of land area
- Jobs-housing balance (JOBHOUS) = 1 - [Absolute Value(total employment - 1.5 x total housing units)]/(total employment + 1.5 x total housing units)
- Accessibility indices for four trip purposes - computed with a standard gravity model and normalized on a scale of 0 to 1
  Home-based work trips (ACCESSHBW)
  Home-based shopping trips (ACCESSHBS)
  Home-based social-recreation trips (ACCESSHBR)
  Home-based other trips (ACCESSHBO)

Land Use Variables Tested for Places of Work (traffic analysis zones in which household members work)
- Gross overall density ($OVERDEN_{work}$) = (population + jobs)/acres of land area
- Accessibility index for nonhome-based trips (ACCESSNHB)

a household's place of residence or its place(s) of work. Also, each relates either to a household's immediate locale or its position in the larger region.

Lest there be confusion, $OVERDEN_{home}$, $OVERDEN_{work}$, ACCESSHBW, and ACCESSNHB measure very different things. $OVERDEN_{home}$ is the density of population and jobs within the traffic analysis zone where a household resides; $OVERDEN_{work}$ is the density of population and jobs within the zone or zones where household members work; ACCESSHBW reflects the distribution of all jobs moving outward from the zone where the household resides, with nearby jobs weighted more heavily than distant ones; and ACCESSNHB reflects the distribution of commercial jobs and other nonhome-based trip attractions moving outward from the zone(s) where household members work.[20]

The use of overall density was dictated by data limitations. We could not compute *net* densities because only total land areas of zones were known (not areas devoted to different land uses). We could have computed gross residential and gross employment densitites, but gross densities have little meaning in mixed-use zones.

Convinced that the *household* (as opposed to the *individual*) is the appropriate unit of analysis in travel research, we wrestled with how best to represent work place variables for households with more than one working member. For want of a better alternative, $OVERDEN_{work}$ and ACCESSNHB were simply averaged for members of such households.

Land Use Variables

	Place of Residence	Place of Work
Local	$OVERDEN_{home}$ JOBHOUS	$OVERDEN_{work}$
Regional	ACCESSHBW ACCESSHBS ACCESSHBR ACCESSHBO	ACCESSNHB

Results

Regression results are presented in the following table. Variables enter the VHT equation at extremely high significance levels, a result in part of the large sample of households represented.

VHT proves significantly related to household size, number of working members, income, and vehicles/person. The fact that income and auto ownership have independent effects on travel may come as a surprise. Travel models usually treat these two variables as interchangeable.

In addition to these household characteristics, two land use variables prove significant. One is the accessibility index for home-based other trips (ACCESSHBO). ACCESSHBO is the broadest of all accessibility measures, accounting for the number of dwelling units, commercial jobs, service jobs, and school enrollments within a given travel time of home.[21] The regression coefficient

VHT Regression Equation
(coefficients with t-statistics in parentheses)

PERSONS	0.95** (8.7)
WORKERS	0.46** (3.4)
INCOME	0.018** (4.2)
AUTOS/PERSON	0.67 (2.3)
ACCESSHBO	-1.81* (-3.2)
$OVERDEN_{work}$	0.28* (3.1)
Constant	0.09
R^2	0.41

** Significant at the 0.001 level or beyond, one-tailed test.
* Significant at the 0.01 level or beyond, one-tailed test.

of ACCESSHBO implies that households living in the most accessible neighborhoods (ACCESSHBO = 1) spend 1.81 fewer hours in travel than do those living in the least accessible neighborhoods (ACCESSHBO = 0), or close to

1 hour per day over the two days of the travel survey.

The other land use variable significantly related to VHT is the overall density at the household's work place(s) ($OVERDEN_{work}$). It enters the equation, somewhat unexpectedly, with a positive sign. This variable is correlated with work place accessibility (ACCESSNHB). Apparently, when work places are accessible to other activities, so many additional trips are generated as to overwhelm the favorable effect of accessibility on trip lengths. Perhaps the opposite would be true if work place accessibility were so good that employees could walk to other activities. As it is, in Palm Beach County, *single-use employment centers* are the rule, *mixed-use activity centers*, the exception. Trips made in connection with work trips are almost always by automobile.

Interpretation

If the goal is vehicular travel reduction, some tentative conclusions relevant to land planning can be drawn from this study.

(1) Development patterns have a significant effect on household travel beyond any relationship they may have to sociodemographic characteristics of households. Placing the same households in more accessible residential locations will cut down significantly on their vehicular travel. This may be an obvious point but is one disputed by skeptics. Development patterns matter even in this era of near-universal auto ownership, superhighways, and low-cost travel.

(2) Good regional accessibility of residences cuts down on household vehicular travel to a far greater extent than does localized density or mixed use, casting doubt on the value of pedestrian pockets or transit-oriented developments in remote locations. Looking at simple correlations, densities and jobs-housing balances at home zones are inversely related to vehicle hours of travel at significant or near-significant levels (referring to the t-statistics of simple correlation coefficients). However, as we control for sociodemographic variables, these relationships become weaker and weaker (referring now to t-statistics of partial correlation coefficients). And they pale beside the relationship of travel to regional accessibility.

(3) Accessibility of residences to a mix of land uses is the key to vehicular travel reduction. Accessibility to shopping by itself is relatively unimportant, as is accessibility to work places. But households with good accessibility to shopping, services, schools, and other households can efficiently link trips for different purposes into tours. In our study area, households living in the most accessible locations spend nearly one hour per day less in vehicular travel than do otherwise comparable households living in the least accessible locations.

(4) Good accessibility of work places to other activities has countervailing effects on vehicular travel; it reduces the average length of work-related trips (which include side trips and intermediate stops on the way to and from work) and reduces the number of trips made independent of work (due to substitution of work-related trips for those otherwise made independently).[22] At the same time, good work place accessibility greatly increases the number of trips made in connection with work. The latter effect overwhelms the former. The balance would likely shift in favor of accessible work places if accessibility were improved to the point where employees could visit other activities on foot, something they cannot do in Palm Beach County's single-purpose employment centers.

ENDNOTES

[1] The material in this appendix is a synthesis of two articles: R. Ewing, P. Haliyur, and G.W. Page, "Getting Around a Traditional City, a Suburban PUD, and Everything In-Between," *Transportation Research Record 1466*, 1994, pp. 53-62; and R. Ewing, "Beyond Density, Mode Choice, and Single-Purpose Trips," *Transportation Quarterly*, Winter Issue, 1996, in press.

[2] S. Van der Ryn and P. Calthorpe, "The New Suburban Fabric," In S. Van der Ryn and P. Calthorpe (eds.), *Sustainable Communities—A New Design Synthesis for Cities, Suburbs, and Towns*, Sierra Club Books, San Francisco, 1986, pp. 54-105; P. Calthorpe, "Pedestrian Pockets: New Strategies for Suburban Growth," In D. Kelbaugh (ed.), *The Pedestrian Pocket Book—A New Suburban Design Strategy*, Princeton Architectural Press, New York, 1989, pp. 7-20; A. Duany and E. Plater-Zyberk, *Towns and Town-Making Principles*, Rizzoli International Publications, New York, 1991; A. Duany and E. Plater-Zyberk, "The Second Coming of the American Small Town," *Wilson Quarterly*, Vol. 16, 1992, pp. 19-48; A. Duany, E. Plater-Zyberk, and R. Shearer, "Zoning for Traditional Neighborhoods," *Land Development*, Vol. 5, Fall 1992, pp. 20-26; P. Calthorpe, *The Next American Metropolis—Ecology, Community and the American Dream*, Princeton Architectural Press, New York, 1993; and articles by Calthorpe and Duany/Plater-Zyberk in P. Katz, *The New Urbanism—Toward an Architecture of Community*, McGraw-Hill, New York, 1994.

[3] P.W.G. Newman and J.R. Kenworthy, "Gasoline Consumption and Cities: A Comparison of U.S. Cities with a Global Survey," *Journal of the American Planning Association*, Vol. 55, 1989, pp. 24-37; G. Harvey, *Relation of Residential Density to VMT Per Resident*, Metropolitan Transportation Commission, Oakland, Calif., 1990; R.J. Spillar and G.S. Rutherford, "The Effects of Population Density and Income on Per Capita Transit Ridership in Western American Cities," *ITE 1990 Compendium of Technical Papers*, Institute of Transportation Engineers, Washington, D.C., 1990, pp. 327-331; J. Holtzclaw, *Explaining Urban Density and Transit Impacts on Auto Use*, Sierra Club, San Francisco, 1991, pp. 18-24; P.W.G. Newman and J.R. Kenworthy, *Cities and Automobile Dependence: A Sourcebook*, Gower Technical, Brookfield,

VT, 1991, pp. 34-68; R. Cervero, "Rail-Oriented Office Development in California: How Successful?" *Transportation Quarterly*, Vol. 48, 1994, pp. 33-44; R.T. Dunphy and K.M. Fisher, "Transportation, Congestion, and Density: New Insights," Paper presented at the 73rd Annual Meeting, Transportation Research Board, Washington, D.C., 1994; L.D. Frank and G. Pivo, "Impacts of Mixed Use and Density on the Utilization of Three Modes of Travel: Single Occupant Vehicle, Transit, and Walking," *Transportation Research Record 1466*, 1994a, pp. 44-52; L.D. Frank and G. Pivo, *Relationships Between Land Use and Travel Behavior in the Puget Sound Region*, Washington State Department of Transportation, Seattle, 1994b, pp. 14-34; and J. Holtzclaw, *Using Residential Patterns and Transit to Decrease Auto Dependence and Costs*, Natural Resources Defense Council, San Francisco, 1994, pp. 20-21.

[4] S.L. Handy, "Regional Versus Local Accessibility: Neo-Traditional Development and Its Implications for Non-Work Travel," Paper prepared for the 1992 Annual Meeting, American Collegiate Schools of Planning, 1992; R. Cervero, "Evidence on Travel Behavior in Transit-Supportive Residential Neighborhoods," *Transit-Supportive Development in the United States: Experiences and Prospects*, Technology Sharing Program, U.S. Department of Transportation, Washington, D.C., 1993, pp. 127-163; Parsons Brinckerhoff Quade Douglas, Inc., *The Pedestrian Environment*, 1000 Friends of Oregon, Portland, Ore., 1993, pp. 29-34; Sasaki Associates, Inc., *Transit and Pedestrian Oriented Neighborhoods*, Maryland-National Capital Park & Planning Commission, Silver Spring, Md., 1993, pp. 47-53; Cambridge Systematics, Inc., *The Effects of Land Use and Travel Demand Management Strategies on Commuting Behavior*, Technology Sharing Program, U.S. Department of Transportation, Washington, D.C., 1994, pp. 3-19 through 3-21; B. Friedman, S.P. Gordon, and J.B. Peers, "Effect of Neotraditional Neighborhood Design on Travel Characteristics," *Transportation Research Record 1466*, 1994, pp. 63-70; and S. Handy, "Understanding the Link Between Urban Form and Travel Behavior," Paper presented at the 74rd Annual Meeting, Transportation Research Board, Washington, D.C., 1995.

[5] Cambridge Systematics, Inc., op. cit., pp. 3-5 through 3-

10; Joint Center for Urban Mobility Research (Rice University), *Houston's Major Activity Centers and Worker Travel Behavior*, Houston-Galveston Area Council, Houston, 1987, pp. V-28 through V-37; R. Cervero, "Land Use Mixing and Suburban Mobility," *Transportation Quarterly*, Vol. 42, 1988, pp. 429-446; R. Cervero, *America's Suburban Centers—The Land Use-Transportation Link*, Unwin Hyman, Boston, 1989, pp. 137-142; and R. Cervero, "Land Use and Travel at Suburban Activity Centers," *Transportation Quarterly*, Vol. 45, 1991, pp. 479-491. Also see Frank and Pivo, op. cit., 1994b.

[6] Cervero, op. cit., 1993, pp. 179-181; Frank and Pivo, op. cit., 1994b; San Diego Association of Governments, "Jobs/Housing Balance and Transportation Corridor Densities," Appendix 3 of *Regional Growth Management Strategy*, San Diego, 1991; and J.C. Levine, "Decentralization of Jobs and the Emerging Suburban Commute," *Transportation Research Record 1364*, 1992, pp. 71-80. Jobs-housing balance has also been related to the proportion of residents living and working in the same community and the proportion walking or bicycling to work. R. Cervero, "Jobs-Housing Balancing and Regional Mobility," *Journal of the American Planning Association*, Vol. 55, 1989, pp. 136-150; and D.M. Nowlan and G. Stewart, "Downtown Population Growth and Commuting Trips - Recent Experience in Toronto," *Journal of the American Planning Association*, Vol. 57, 1991, pp. 165-182.

[7] A. Downs, *Stuck in Traffic—Coping with Peak-Hour Traffic Congestion*, Brookings Institution, Washington, D.C., 1992, pp. 79-120; and H.W. Richardson and P. Gordon, "Market Planning—Oxymoron or Common Sense?" *Journal of the American Planning Association*, Vol. 59, 1993, pp. 347-349.

[8] P. Gordon, A. Kumar, and H.W. Richardson, "The Influence of Metropolitan Spatial Structure on Commuting Time," *Journal of Urban Economics*, Vol. 26, 1989, pp. 138-151; P. Gordon and H.W. Richardson, "Gasoline Consumption and Cities—A Reply," *Journal of the American Planning Association*, Vol. 55, 1989, pp. 342-346; P. Gordon, H.W. Richardson, and M. Jun, "The Commuting Paradox—Evidence from the Top Twenty," *Journal of the American Planning Association*, Vol. 57, 1991, pp. 416-420; and C.C.

Bae and H.W. Richardson, "Automobiles, the Environment and Metropolitan Spatial Structure," *Metropolitan America in Transition: Implications for Land Use and Transportation Planning*, Lincoln Institute of Land Policy, Cambridge, Mass., 1993.

[9] G. Giuliano, "Research Policy and Review 27. New Directions for Understanding Transportation and Land Use," *Environment and Planning A*, Vol. 21, 1989, pp. 145-159; G. Giuliano, *Literature Synthesis: Transportation and Urban Form*, Federal Highway Administration, Washington, D.C., 1989; G. Giuliano, "Is Jobs-Housing Balance a Transportation Issue?" *Transportation Research Record 1305*, 1991, pp. 305-312; G. Giuliano and K. Small, "Is the Journey to Work Explained by Urban Structure?" *Urban Studies*, Vol. 30, 1993, pp. 1485-1500; and G. Giuliano, "Transportation and Land Use: Theories, Evidence and Policy Dilemmas," Paper presented at the FAU/FIU Joint Center Distinguished Speaker Series, Ft. Lauderdale, April 4, 1994.

[10] This criticism is legitimate in some cases. See A. Gomez-Ibanez, "A Global View of Automobile Dependence," *Journal of the American Planning Association*, Vol. 57, 1991, pp. 376-379. However, a few studies have controlled for sociodemographic variables and still found significant relationships between land use patterns on household travel behavior. See Ewing, op. cit., in press; Frank and Pivo, op. cit., 1994a; Frank and Pivo, op. cit., 1994b; and Parsons Brinckerhoff Quade Douglas, op. cit.

[11] A. Karlqvist, "Some Theoretical Aspects of Accessibility Based Location Models," In A. Karlqvist et al. (eds.), *Dynamic Allocation of Urban Space*, Lexington Books, Lexington, Mass., 1975, pp. 71-88.

[12] H. Kim et al., "Shopping Trip Chains: Current Patterns and Changes Since 1970," Paper presented at the 73nd Annual Meeting, Transportation Research Board, Washington, D.C., 1994; and P.B. Lockwood and M.J. Demetsky, "Nonwork Travel—An Evaluation of Daily Behavior," Paper presented at the 73nd Annual Meeting, Transportation Research Board, Washington, D.C., 1994.

[13] This way of conceptualizing household travel-activity patterns dates back to O. Westelius, *The Individual's Pattern of Travel in an Urban Area*, National Swedish Institute for Building Research, Stckholm, 1972. The "peg" terminology comes from I. Cullen and V. Godson, *Urban Networks: The Structure of Activity Patterns*, Pergamon Press, London, 1975.

[14] To control for differences in household income, 18 households, reporting annual incomes of less than $20,000, had to be dropped from the samples. They are nearly all from West Palm Beach, Jupiter/Tequesta, or West Boca. Three additional households that refused to disclose household income and reported owning no automobile were also dropped. They almost certainly fall into the lowest income categories. With these households out, samples from the six communities show no significant differences in household income or household size (in chi-square tests).

[15] VHT per person was computed assuming standard vehicle occupancies: 2.5 persons/vehicle for carpools and 30 persons/vehicle for transit.

[16] An accessibility index is the denominator of the gravity model, used in the standard "4-step" regional travel modeling process to distribute trips. The index represents the distribution of trip attractions around each zone producing trips. The higher the index, the more accessible the attractions. The index is computed by multiplying the number of trip attractions by the interzonal friction factor (which declines with interzonal travel time), and summing the result over all attraction zones.

[17] Parenthetically, it would have been instructive to model vehicle miles of travel (VMT) by household members as well as vehicle hours of travel (VHT). Unfortunately, trip lengths were not recorded in household travel diaries and could not be estimated consistently because destination locations were not geocoded for a third of all trips. Variations in VMT are almost certainly even more pronounced than variations in VHT since vehicle travel speeds are highest in areas of high VHT and lowest in areas of low VHT.

[18] Ewing, op. cit., 1995.

[19] The possibility of multicollinearity (extreme collinearity of explanatory variables) was checked in all regressions. It proved a problem in a couple cases, but not in connection with sociodemographic variables.

[20] An accessibility index is the denominator of a gravity model used in the standard "4-step" regional travel modeling process to distribute trips for a given purpose. The higher the index, the more accessible are trip attractions. The index is computed for each production zone by multiplying the number of attractions in each attraction zone by the interzonal friction factor (which declines with interzonal travel time between production and attraction zones), and summing the result over all attraction zones.

[21] The attraction measure for home-based other trips is:

Home-Based Other Attractions = 0.2 x Total Dwelling Units + 1.3 x Commercial Employment + 1.3 x Service Employment + 1.3 x School Enrollment

[22] See Ewing, op. cit.